MUHAMMAD AND THE BELIEVERS

Muhammad

and the

Believers

At the Origins of Islam

Fred M. Donner

THE BELKNAP PRESS OF
HARVARD UNIVERSITY PRESS
Cambridge, Massachusetts
London, England
2010

Library of Congress Cataloging-in-Publication Data

Donner, Fred McGraw, 1945–
Muhammad and the believers: at the origins of Islam / Fred M. Donner.
    p.   cm.
Includes bibliographical references and index.
ISBN 978-0-674-05097-6
1. Islam—Origin.   2. Islam—History.   3. Islamic Empire—History—622–661.
    4. Muhammad, Prophet, d. 632.   I. Title.
        BP55.D66   2010
    297.09'021—dc22   2009052195

For Alex and Lucy

Contents

Maps

Preface

A little over a century ago, renowned French scholar Ernest Renan (1823–1892) wrote the following summation of his findings on the origins and early history of Islam: "We arrive, then, from all parts at this singular result: that the Mussulman movement was produced almost without religious faith; that, putting aside a small number of faithful disciples, Mahomet really worked with but little conviction in Arabia, and never succeeded in overcoming the opposition represented by the Omeyade party."

While Renan's statement admittedly represents an extreme and harsh formulation of the ideas he advances, for many years Western scholars who were studying Islam's beginnings continued to hold many of those ideas. The notions that the prophet Muhammad (died 632 C.E.) and his followers were motivated mainly by factors other than religion, and that the Umayyad family, which ruled from 661 to 750, were fundamentally hostile to the essence of Muhammad's movement, is even today widespread in Western scholarship. Renan's most cynical comment—that the movement that grew into what we know as Islam "was produced almost without religious faith"—has, in subtler guise, been embraced by many subsequent scholars, usually through a process of reductionism whereby the driving force of the movement begun by Muhammad is identified as having been "really" something other than religious conviction. At the end of the nineteenth century, Hubert Grimme sought to prove that Muhammad's preaching was first and foremost that of a social, not a religious, reformer; W. Montgomery Watt, reflecting the regnant position of the social sciences in the middle of the twentieth century, argued that the movement was engendered by social and economic stresses in the society in which Muhammad lived; and numerous others, including L. Caetani, C. H. Becker, B. Lewis, P. Crone, G. Bowersock, I. Lapidus, and S. Bashear, have argued that the movement was really a kind of nationalist or "nativist" political adventure, in which religion was secondary (and, by implication, merely a pretext for the real objectives).

In the following pages I attempt to present almost the exact opposite of Renan's views. It is my conviction that Islam began as a religious movement—not as a social, economic, or "national" one; in particular, it embodied an intense concern for attaining personal salvation through righteous behavior. The early Believers were concerned with social and political issues but only insofar as they related to concepts of piety and proper behavior needed to ensure salvation.

Moreover—and again in sharp contrast to Renan and many subsequent Western (and Muslim) scholars—I see the rulers of the Umayyad dynasty (660–750) not as cynical manipulators of the outward trappings of the religious movement begun by Muhammad but as rulers who sought practical ways to realize the most important goals of the movement and who perhaps more than anyone else helped the Believers attain a clear sense of their own distinct identity and of their legitimacy as a religious community. Without the contributions of the Umayyads, it seems doubtful whether Islam, as we recognize it today, would even exist.

A proper historical understanding of Islam's beginnings requires that we see it against the background of religious trends in the whole of the Near East in late antiquity—not only in an Arabian context, even though Arabia was where Muhammad lived and acted. By the sixth century C.E., Arabia was thoroughly penetrated by trends of religious thought current in neighboring lands. I shall therefore begin with a brief review of this pre-Islamic Near Eastern background (Chapter 1), after which I shall consider how a Believers' movement began in Arabia with Muhammad (Chapter 2), the rapid expansion of the Believers' movement in the decades following Muhammad's death (Chapter 3), the internal divisions that tore the movement during its first century (Chapter 4), and the emergence from the Believers' movement of something we can clearly recognize as Islam about two generations after Muhammad's death (Chapter 5).

Acknowledgments

It is a pleasure to recognize many institutions and individuals who facilitated the writing of this book. I am grateful to the National Endowment for the Humanities, an agency of the U.S. federal government, and to the American Center for Oriental Research in Amman, Jordan, for granting me an NEH/ACOR Fellowship during part of 2001, which enabled me to spend most of the first half of that year drafting parts of this work in the calm, supportive environment of ACOR's library in Amman. The Director of ACOR at that time, Dr. Pierre Bikai, Dr. Patricia Bikai, and the ACOR staff, especially its librarian Humi Ayoubi, made my stay there both productive and pleasant. The former Dean of Humanities at the University of Chicago, Professor Janel Mueller, generously allowed me to dodge my responsibilities as department chair so that I could take those months on leave, as well as another stretch of ten weeks in spring 2002, in order to draft the book. The latter period was spent mostly at the Jafet Library of the American University of Beirut, and I extend my thanks also to the helpful staff of that fine institution. Among libraries and librarians, however, my greatest debt is to the University of Chicago's Regenstein Library, and to its Middle East bibliographer,

Bruce Craig, who with his staff has built a collection that is peerless in its comprehensiveness and ease of use.

Readers owe a debt of gratitude to numerous friends and colleagues who read all or part of this work in manuscript and offered generous critical comments and suggestions. These saved me from a number of gaffes and contributed much to the book's clarity, cogency, and balance. Needless to say, the shortcomings that remain reflect my stubbornness, not their lack of insight. In alphabetical order, they are Mehmetcan Akpinar, Fred Astren, Carel Bertram, Paul M. Cobb, Hugo Ferrer-Higueras, Mark Graham, Walter E. Kaegi, Khaled Keshk, Gary Leiser, Shari Lowin, Chase Robinson, Roshanak Shaery-Eisenlohr, and Mark Wegner. The enthusiastic encouragement of Drs. Leiser and Shaery-Eisenlohr was especially heartening. I also wish to thank the twenty-five college teachers who participated in the NEH Summer Institute on "Islamic Origins" that I directed during summer 2000; it was in that setting that I was first able to try out some of the ideas presented here, and their responses helped sharpen my thinking and emboldened me to try formulating them as a book of this kind. I am most grateful, too, to my esteemed colleagues at the University of Jordan, Professors ʿAbd al-ʿAziz al-Duri, Saleh Hamarneh, and Faleh Husayn, for their friendship and unwavering support for this project, which helped reenergize me when I had for various reasons lost momentum. My colleagues Touraj Daryaee (University of California, Irvine) and Gerd-R. Puin (Saarbrücken) assisted me in securing photographs. Finally, I owe an unpayable debt to my wife, Carel Bertram, for her sage advice, love, and encouragement in everything I do, this book included.

A Note on Conventions

This book is meant mainly for nonspecialists—introductory students and general readers with an interest in the beginnings of Islam. It is not intended to be a work of technical scholarship, although I hope that scholars will find some of the ideas I present in it novel and worthy of serious consideration. Readers new to the subject who wish to know where to find more information on a particular subject, or specialists who wonder about the supporting evidence for something I say, will usually find what they need in the section "Notes and Guide to Further Reading." This is organized by chapter and contains bibliographical suggestions and references to specific points, organized more or less in the sequence in which they occur in the body of the book.

I have generally omitted diacritical marks when converting words from Arabic and other Near Eastern languages to Roman letters— the general reader is confused or put off by them, the specialist generally does not need them, and the publisher abhors them as cumbersome and costly. The only exception is that I have retained the signs for *'ayn* (') and *hamza* (').

Names of persons are given in strict transliteration (but without diacritics): thus, Muhammad, ʿAʾisha, Sulayman, and so on. On the other hand, whenever possible I have given most place-names in familiar English forms: thus, Mecca (not Makka), Damascus (not Dimashq), and so on. In most cases, I have dropped the Arabic article al- before the names of persons, groups, and towns, while usually retaining it within compound names (for example, ʿAmr ibn al-ʿAs). Most Arabic names are patronymic and include the word "ibn" ("son of"), so "ʿAmr ibn Qays" might also appear as "Ibn Qays," or simply as "ʿAmr."

The abbreviation "Q." is used to indicate quotations from the Qurʾan, Islam's holy book, throughout the text.

Some dates are given first in the years of the Islamic or *hijra* calendar (AH), followed after a slash by the Common Era (C.E.) date—so, for example, Muhammad is said to have died in 11/632, which means year 11 in the Islamic (lunar) calendar and 632 C.E.

The Muslim calendar is a lunar one of 354 days; consequently, a given month and day slowly cycle through the C.E. calendar. The twelve months of the Muslim calendar are alternately 29 or 30 days long:

Muharram	30 days
Safar	29
Rabiʿ I	30
Rabiʿ II	29
Jumada I	30
Jumada II	29
Rajab	30
Shaʿban	29
Ramadan	30
Shawwal	29
Dhu l-Qaʿda	30
Dhu l-Hijja	29

MUHAMMAD AND THE BELIEVERS

1

The Near East on the
Eve of Islam

The roots of the religion of Islam are to be found in the career of a man named Muhammad ibn ʿAbd Allah, who was born in Mecca, a town in western Arabia, in the latter part of the sixth century C.E. Arabia at this time was not an isolated place. It was, rather, part of a much wider cultural world that embraced the lands of the Near East and the eastern Mediterranean. For this reason, to understand the setting in which Muhammad lived and worked and the meaning of the religious movement he started, we must first look far beyond his immediate surroundings in Mecca.

Muhammad lived near the middle of what scholars call "late antiquity"—the period from roughly the third to the seventh or eighth centuries C.E.—during which the "classical" cultures of the Greco-Roman and Iranian worlds underwent gradual transformation. In the Mediterranean region and adjacent lands, many features of the earlier classical cultures were still recognizable even as late as the seventh or eighth century, albeit in new or modified form, while others died out, were changed beyond recognition, or were given completely new meaning and function. For example, in the sixth century C.E. the literate elites of the lands of the old Roman Empire

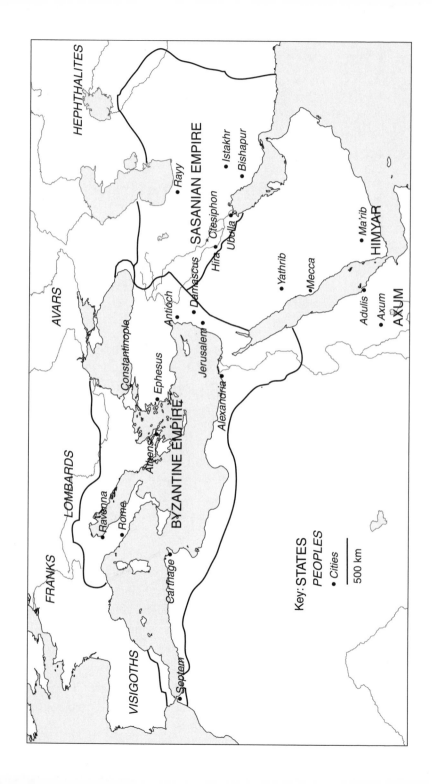

HEPHTHALITES

SASANIAN EMPIRE

Rayy

Istakhr
Bishapur

Ctesiphon
Hira Damascus
Ubulla

Ma'rib
HIMYAR

Yathrib

Mecca

Antioch

Constantinople

Jerusalem

Adulis
Axum
AXUM

AVARS

Ephesus

Athens

BYZANTINE EMPIRE

Alexandria

FRANKS

LOMBARDS

Ravenna
Rome

Carthage

VISIGOTHS

Septem

Key: STATES
PEOPLES
• Cities
500 km

around the eastern Mediterranean still cultivated knowledge of Greek philosophy and Roman law and of Greek and Latin literature, even though the pursuit of these arts was less widespread and often dealt with new and different issues than in Roman times. At the same time, most people had by this time given up their former pagan cults for Christianity. Similarly, the public and civic rituals of classical times, focused on the amphitheatre, the public bath, and the performance of civic duties, were beginning to atrophy—especially in smaller towns—and, after the fifth century, were gradually being replaced by more private pursuits of a religious and introspective kind. With the spread of Christianity in the eastern Mediterranean lands came also the emergence—alongside Greek and Latin—of new liturgical, and eventually literary, languages such as Syriac, Coptic, Armenian, and Ethiopic, which had formerly been unwritten. We can see in retrospect, then, that the late antique period in the eastern Mediterranean was one of transition between the preceding classical era, with its well-articulated civic life and Greco-Latin focus, and the subsequent Islamic era, with its emphasis on personal religious observance and the development of a new literary tradition in Arabic.

The Empires of the Late Antique Near East

In the latter half of the sixth century c.e., the Near East and Mediterranean basin were dominated politically by two great empires—the Byzantine or Later Roman Empire in the west and the Sasanian Persian Empire in the east. The Byzantine Empire was actually the continuation of the older Roman Empire. Its rulers called themselves, in Greek, *Rhomaioi*—"Romans"—right up until the empire's demise in 1453. For this reason it is also sometimes called the "Later

---

Map 1. The Byzantine and Sasanian Empires, ca. 565 c.e. (borders approximate)

Roman Empire," but I shall refer to it here as the Byzantine Empire, after Byzantium, the village on the Bosporus on which the capital city, Constantinople, was founded.

In the late sixth century, the Byzantine Empire dominated the lands on the eastern and southern shores of the Mediterranean basin (today's Turkey, Syria, Egypt, and so on). The other great empire, that of the Sasanians, was centered on the mountainous Iranian plateau and the adjacent lowlands of what is today Iraq, the rich basin of the Tigris and Euphrates rivers. Just as the Byzantines preserved the Roman heritage, the Sasanians were heirs to the long imperial traditions of ancient Persia. Most of the vast region from Afghanistan to the central Mediterranean was under the direct rule of one or the other of the two empires. Even those areas in the region that were outside their direct control were either firmly within the sphere of influence of one or the other power or were the scene of intense competition between them for political allegiance, religious influence, and economic domination. This contested terrain included such areas as Armenia, the Caucasus, and, most important for our purposes, Arabia. A third, lesser power also existed in the Near East—the kingdom of Axum (sometimes Aksum). The Axumite capital was situated in the highlands of Ethiopia, but Axumites engaged in extensive maritime trade from the port city of Adulis on the Red Sea coast. By the fourth century, Axum had been converted to Christianity and for that reason was sometimes allied with Byzantium; but in general our knowledge of Axum is very limited, and in any case, Axumite culture did not contribute much to Islamic tradition, whereas both Byzantium and Sasanian Persia did. Hence, most of our attention hereafter will be devoted to describing the Byzantine and Sasanian empires.

The Byzantine Empire

The Byzantine emperors ruled from their capital city at Constantinople (modern Istanbul) on the Bosporus; the city was dedicated in

> ### JUSTINIAN'S EDICT OF 554 C.E. TO THE PEOPLE OF CONSTANTINOPLE, NOVEL CXXXII
>
> We believe that the first and greatest blessing for all mankind is the confession of the Christian faith, true and beyond reproach, to the end that it may be universally established and that all the most holy priests of the whole globe may be joined together in unity. . . .

330 C.E. by the Roman emperor Constantine as the "Second Rome." From Constantinople, the Byzantine emperors attempted to hold their far-flung possessions together through military action and a deft religious policy. The Byzantine emperors subscribed to a Christianized form of the vision of a united world order first advanced in the West by Alexander the Great (d. 323 B.C.E.) and later adopted by the Romans. Those who held to the Byzantine variant dreamed of a universal state in which all subjects were loyal politically to the emperor and religiously to the Byzantine ("Orthodox") church headed by the patriarch of Constantinople, in close association with the emperors.

The Byzantine emperors faced at least two main problems—over and above the challenge of their Sasanian rival—in trying to realize this vision. The first problem was maintaining the strength and prosperity of the vast territory they claimed to rule, and their effective control of it, given the rudimentary technologies of communication and management available in that age—in short, the problem of government. In its heyday during the first century B.C.E. and first century C.E., the Roman Empire had extended from Britain to Mesopotamia and Egypt, a span of roughly 4,000 kilometers (km), or 2,500 miles (mi). It included people speaking a dizzyingly wide array of languages—Latin and Greek in many cities around the Mediterranean, Germanic and Celtic dialects in Europe, Berber

Land Walls of Constantinople. The city's magnificent defenses, still impressive today, permitted it to withstand the onslaughts of many enemies from the fourth until the fourteenth century C.E.

dialects in North Africa, Coptic in Egypt, Aramaic and Arabic in Syria, Armenian and Georgian and dozens of other languages in the Caucasus and Anatolia, and Albanian and Slavic dialects in the Balkans. The sheer size of the empire had caused the emperor Diocletian (284–305) to create a system of two coordinate emperors, one in the west and one in the east—so that each could better control his respective half of the empire, suppressing efficiently any uprisings or unrest in his domain and warding off any invasions from the outside. However, during the fourth and fifth centuries, the invasions and migrations of the Germanic peoples and other "barbarians," such as the Avars and the Huns, were simply too much for the emperors in Italy, who were overwhelmed by them. By the early sixth century, much of the western half of the empire had become the domains of various Germanic kings—the Visigoths in Spain, the Vandals in North Africa, the Franks in Gaul, the Ostrogoths in Italy. Paralleling this political disintegration was a widespread economic contraction in many of the western Mediterranean lands.

The eastern half of the empire, by contrast, managed to live on as a political entity, and its economy remained much more vibrant than that of the West. The Byzantine emperors in Constantinople, despite some close calls at the hands of the Avars, Bulgars, and Slavs, were able to ward off repeated barbarian onslaughts. Moreover, they always thought of themselves as the rightful rulers of the former empire in its full extent. Some even dared to dream of restoring the empire's glory by reclaiming lost lands in the west. This was especially true of the Byzantine emperor Justinian I (ruled 527–565)—who, depending on one's point of view, might be considered either "The Great" or merely megalomaniac. Justinian marshaled the full power of the Byzantine state, including its powers of taxation, in an attempt to reconquer the lost western provinces. His brilliant general Belisarius did in fact succeed in reestablishing Byzantine (Roman) rule in parts of Italy, Sicily, North Africa, and parts of Spain. Justinian also spent lavishly on great buildings, of which the magnificent church of Hagia Sophia in Constantinople is the finest surviving example. But the cost of this was high, as his efforts to restore Rome's lost glory through conquest and construction left the empire's populations impoverished and resentful, its treasury depleted, and its armies stretched thin.

Urban centers in the eastern Mediterranean were much stronger than those in the West, where cities had almost vanished, but their prosperity was also weakened during the late sixth century. One factor was a series of severe earthquakes that shook the eastern Mediterranean lands repeatedly in this period; another was the plague. Plague, which arrived in the 540s and returned every several years thereafter, regularly harvested off part of the population

Hagia Sophia. Justinian's great church in Constantinople, dedicated to "Holy Wisdom," symbolized the intimate nexus between the Byzantine emperor and the church.

and further sapped the empire's ability to recover its vitality. By the late sixth century, the Byzantine Empire was ripe for devastating onslaughts by the Sasanians—the final chapters in the long series of Roman-Persian wars stretching back to the first century c.e. Resurgent under their powerful great king Khosro I Anoshirwan (ruled 531–579), the Sasanians attacked the Byzantine Empire several times during the 540s and 550s. They invaded Byzantine-controlled Armenia, Lazica, Mesopotamia, and Syria and sacked the most important Byzantine city of the eastern Mediterranean, Antioch. Later, starting in 603, the Sasanian great king Khosro II Parviz (ruled 589–628) launched an even more devastating attack that resulted in the Persian conquest of Syria, Egypt, and much of Anatolia. Like the attacks of the mid-sixth century, that war was

Sinews of empire: A surviving stretch of Roman road in northern Syria. Built to facilitate the movement of Roman legions, these roads not only permitted the emperors to send troops promptly to distant provinces but also served as vital ways for overland commerce.

possible in part because the Byzantine Empire was in a weakened state.

The other major challenge faced by the Byzantine emperors between the third and seventh centuries had to do with religion. In 313 C.E., Emperor Constantine I (ruled 306–337) declared Christianity a legal religion in the Roman Empire in the Edict of Milan; it was established as the official faith by Emperor Theodosius I ("The Great," ruled 379–395). Since that time, the emperors had dreamed of realizing the vision of an empire that was not only universal in its extent but also completely unified in its religious doctrine—with the Byzantine emperor himself as the great patron and protector of the faith that bound all the empire's subjects, both to one another and in loyalty to the state and emperor. In the earlier Roman Empire, the official cult of the deified emperor had served this purpose, while allowing people to continue to worship their local pagan gods as well; but when Christian monotheism became the empire's official creed, the emperors demanded a deeper, exclusive religious obedience from their subjects.

This dream of religio-political unity, however, proved impossible to attain. Not only did diverse groups of pagans, Jews, and Samaritans in the empire stubbornly resist Christianity; even among those who recognized Jesus as their savior, there arose sharp differences over the question of Christ's true nature (Christology) and its impli- cations for the individual. Was Jesus primarily a man, albeit one filled with divine spirit? Or was he God, essentially a divine being, merely occupying the body of a man? Since he died on the cross, did that mean that God had died? If so, how could that be? And if not, how could it be said that Jesus died at all? Since Christians believed passionately that their very salvation depended on getting the credal formulation of such theological issues right, debates over Christ's nature were intense and protracted. In the end, it proved impossible to resolve these issues satisfactorily, even though the emperors expended a great deal of thought, money, and their subjects' good will in the effort to mediate disputes in search of a theological middle ground acceptable to all sides. It must also be said that these debates over doctrine often pitted powerful factions within the church against one another for reasons that were as much personal and political as doctrinal. Particularly important in this respect was the old rivalry between the patriarchs of the ancient sees of Alexandria and Constantinople, though the bishops of Rome, Antioch, and other centers also played a part.

Orthodoxy thus came to be defined through a series of church councils—intensely political gatherings of Christian bishops, sometimes supervised by the imperial court—that, among many other items of business, successively declared specific doctrines to be heresies. The result was that by the sixth century, the Christians of the Near East had coalesced into several well-defined communities, each with its own version of the faith. The official Byzantine church—"Greek orthodox," as it is called today in the United States—was, like the Latin church in Rome, *dyophysite*; that is, it taught that Christ had two natures, one divine and one human, which were separate and distinct but combined in a single person. (This separation enabled them to understand Christ's crucifixion as the death of his human nature, while his divine nature, being divine, was immortal.) Byzantine Orthodox Christians were predominant in Anatolia, the Balkans, Greece, and Palestine, and in urban centers elsewhere where imperial authority was strong. On the other hand, in Egypt, Syria, and Armenia most Christians, particularly in the countryside, were monophysite, that is, they belonged to one of several churches that considered Christ to have had only a single nature that was simultaneously divine and human. (From their perspective, the key point about Christ was that in him God had truly experienced human agony and death, but being God he was able to rise from the dead.) The emperor's efforts to heal this rift by convening the Council of Chalcedon (451) backfired when the resultant formula was rejected by the monophysites, who clung tenaciously to their creed despite sometimes heavy-handed efforts by the Byzantine authorities to wean them of it. A third group, largely driven out of Byzantine domains by the sixth century but numerous in the Sasanian Empire and even in Central Asia, were the Nestorians, named after Bishop Nestorius of Constantinople, whose doctrine was condemned at the Council of Ephesus in 431. Although dyophysite, the Nestorians placed, in the eyes of both the "orthodox" Byzantine church and the monophysites, too much emphasis

Mar Saba. This great monastery, in the semi-desert east of Jerusalem, like others in Egypt, Syria, and Mesopotamia, was a product of the surge of Christian religiosity that swept the Byzantine empire between the fourth and sixth centuries C.E.

on Christ's human nature and understated his divinity. North Africa was home to yet another sect deemed heretical, the puritanical Donatists, who rejected any role of the Byzantine emperor in their affairs. Although in retreat after the fourth century, particularly after Augustine's stringent efforts to refute them, the Donatists remained active in North Africa as a minority beside the regionally dominant Roman church.

These differences over doctrine, and their hardening into discrete sectarian communities, plagued the Byzantine emperors' efforts to build a unified ideological base of support for themselves and generated widespread resentment in the eastern provinces (and sometimes in the west) against the Byzantine authorities—a resentment that we can glimpse in the numerous polemical tracts in which members of one Christian community attacked the beliefs of others. The early stirrings of Christian anti-Semitism are also to be found in tracts directed explicitly against Judaism or in tracts in which Nestorians are denigrated by other Christians who liken them, because of their emphasis on Jesus' human nature, to Jews, who of course denied Jesus' divinity altogether. Various Christian sects also directed some polemical writings against Zoroastrianism, the official faith of the Sasanian Empire (see below). Christian chauvinism was sometimes pursued in less academic ways as well. Their refusal to build on the Temple Mount in Jerusalem, for example, was partly to affirm Jesus' supposed saying that no stone of the Temple would be left standing on another (Mt. 24:2), but the Byzantine authorities' use of the place as a dumping ground was presumably in order to symbolize their view that Judaism and its temple had been transcended by Jesus' preaching and belonged in "the dustbin of history." From the time of Theodosius, there were, in addition to intermittent bouts of popular anti-Jewish agitation, episodes of official discrimination, dispossession, persecution, closure of synagogues, and forced conversion of Jews by the Byzantine authorities.

Another feature of Christianity in the Byzantine Near East—one that seems to have been shared by different Christian denominations—was an inclination toward asceticism. Asceticism had deep roots in the ancient world but seems to have become increasingly prevalent during the fifth and sixth centuries. Its most extreme practitioners indulged in spectacular—sometimes theatrical—forms of self-denial. Some suspended themselves for long periods from trees, secluded themselves in caves, or, like the famous St. Simeon the Stylite (died 459), perched atop pillars, exposed to the elements, to pray and preach, sometimes for years on end, drawing pilgrims in large numbers. Most minimized their intake of food or sleep, sometimes to virtually nothing; others wandered the countryside almost naked to pray and live on what the Lord, and sympathetic villagers, might provide. Less sensational but far more widespread was the establishment of monasteries and convents, in which people took up an abstemious life of prayer far removed from the temptations of this sinful world. The monastic movement had begun in the early fourth century in the Egyptian deserts, but the building of such communal refuges spread rapidly into Syria, Anatolia, and Mesopotamia. The famous monasteries of St. Pachomius in Egypt, Mar Saba in Palestine, St. Simeon in Syria, and Qartmin in Mesopotamia were merely the most celebrated examples of a widespread trend.

Whatever its particular form, this tendency to ascetic self-denial was motivated by a conviction that salvation in the afterlife was to be achieved not only through right belief, but also by strictly righteous behavior. This involved, in particular, continuous prayer and a refusal to succumb to the temptations of physical desires, such as the need for sleep, food, shelter, sexual gratification, or human companionship, which were viewed by some, at least, as snares of the devil. Most people, of course, lacked the commitment or the discipline needed to engage in such heroic self-denial, but many acknowledged that it represented a kind of ideal and were supportive of those saintly individuals who could master their appetites sufficiently to attain it—hoping, perhaps, that by aiding them they would themselves gain some of the sanctity that the ascetic was presumed to have acquired. The ascetic movement thus belonged to a broader trend in the Byzantine Christianity of the fourth to sixth centuries that saw the articulation of a range of popular religious practices that helped bridge the divide between clergy and laity. These included pilgrimages, processions, the worship of saints' shrines, the veneration of icons, and new forms of liturgy, in all of which both clergy and laity could be involved or in which lay persons could have tangible contact with the sacred even in the absence of ordained clergy.

Another dimension of the religious mood of the Byzantine domains in the sixth century, and one not unrelated to asceticism, was

St. Simeon. Ruins of the great cathedral constructed around the pillar on which St. Simeon the Stylite sat for forty years; his asceticism attracted crowds of the devout and the curious to hear his sermons and resulted in the establishment of the cathedral and an adjoining monastery.

the widespread appeal of apocalyptic ideas—that is, predictions of the approaching end of the world, or End of Days. These usually anticipated an imminent, cataclysmic change in the world that would end current oppression or distress and usher in a new era in which the righteous would be vindicated (the identity of "the righteous" varying, of course, depending on who was spreading the predictions). In this new era or eon, they would vanquish their former persecutors and enjoy happiness and prosperity for a time before the dawning of the Last Judgment. With the Judgment, the righteous would finally be delivered by attaining everlasting salvation in heaven. A number of such apocalyptic scenarios were generated by members of religious communities that faced Byzantine oppression or harassment, such as the monophysite churches of Egypt, Syria, and Armenia, and have an unmistakably vindictive quality. But apocalyptic ideas were almost infinitely malleable and could also be advanced by the orthodox, who portrayed the coming cataclysm as one in which their faith would finally triumph over its stubborn opponents; in their eyes, the struggle to convert all of mankind to orthodoxy was a precursor to the Last Judgment. Indeed, one apocalyptic notion linked the Byzantine emperor himself directly to the events of the Last Judgment. According to this theory, which is a kind of Byzantine variant of Jewish messianism, the Last Emperor, after vanquishing the enemies of Christianity in battle and establishing an era of justice and prosperity, would hand over royal authority to Jesus at the Second Coming—an event predicted to happen in Jerusalem—and thus dissolve the Byzantine Empire and inaugurate the millennial era immediately preceding the Last Judgment. Regardless of who advanced them, these various apocalyptic ideas gave many people, even (perhaps especially) those suffering from poverty or oppression, some hope for the future and also served as a call for people to make greater efforts to live righteously, in order to be sure to be counted among the saved when the Judgment came.

As in antiquity, daily life for most people in the sixth-century Byzantine Empire was brutally harsh—so harsh that most of us alive today, in the West at least, could hardly endure it. Members of the elite—large landowners and high officials of church and state (entirely male)—were extremely wealthy, sometimes highly educated, and lived lives of leisure, but they constituted only a tiny fraction of the total population. This male elite held virtually all formal authority and dominated slaves, women, children, and men of common class. A middling group of prosperous farmers and petty officials or of moderately to very wealthy merchants existed but was relatively small. The overwhelming majority of the population lived in dire poverty as sharecroppers or peasants, poor urban laborers and artisans, or beggars. Slavery was still legal as an institution and widespread as a social phenomenon. There were few social services for the population and early deaths from disease, starvation, exposure, exhaustion, abuse, and violence must have been commonplace, particularly in periods of civil unrest, which were frequent. One of the very few ways to move up in society was through the imperial service, particularly the army—some soldiers of peasant origin even rose to be emperor—but this route was only open to a small number of men.

The emergence by the sixth century of bishops as the leading figures in the civic life of most towns of the Byzantine Near East may have tempered the harshness of life slightly, for the bishops at least acknowledged the poor, orphans, and widows in their midst as part of their communities and recognized their responsibility to alleviate the tribulations of such unfortunates. Unlike paganism, Christianity saw every individual as having the potential to attain sainthood through virtuous living and thus opened up vistas of a new kind of egalitarianism. Because this egalitarian vision was far from being realized in society, however, it is easy to understand how the ascetic tendency in Christianity and apocalyptic hopes for deliverance could become widespread in the Byzantine domains.

The Sasanian Empire

We know far less about the other great power of the Near East in the sixth century—the Persian Empire under the great kings of the Sasanian dynasty (226–651)—than we do about the Byzantines. It, too, encompassed vast territories, from the rich lowlands of the Tigris and Euphrates rivers in the west, its greatest source of tax revenues and the site of its capital, Ctesiphon (near modern Baghdad), to

Afghanistan and the fringes of Central Asia in the east. The population of this huge area spoke a variety of languages. Several Iranian languages (Middle Persian or Pahlavi, Soghdian, Bactrian, Khwarizmian) dominated the highlands and the empire's Central Asian fringes in the northeast; the lowlands of Mesopotamia were the domain of Aramaic and Arabic; and Armenian, Georgian, and probably a score of other languages were dotted throughout the inaccessibly tangled terrain of the Caucasus region.

In spite of the splendor of its impressive capital at Ctesiphon, for much of its earlier history the Sasanian Empire was poorly centralized and poorly integrated, with power diffused among a number of aristocratic families of the Iranian plateau who frequently contested the Sasanian family's leadership (and usually held some power via important posts in the government). The great king's very title—*shahanshah*, literally "king of kings"—hints at the Sasanian family's uncertain claim to preeminence over these rival noble families, who obviously also claimed kingship. In the sixth century, however, Great King Khosro I Anoshirwan (ruled 531–579) succeeded in asserting the royal prerogative against the nobility by reorganizing the state, imposing a greater degree of centralization through the efforts of his standing army and its garrisons and via an extensive bureaucracy. His successor Khosro II Parviz (ruled 589–628) was the main beneficiary of his policies, which enabled him to launch the great campaign against the Byzantine empire that began in 603.

Like the Byzantines, the Sasanians ruled a population that was not only polyglot but also religiously diverse. Zoroastrianism (Mazdaism), a version of the ancient traditional religion of Iran, was the most important faith in the empire and dominant especially on the Iranian plateau. Zoroastrianism was essentially a dualistic faith that conceived of the universe as the arena of a cosmic struggle between the forces of good and evil, embodied in the gods Ohrmazd (Ahura Mazda) and Ahriman, respectively. These primal forces

The Sasanian Throne-Hall at Ctesiphon, Iraq. In their capital at Ctesiphon (in the south suburbs of modern Baghdad), the Sasanians constructed a large palace with a soaring throne room, an amazing feat of brick construction. Although a large part of the two wings that flanked the central arch have now collapsed, the arch itself still stands.

were symbolized by light (particularly fire and the sun) and darkness, a symbolism that traveled westward—it is, for example, the ultimate source of the use of the halo to distinguish sacred figures in European religious iconography. Zoroastrians said special prayers at the moments of sunrise and sunset to mark their reverence for the sun, and many key rituals were performed in fire temples where an eternally burning sacred flame was tended by Zoroastrian priests. Most of the major fire temples were located on the Iranian plateau.

Zoroastrianism had long been associated with the Iranian monarchy, and during the Sasanian period became the quasi-official religion of the Sasanian state, although the relationship between the Sasanian great kings and the Zoroastrian priests (*herbeds*) and high priests (*mobeds*) was sometimes contentious. Zoroastrianism did not display the same number of internal divisions as did contemporary Christianity with its many rival sects, but there was a debate among Zoroastrians over Zurvanism, which may have been virtually a form of monotheism; it focused on the figure of Zurvan, considered by some a manifestation of eternal time and the father of both Ohrmazd and Ahriman. A few great kings flirted with rival forms of religious expression, such as Manichaeism (founded by the prophet Mani in the third century C.E.), Mazdakism (late fifth century C.E.), or Christianity. The special relationship of the Sasanians to Zoroastrianism, however, endured until the end of the dynasty, and with good reason, for Zoroastrianism bolstered the Sasanians' ideology of universal rule because the great king was considered to represent the dominion of Ahura Mazda over the world. This, and the Sasanians' sense that they were heirs to great Aryan empires of times gone by, led them to consider themselves superior to all other earthly powers (such as the Byzantines) who were, in their view, mere upstarts and qualified only to be their tributaries.

The Sasanian Empire also included large communities of non-Zoroastrians, however; some great kings subjected these to bitter persecutions, while others seem to have tolerated them somewhat less grudgingly than the Byzantine emperors did their religious minorities. Particularly noteworthy were large communities of Jews in Iraq (Babylonia), which with its famous Jewish academies was probably the greatest center of Jewish life and learning in the world at this time. Also important were Christian communities, both monophysite and Nestorian. The Nestorians had been welcomed into Sasa-

Triumph of Shapur. This central panel from a wall relief engraved by the Sasanians at Bishapur, Iran, commemorates the great king Shapur I's victory over three Roman emperors. The great king, mounted on his horse, holds the wrist of the emperor Valerian in an age-old symbol of captivity. Meanwhile, the emperor Philip the Arab submits by kneeling before him to request mercy, while two attendants look on. The emperor Gordian III lies on the ground, trampled by the great king's steed. Overhead, a small angel bears a beribboned diadem symbolizing divine favor for the great king.

nian territory after they had been condemned as heretics at the Council of Ephesus in 431 and forced to flee; Ctesiphon, the Sasanian capital, was the seat of the Nestorian patriarch. Whereas most monophysite Christians in the Sasanian domains were concentrated in northern Mesopotamia, Persian Armenia, Iraq, and the western-most fringes of the Iranian plateau, the Nestorians spread more widely and established small colonies in many areas, especially along the trade routes to, and through, Central Asia, even far beyond the Sasanian borders.

Zoroastrian society under the Sasanians was marked by a hierarchical order that was, if anything, even more rigidly defined than that of Byzantine society. The traditional Iranian social order divided the population into distinct strata, with religious leaders and the small political elite of landowners and warriors forming an upper stratum that was strictly differentiated from a commoners' stratum of peasants, artisans, and merchants (another scheme identifies the strata as priests, soldiers, scribes, and farmers). Slaves, of course, were at the bottom of the heap. This strict social hierarchy was reinforced by Zoroastrian orthodoxy, which established separate fire temples for the different strata. This system was probably most clearly in place on the Iranian plateau; in Mesopotamia and Iraq—where Zoroastrians, although politically important, were fewer in number than Jews and Christians—the social order may have been somewhat more fluid, but even there stratification between elites and commoners prevailed. The rigidity of this social order helped create the conditions in which movements such as Manichaeism or Mazdakism, which aimed at creating a more equitable society, found popular support; it was only partly tempered by reforms initiated by Great King Khosro Anoshirwan in the early sixth century.

For all their differences, the Byzantine and Sasanian empires shared certain common features and faced similar challenges. Their rulers struggled to unify vast domains and fragmented populations by the use of force, when necessary, and by recourse to a religious ideology that they tried to impose on their subjects, which bolstered their claim to rule. Both, perhaps inadvertently, fostered movements with egalitarian tendencies that used religious ideas to blunt the harshness of existing social norms. Both also faced the challenge of warding off external enemies on their frontiers, many of them nomadic groups from the Eurasian steppes: The Byzantines faced the Goths, Huns, Slavs, and Avars, whereas the Sasanians had to deal with the Kushans, Chionites, Huns, Hephthalites (White Huns), and Turks.

Above all, however, the two empires faced the challenge of each other. As the two great competitors for dominance in the Near East in the sixth century, their political rivalry had religious, cultural-ideological, and economic dimensions, the last-mentioned including competition for sources of metals and other resources, for trade revenues, and for taxable lands in an overwhelmingly semiarid region, the Near East, that had relatively few of them. At stake was not merely Byzantine versus Sasanian political control and economic influence, but also Christianity as opposed to Zoroastrianism and Hellenic as opposed to Iranian cultural traditions. We must not forget, either, that both empires laid claim to universal dominion and only grudgingly (and provisionally) recognized the other as its equal—an attitude that had very deep roots, going back at least as far as the clash between the Persians and Alexander the Great in the fourth century B.C.E.

This rivalry, on the political, cultural, and economic planes at least, went back to early Roman times and was played out throughout the Near East, including (as discussed below) the Arabian peninsula. It manifested itself in periodic diplomatic maneuvering between the two powers in an attempt to secure political allegiance and cultural and economic advantage in those border areas that the empires did not already rule directly or did not wish to bother to rule directly, such as Arabia.

Rivalry over trade was a significant component of this contest. Chinese silk, Indian cotton, pepper and other spices, South Arabian incense, leather (heavily in demand by the imperial armies), and other commodities had been important items of trade for the Romans, who had even established commercial colonies in South India, and they continued to be important for the Byzantines. Silk, in particular, was prized and came via the routes known collectively as the famous "Silk Road" through Central Asia and Iran to the

Mediterranean. Goods from the Indian Ocean could reach Byzantine territory either through the Persian Gulf and the Tigris-Euphrates valley or via the Red Sea. The Sasanians, who had extensive commercial contacts of their own in the Indian Ocean basin and who may have maintained commercial colonies in India, were keen to monopolize the flow of eastern luxury goods into Byzantine territory in order to levy taxes on them. A recurring feature of Byzantine-Sasanian peace agreements was the establishment of official customs stations where goods were required to cross the border.

Frequently, the two empires grew impatient with diplomacy and engaged in a long series of wars that were very costly to both sides. In particular, between 500 C.E. and the collapse of the Sasanian state in the 630s, the Byzantines and Sasanians fought five wars and were at war almost continuously for the final ninety years of that period, periodically trading control of key border areas, such as northern Mesopotamia and parts of Armenia and the Caucasus. The last of these wars (603–629) involved unusually dramatic shifts of fortune for both sides and was part of the immediate background against which Muhammad and his Believers' movement first appeared.

This final Byzantine-Sasanian war began shortly after the Byzantine emperor Maurice was murdered by the usurper Phocas in a military coup in 602. This event elicited a swift reaction from Great King Khosro II. Khosro either saw it as an opportunity to take advantage of a moment of Byzantine disarray or to exact revenge for Maurice, who, in 591, had helped him regain the Sasanian throne from a military usurper in Ctesiphon in exchange for border concessions in Armenia and Mesopotamia. In any case, beginning in 603, Khosro launched a series of attacks against Byzantine positions in Mesopotamia and Armenia and by the end of the decade had brought all lands up to the Euphrates firmly under Sasanian control.

Meanwhile, an internal rebellion against Phocas was building in the Byzantine Empire, led by the governor of North Africa and his son Heraclius. This led to widespread unrest and eventually the fall of Phocas as Heraclius was proclaimed emperor in Constantinople in 610. Khosro took advantage of this unrest to press his assault on the Byzantines further; he may have been aiming to finish them off completely. Sasanian forces crossed northern Syria to the Mediterranean coast, seized Antioch, and used this as a base to push into Anatolia to the north and Syria to the south. Between 610 and 616, all of Syria and Palestine was occupied and Persian garrisons installed in the major cities. Jerusalem, where the Persians appear to have been supported by the local Jews, was captured in 614, many citizens were massacred, and fragments of the True Cross, a relic of unequalled symbolic significance, were carried off to Ctesiphon. Farther to the south, Egypt, a key provider of grain for Constantinople, was seized by the Sasanians between 617 and 619. In the north, meanwhile, Sasanian armies from Syria had seized Cappadocia and its main center, Caesarea (modern Kayseri), while another army marched from Armenia as far as Galatia (around modern Ankara). By 621, fully half of Anatolia, the traditional heartland of the Byzantine Empire, was in Sasanian hands, as well as all of the Caucasus, Armenia, Syria, and Egypt; to make matters worse, Khosro had concluded an alliance with the chief of the nomadic Avars, who were simultaneously attacking Constantinople from the northwest.

The survival of the Byzantine Empire, which under the circumstances must be considered almost miraculous, can be attributed to Heraclius's determination and to his skill and daring as military commander and diplomat—and also, perhaps, to the magnificent defensive walls of Constantinople, which withstood a siege by the Avars in the summer of 626, when Heraclius and his army were campaigning far away. Despite renewed challenges from the Avars and stiff Sasanian opposition, he rallied the Byzantine troops to save the Christian empire and to restore the True Cross to Jerusalem, perhaps the first instance of a religiously legitimized imperial war. In 624 he marched his armies through central Anatolia into Armenia and the Caucasus; it may have helped that Heraclius's family was itself of

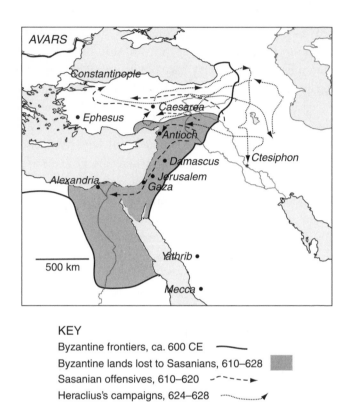

Map 2. The last Byzantine-Sasanian War, ca. 610–628 C.E.
(Adapted from W. Kaegi, *Heraclius*.)

Armenian origin. There he made contact with the Sasanians' steppe enemy, the Turks, and with their assistance broke the Sasanian grip on this strategically important region, which was nearly in the Sasanians' backyard. In 625 he further consolidated his control over Anatolia. In the autumn and winter of 627–628, Heraclius marched his army into northern Mesopotamia and then toward the Sasanian capital, Ctesiphon. His unexpected raid into the heartland of the empire caused Khosro to lose support at court, and the great king was overthrown in a coup early in 628; his successor (Khosro's son

Kavad II, ruled 628–629) sued for peace and ordered the withdrawal of remaining Sasanian forces from Anatolia, Armenia, Syria, and Egypt. By 629 the Sasanians had withdrawn behind new borders, which left the Byzantines in control of all of their former possessions as well as Armenia and northern Mesopotamia. The Sasanians entered a prolonged period of political instability, with numerous pretenders, including two Sasanian princesses, vying for the throne over the next decade. Heraclius triumphantly restored the relic of the True Cross to Jerusalem in 630, but after more than a decade of Sasanian rule, the Byzantine political infrastructure in Syria and Egypt was shaken, and many towns and communities had become used to making their own decisions.

These dramatic events, then, which left both great empires in a weakened state after decades of war, formed the wider background against which the career of Muhammad took place in Arabia.

Arabia between the Great Powers

Arabia was wedged between the two great empires on their southern desert edges. It is a vast and overwhelmingly arid land, extending in the north into the edges of the modern countries of Jordan, Syria, and Iraq. Much of Arabia consists of sandy or, more commonly, rocky desert—the main exceptions being the Yemen in the Arabian deep south and parts of Oman in the southeast, which are blessed with some moisture from the Indian Ocean and water from mountain springs. Elsewhere, rainfall is scant and irregular. For the most part, adequate water for agriculture can be found only where artesian wells bring underground water to the surface, forming an oasis with groves of palm trees, amid which crops of cereals, fruits, and vegetables could be raised. Most Arabian oases are small, but a few large oasis towns can be found in northern and eastern Arabia: in the north, Palmyra (actually in Syria), Azraq (in Jordan),

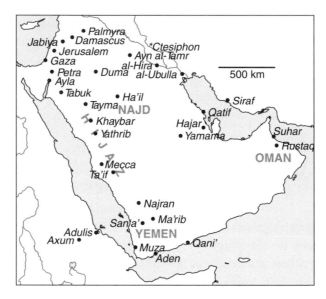

Map 3. Arabia, ca. 600 C.E.

Dumat al-Jandal, Tayma, Khaybar, and Yathrib (Medina); and in the east, al-Yamama (modern Riyadh), Hajar (modern al-Hasa), and Ha'il.

The Yemen, being fairly well watered, supported the rise of more highly developed forms of political organization than the rest of Arabia. Several early South Arabian kingdoms, which thrived in the first millennium B.C.E.—Saba' (Sheba), Ma'in, Qataban, Hadramawt—eventually gave way to an even larger polity, the kingdom of Himyar, which dominated most of Yemen from the first to the sixth centuries C.E.

In most of Arabia, however, the meager agricultural resources meant that the social and political order was structured around family and kinship groups ("tribes") that bound people together in solidarity and mutual defense. (Indeed, even in South Arabia the kingdom was only a thin veneer over an essentially tribal society.) There

Bar'an Temple, Ma'rib. The ancient South Arabian kingdoms constructed large shrines such as this one to their various astral deities.

was no "law" in the sense we understand it; rather, an individual's tribe or extended family provided him or her with day-to-day security, because any affront to a member of the tribe, particularly a homicide, would bring rapid retaliation against the offender's tribe. Both settled and nomadic people organized themselves this way; indeed, many groups had both settled and nomadic sections within one and the same tribe.

Arabia's political and social fragmentation was matched by its religious diversity on the eve of Islam. The traditional religion of Arabia was polytheism—a paganism that revered astral deities (the sun, moon, Venus, and so on), among others, and which existed in numerous variants as local cults, late survivals of the pagan religions of the ancient Near East. This local polytheism was peculiarly well suited to the Arabian social environment, for Arabian tribes not only considered themselves blood relatives (whether or not they actually were), they also usually joined in worshipping a particular local idol or god, whom they considered their divine protector, so that their social identity also had a religious component. These Arabian gods were honored at local shrines, called *harams*, often centered on a sacred tree, rock, spring, or other feature, which the deity was thought to inhabit. The *haram* consisted of a sacred area with definite boundaries around the shrine proper, in which it was forbidden for members of the cult to engage in bloodshed or violence—a ban that was enforced by the other groups that worshipped the same deity and by the family or tribe that served as the shrine's caretakers. This feature made the *haram* a place where people from different tribes could mingle safely, whether to visit a marketplace, to settle outstanding quarrels, or to arrange marriages and alliances. If there was sufficient water, a *haram* thus grew into a sizable settlement, because it tended to attract as settlers merchants and others for whom security of property was essential. Most of the larger towns of northern Arabia had a *haram* at their core—as well as a good supply of fresh water.

By the sixth century C.E., however, this residual Arabian paganism was apparently receding in the face of a gradual spread of monotheism. Judaism had come to Arabia very early—probably immediately after the Roman destruction of the Second Temple in Jerusalem in 70 C.E. Communities of Arabic-speaking Jews were found in most parts of Arabia, particularly in the Yemen and in the oasis towns of northwestern Arabia—Tabuk, Tayma', Khaybar, Yathrib (Medina), and so on. These may have been descendants of Jewish migrants or refugees from Palestine or Babylonia, local converts, or an amalgam of both. Christianity was also found in Arabia, especially in Yemen (where it had become established in the fourth century through Byzantine proselytizing), in eastern Arabia, and on Arabia's northern fringes bordering on Syria and Iraq, where it seems to have gained a following even among some pastoral nomadic groups. There is less agreement among scholars on the prevalence of Christians in the Hijaz (the mountainous western side of Arabia), although some stray references show that Christians were not unknown there. Arabia may also have been home to some communities of Jewish Christians called Nazoreans, who recognized Jesus as messiah but adhered to bans on consuming pork and wine. We have, unfortunately, very little firsthand information about these diverse Jewish and Christian communities in the sixth century. It seems plausible to suppose, however, that they were affected by the tendencies to asceticism and apocalypticism that were current in the wider Near Eastern world at that time.

A final aspect of religious life in Arabia that is worthy of mention is the survival there of the tradition of active prophecy, even though by the sixth century it had largely died out elsewhere in the Near East. Although by that time mainstream Jews and many Christians considered active prophecy to be a thing of the past, prophecy continued to be practiced by a few groups like the Montanists, a small Christian sect found mainly in Asia Minor. The religious teacher Mani, founder of Manichaeism, who lived in southern Iraq during the third century C.E., also claimed to have been a prophet. At the time of Muhammad's preaching in the early seventh century, moreover, there were a number of other figures in Arabia who, like him, presented themselves as prophets bearing a divine message. All of this points to the vitality of the tradition of active prophecy, particularly in Arabia, and helps us understand the way in which people in Arabia may have received Muhammad's claims to be a prophet.

For both political and economic reasons, the Byzantines and Sasanians felt a need to maintain a presence in Arabia—if only to thwart the other from gaining too much influence there. Yet, the dearth of resources in northern Arabia discouraged them from trying to establish direct control over this area, for it would have cost more to garrison and administer it than they could hope to secure in taxes. Instead, they adopted the stratagem of establishing alliances with the chiefs of Arabian tribes, who then served the empires' interests in exchange for cash subsidies, weapons, and titles; such indirect rule was much cheaper, in money and men, than trying to control the area directly with their own troops. The Sasanians established such an alliance with the "kings" of the Nasrid family of the tribe of Lakhm, whose base was al-Hira in lower Iraq; the Nasrids contributed troops to the Sasanian army and proved a thorn in the side of the Byzantines because of their periodic raids against Byzantine Syria. The Sasanians also had alliances with other chieftains along the Arabian coasts of the Persian Gulf. In northern Oman, they not only allied themselves with the local rulers, the Julandas, but established a more direct presence, appointing a Sasanian governor, with a permanent garrison of Sasanian troops based in Rustaq, to keep an eye on this region of strategic and agricultural importance. The Sasanians thus cast a large shadow over the gulf coasts of Arabia in the late antique period.

The Byzantines pursued a similar policy in northwest Arabia. The chiefs of the Jafnid family of the tribe of Ghassan, who resided at al-Jabiya in the Jawlan plateau overlooking Lake Tiberias, were recognized by the Byzantine emperors as "phylarchs," or tribal affiliates of the empire during the sixth century, and were outfitted with weapons and cash as well as with titles. Other tribes had, in earlier centuries, played the same role. Like their Sasanian counterparts the Nasrids, the Jafnids gave military assistance to their imperial patrons and participated in a number of major Roman campaigns against the Sasanians and even once (570) attacked the Nasrid capital at al-Hira in central Iraq. When not engaged in open hostilities, the Nasrid and Jafnid clients of the two empires were special rivals for influence among the nomadic people and oasis settlements of northern Arabia and served generally as agents of Sasanian and Byzantine interests. In particular, the Jafnids were expected to prevent other nomadic groups on the fringes of Byzantine Syria from raiding or plundering settled communities in taxable districts.

There is some evidence that mining of gold and other ores may have contributed to the economic vitality of the Arabian peninsula in the century before the rise of Islam. Recent work suggests, however, that Arabia's main resource of interest to the empires may have been leather, which was used by their armies for saddles, harnesses, boots, shields, tents, and other equipment.

Arabia was also significant economically because it lay on the Byzantines' path to the Indian Ocean basin and its rich commerce. Indian cotton, pepper and other spices, South Arabian incense, and other commodities came to the Mediterranean world either on ships that traveled sea routes that skirted Arabia and called at its ports—particularly Muza (Mocha) and Kane, in South Arabia—or by caravan through the towns of western Arabia, including Mecca. In the Red Sea, a good part of this sea trade was carried in Byzantine times by Axumite shippers hailing from their main port, Adulis. The Byzantine and Sasanian empires both aspired to control this commerce and the taxes that they could collect on it, with the result that Arabia became a focus of serious competition between the empires. The Byzantines, for example, maintained a customs station on the island of Iotabe in the straits of Tiran (at the mouth of the Gulf of Aqaba), and a few stray reports hint that both the Byzantines and the Sasanians attempted, and perhaps succeeded, in establishing special ties with local leaders to collect taxes in Yathrib or Mecca on the eve of Islam in an effort to draw this region into their spheres of influence.

Yemen became a special focus of this Byzantine-Sasanian competition, partly for religious reasons and partly because it occupied a particularly pivotal place in their rivalry over Arabian trade. During the first three-quarters of the sixth century, the Byzantines exercised some indirect influence in Yemen, which, though distant (3,500 km, or 2,175 mi, from Constantinople), was their direct gateway to the Indian Ocean via the Red Sea. For the Byzantines, this route had the advantage of circumventing the Sasanians, who sat astride the other trade routes to the Indian Ocean basin and East Asia, which passed either through Iran—the famous "Silk Road"—or, via the Persian Gulf, through Iraq.

The Byzantine political presence in Yemen was mainly established through the intermediary of their ally, the Christian kingdom of Axum. On the urging of the Byzantine emperor Justin, the Axumite king Ella Asbeha invaded Yemen around 523 C.E. and established a Christian ruler there. This invasion may have been in part a reaction to the activities of a Jewish king of the Himyarites, Dhu Nuwas, who had just beforehand engaged in a series of bloody clashes with Yemenite Christians, or it may have been mainly in order to facilitate Byzantine commerce with India. This Ethiopian regime in Yemen, which soon became independent of Axum, dominated the country for a half-century; its most important leader was the king Abraha, who attempted to extend his rule into north-central Arabia and is reported by tradition to have mounted an unsuccessful siege on Mecca around the time of Muhammad's birth.

The Sasanians were not about to allow this indirect Byzantine presence in South Arabia to stand unchallenged, however. In the 570s, Great King Khosro II sent an expeditionary force that occupied Yemen and made it a province of the empire, administered directly by a Sasanian governor with a strong garrison. By the end of the sixth century, then, the Sasanians had enclosed Arabia almost completely on its eastern and southern sides; only the Red Sea littoral and its extension into southern Syria was free of their control. The Byzantine Empire, on the other hand, was especially influential in northwestern Arabia.

Mecca and Yathrib (Medina)

The two towns where Muhammad spent his life, Mecca and Yathrib (later usually called Medina), were about 325 km (200 mi) apart from one another in the rugged region known as the Hijaz in western Arabia. The two towns were very different from one another. Yathrib was a typical large date-palm oasis, actually a loose cluster of contiguous villages, with mud-brick houses and fields of barley and other crops scattered under and between the date groves that grew around perennial springs. In each village or quarter was one or more mud-brick towers (*atam;* singular, *utm*) to which the villagers could repair if threatened by robbers or hostile nomads. In Muhammad's day the residents of Yathrib were from several different tribes or clans. The original inhabitants of the oasis seem to have been from upward of a dozen Jewish families or clans, among which the clans of Qaynuqaʾ, Nadir, and Qurayza were especially prominent. Many of these were farmers and held rich lands, but others—such as the Qaynuqaʾ, who were goldsmiths—engaged in trade or artisanship. By Muhammad's time in the late sixth century, however, the town was dominated by roughly ten clans of pagans (polytheists), who had settled in Yathrib several generations earlier and lived mainly from agriculture. Among these, the clans of Aws and Khazraj were the most powerful and engaged in sometimes bitter rivalry and feuds for leadership of the town, struggles in which the Jewish tribes were closely involved.

Mecca, on the other hand, was not an oasis town and had very little agricultural potential. The well of Zamzam did provide sufficient freshwater for drinking and for small garden plots, but the town's location in stony hills did not permit extensive cultivation, and in Muhammad's day some of its staple foodstuffs were imported from elsewhere in Arabia or from Syria. Mecca owed its prominence not to cultivation but to religious cult and commerce: It was a typical Arabian *haram* in which violence and bloodshed were forbidden. At the center of the town was the shrine called the Kaʿba—a large, cubical building with a sacred black stone affixed in one corner—that was the sanctuary to the pagan god Hubal. The custodians of this shrine belonged to the tribe of Quraysh, whose different clans made up most of the population of Mecca and shared the various cult responsibilities, such as providing water and food to the pilgrims,

An Arabian oasis. This photograph of the oasis of Jabrin, in Oman, conveys
some idea of the general appearance of palm oases such as Yathrib, with
houses of mud-brick and garden plots scattered loosely among large groves
of date palms.

preparing and selling special pilgrimage garb, and supervising particular rituals. People from other tribes, particularly pastoral nomads
who lived near Mecca, also joined its cult, sometimes bringing their
own idols into the shrine for safekeeping.

The tribe of Quraysh in Mecca were also heavily involved in commerce and organized caravans that carried goods between Mecca
and trading centers in Yemen, eastern Arabia, and southern Syria,
and they doubtless had contact with Axumite shippers as well. They
also participated in an annual trade fair held at a place called ʿUkaz,
near Mecca, at which merchants from many parts of Arabia gathered. It was once thought that Mecca was the center of a booming
trade in luxury items from east Africa, India, and Yemen, such as
ivory, slaves, and spices, but work since the 1970s reveals that much
of the trade was in more modest staple commodities such as ani-

The Ka'ba in Mecca. Although the structures around the Ka'ba had been rebuilt numerous times over the centuries, this photo from the late nineteenth century may give some idea of what the shrine looked like in the early Islamic centuries, before the tremendous expansions and rebuildings of the second half of the twentieth century.

mal hides and basic foodstuffs. The presence of gold mines in the Hijaz suggests that there may also have been some trade in this precious metal. Whatever commodities were involved, Mecca's commercial activity seems to have drawn people from outside Mecca into the town's cult, so that by the later years of the sixth century, when Muhammad was growing up in Mecca, its *haram* seems to have become one of the most important shrines among the many in western Arabia, and its custodians, Muhammad's tribe of Quraysh, had considerable experience in organization and management of joint commercial ventures and a network of contacts throughout

Arabia. It was in this environment of modest commercial activity and diverse religious ideas coming from both Arabian paganism and from the monotheistic traditions of the wider Near East that Muhammad ibn 'Abdullah, the prophet of Islam, was born and raised.

2

Muhammad and the Believers' Movement

Islamic tradition provides a richly detailed narrative of the life of Muhammad, the man all Muslims recognize as their prophet. This narrative is not contemporary but, rather, based on reports that were circulated and collected within the Muslim community during the several centuries following Muhammad's death. As this chapter explores in more detail, these reports contain material of many kinds. Some of them appear to be sober recountings of events, based ultimately on the testimony of eyewitnesses. Others offer miracle stories or improbable idealizations and seem to belong to the realm of legend or religious apologetic. The following pages present, first, a very condensed summary of the traditional biography of Muhammad, setting aside those reports that are clearly legendary. Thereafter, we will discuss some of the problems of this traditional picture and offer an alternative reading of Muhammad's life that takes these problems into account.

The Traditional Biography of Muhammad the Prophet

According to Muslim tradition, Muhammad ibn ʿAbdullah was born in the West Arabian town of Mecca in the second half of the sixth century C.E. (some reports say around 570, but different accounts give different dates). He belonged to the clan of Hashim within the tribe of Quraysh that dominated Mecca. He was orphaned at an early age and subsequently raised to adulthood by his paternal uncle, Abu Talib, who was at this time the chief of the Hashim clan.

As discussed earlier, in Muhammad's day Mecca was a town whose inhabitants were heavily involved in two activities: commerce and religion. The caravans organized by Quraysh, and the participation of Quraysh in various trading fairs, brought them into contact with other tribes and communities throughout Arabia. The Quraysh tribe's role as stewards of Mecca's religious rituals, centered on the Ka'ba and other holy sites around Mecca, also gave them contacts with many groups who came to the Ka'ba to do their devotions there, particularly by performing ritual circumambulations in the open area surrounding it. The security that came with Mecca's status as a *haram* was obviously good for commerce, so Quraysh's dual roles, as merchants and stewards of the shrine, were intimately intertwined.

As a young man, Muhammad entered into the commercial and cultic life of Mecca. He married a well-to-do widow, Khadija, who was some years older than he, and managed her caravan trading ventures. As he entered maturity, he became highly esteemed by his fellow tribesmen of Quraysh for his intelligence, honesty, and tactfulness. He also began to feel a periodic need for meditation and took to secluding himself now and then in order to contemplate his life. According to tradition, it was during such a personal retreat, around 610, that Muhammad first began to receive revelations from God, carried to him by the archangel Gabriel. The revelations came to him as intense sounds and visions that so overcame him that he could only lie on the ground, shaking and perspiring, until they were over, after which the words that had been revealed to him were burned indelibly into his memory. These words were eventually written down by his followers and edited together to form the Qur'an

(Koran), Islam's sacred scripture—which is, thus, literally a transcription of the spoken word of God in the view of believing Muslims.

Muhammad was at first terrified by what he had experienced and reluctant to take up the mantle of prophecy that God had thrust on him; but his religious experiences continued and it became clear to him that he could not evade this responsibility. He was also comforted by his wife Khadija, who accepted the veracity of his experiences and so became the first person to believe in his prophetic calling. Muhammad then began to preach publicly the message that was being revealed to him: the oneness of God, the reality of the Last Judgment, and the need for pious and God-fearing behavior. Gradually he began to win the support of some people, who abjured their pagan beliefs and recognized instead the absolute oneness of God and Muhammad's role as a prophet. Some of his earliest followers were close kinsmen, such as his cousin ʿAli, son of Abu Talib, and Saʿd ibn Abi Waqqas, possibly a relative of Muhammad's mother. Other early followers seem to have been people from the weaker clans of Quraysh and of marginal social groups. A number of prominent Meccans also became early adherents to his message, and many of these came to play central roles in the later life of the community. Notable among them were two men: Abu Bakr, a merchant of the clan of Taym, who became Muhammad's closest confidant; and Abu Bakr's kinsman Talha ibn ʿUbaydallah. Others included ʿUthman ibn ʿAffan, a very wealthy member of the powerful clan of Umayya, whose generosity was often put at the prophet's service and who married the prophet's daughters Ruqayya and (after the former's death) Umm Kulthum; and ʿAbd al-Rahman ibn ʿAwf of the clan of Zuhra and Zubayr ibn al-ʿAwwam of the clan of Asad. All of these people would play pivotal roles in the events following Muhammad's death.

Many tribesmen of Quraysh were shocked or disturbed by Muhammad's attack on their ancestral polytheism, the "faith of their fathers," and subjected him and his followers first to ridicule and then to more serious abuse. For a time he was sheltered from this by the resolute support of Abu Talib, who, as his uncle and head of the clan of Hashim, stood firm in protecting Muhammad. Even a boycott of Hashim by other clans of Quraysh, organized particularly by "Abu Jahl" (the name may be pejorative—"Father of Folly"), chief of the powerful clan of Makhzum, did not cause Abu Talib to hand Muhammad to them as they wished. However, Muhammad's situation in Mecca was becoming increasingly precarious, and a number of his followers reportedly took refuge at this time with the Christian king of Abyssinia to escape persecution.

Muhammad's position in Mecca deteriorated rapidly after the deaths, in close succession, of both Khadija and Abu Talib, his main sources of emotional and social support. Abu Talib was succeeded as head of the Hashim by another of Muhammad's uncles, "Abu Lahab" (perhaps another pejorative—"Father of Flame"), but the latter was not supportive of his nephew and after a time withdrew his protection. This happened probably around 619 C.E. Realizing that most of Quraysh would not soon be won over, Muhammad began to preach his message at periodic markets outside Mecca in order to find other supporters. Initially he met with little success, and he was rebuffed by the leaders of the town of al-Ta'if, about 100 km (about 60 mi) west of Mecca. Around that time, however, he was contacted by a small group of men from the town of Yathrib, a cluster of date-palm oases situated about 325 km (200 mi) north of Mecca. As discussed earlier, Yathrib had long been torn by political strife between the Aws and the Khazraj, rival clans of its dominant tribe, the Banu Qayla. Yathrib's three major Jewish clans, the Nadir, Qurayza, and Qaynuqa', may also have been involved in this strife. The people of Yathrib who sought out Muhammad were yearning for someone to reunify and heal their town; they were impressed by Muhammad's message and embraced it, promising to return to the fair the following year with more people. The next year, a larger group met with Muhammad and invited him to come to Yathrib with his Meccan supporters so that they could establish themselves there as a new community dedicated to living and worshipping as God demanded, without interference. Shortly thereafter, in 622 C.E., Muhammad and his followers from Mecca made their *hijra* ("emigration" or "taking refuge") to Yathrib—which I will henceforth refer to by its later name, Medina (from *madinat al-nabi*, "city of the prophet"). Muhammad's *hijra* to Medina, because it came to be considered the inception of a politically independent community of Believers, was adopted within a few years of Muhammad's death as marking the beginning of the Islamic calendar (AH 1). The Meccans who had made *hijra* with Muhammad were called *muhajirun*, "Emigrants," while the Medinese who received them came to be known as *ansar*, "Helpers."

Traditional accounts describe Muhammad's life in Medina in great detail, informing us of some events of a personal nature, such as his numerous marriages and the births (and deaths) of his children. Particularly noteworthy among these personal matters was his marriage to the young 'A'isha, daughter of his stalwart supporter Abu Bakr (whom Islamic tradition remembers as his favorite wife of the fifteen or so he eventually took). Also important was his close relationship with his cousin 'Ali ibn Abi Talib, one of the first to follow his message, who married Muhammad's own daughter Fatima. The traditional sources also emphasize Muhammad's founding in Medina of an independent community, including many notices about how he established ritual practices and laid down social guidelines and legal principles for the new community.

But above all the traditional narratives describe the course of Muhammad's political activities in Medina, which by the end of his life resulted in the creation of an autonomous political community that we can consider an embryonic state. There are two grand themes of this process. One is the story of Muhammad's consolidation of political power over Medina itself, which posed a number of distinct challenges to him. These included occasional tensions between the *muhajirun* and the *ansar*, stubborn opposition by some Medinese (called *munafiqun*, "hypocrites"), lukewarm supporters who seem to have worked against him behind the scenes, and his troubled relations—at once religious, social, and political—with Medina's Jews. The second grand theme of Muhammad's political life in Medina is the story of his prolonged but ultimately victorious struggle with his former hometown, Mecca, and with those members of Quraysh who had resisted his preaching, led now by Abu Sufyan, the new chief of the clan of Umayya. Clearly related to these two themes is a third, the story of his struggle to win the support of pastoral nomadic groups that resided in the vicinity of Medina and, as time went on, with nomadic and settled communities farther afield. They were to prove a crucial component in his construction of a victorious coalition in western Arabia.

Early in his stay in Yathrib/Medina, Muhammad concluded an agreement (or first in a series of agreements) with various clans of the town. This established mutual obligations between him and the Quraysh Emigrants on the one hand and Medinese Helpers on the other, including the Jewish clans affiliated with the latter, binding them all together as belonging to a single community *(umma)*. We can, following several recent authors, call this agreement the "*umma* document." It has many remarkable features, some of which we will discuss more fully below, but in general it established guidelines for cooperation of the various groups in Medina, including mutual responsibilities in times of war, the payment of blood money and ransoming of prisoners, and above all, the parties' commitment to support one another in times of conflict. (See Appendix A for the full text of the *umma* document.)

Immediately after his arrival in Medina, according to tradition, Muhammad and his followers are said to have marked out a place for collective prayer—the first mosque. (The English word is derived from Arabic *masjid*, "place for prostrations"—pronounced *mesgid* in some Arabic dialects—via Spanish *mezquita* and French *mosquée*.) At first Muhammad and his Believers faced toward Jerusalem in prayer, as the Jews did, but after some time Muhammad ordered that the Believers should conduct prayers facing Mecca instead. This change of *qibla* (prayer orientation), which is mentioned in the revelation (Q. 2:142–145), may reflect Muhammad's deteriorating relations with the town's Jews, who according to traditional sources were for the most part not won over to his movement.

One source of Muhammad's difficulties with Medina's Jews, who controlled one of Medina's main markets, may have been his desire to establish a new market in Medina to assist the Meccan Emigrants. In spite of this, some of the Emigrants, uprooted from their livelihoods and cut off from the bulk of the network of close kinsmen that would have sustained them at home in Mecca, soon found themselves on the verge of destitution, and there was only so much that the Medinese Helpers could do for them. In desperation, Muhammad sent a few Emigrants out as a raiding party, which ambushed a Mecca-bound caravan at the town of Nakhla. The booty gained was welcome, but the Nakhla raid opened a long struggle between Muhammad and Quraysh and aroused much criticism even among some of his supporters, because it was undertaken during one of the sacred months, when by local tradition violence was supposed to be forbidden—a controversy resolved (among Muhammad's followers, at least) only by the arrival of a Qur'anic revelation justifying it (Q. 2:217).

TEXT OF QUR'AN 2 (BAQARA/THE COW): 217

They ask you about fighting in the sacred months. Say: fighting in it is a serious [sin], but barring [people] from the way of God, and disbelief in Him and in the sacred mosque, and expelling its people from it are more serious in God's eyes. Spreading discord is more serious than killing. They will continue to fight you until they turn you from your religion, if they can. Whoever of you turns back from his religion and dies an unbeliever—their works in this world and the next are to no avail, and they are the companions of the fire, they shall be in it eternally.

A larger group of Muhammad's followers attacked a sizable Quraysh caravan again at a place called Badr (year 2/624), overcoming the contingent of Meccans guarding it and taking much booty despite being outnumbered. This victory must have strengthened both the morale and the economic position of Muhammad's followers and may mark the beginning of a virtual blockade of Mecca by Muhammad and the Medinese. It also evidently left Muhammad feeling secure enough to make the first open attack on Jews who opposed him. A Jewish leader who had mocked him was murdered by Muhammad's followers; then the important Jewish clan of Qaynuqa', who ran Medina's main market, were besieged in their quarter and ultimately, after negotiations, expelled from the city, leaving behind most of their property, which was taken over by Muhamad's followers. The Qaynuqa' withdrew to Wadi al-Qura, north of Medina, and then to Syria.

After their defeat at Badr, the Meccans were more determined than ever to settle scores with Muhammad and his followers. After trading small raids with him, they organized an alliance that attacked Medina itself. In this clash, called the battle of Uhud (3/625), Muhammad's forces suffered defeat and loss of life. Muhammad himself was slightly wounded, but the Meccan alliance came apart on the brink of victory and had to withdraw, leaving Muhammad and his followers shaken but still standing. Following Uhud, the two sides again traded raids, particularly to thwart each other's attempts to win support among nomadic tribes living nearby. Some of these raids were successful for the Medinese; others, such as that against a place called Bi'r Ma'una, resulted in casualties. In his efforts to win tribal allies, Muhammad sometimes had to allow a pagan tribe to cling to its ancestral religion, but many of his allies also embraced his message of monotheism. Muhammad took advantage of the withdrawal of the Meccan forces to turn against a second major Jewish group of Medina, the clan of Nadir, reportedly because some of them had been plotting to kill Muhammad. His followers besieged the

Nadir, who eventually capitulated and withdrew, most of them going to the largely Jewish oasis town of Khaybar, about 230 km (143 mi) north of Medina.

The traditional sources place at this time a long-distance expedition by the Believers in Medina to the north Arabian oasis and trade center at Dumat al-Jandal—fully 700 km (435 mi) north of Medina—but whatever its goal was, it seems to have been inconclusive. More important, Quraysh had once again organized an alliance, even larger than the previous one, and launched another offensive, including a contingent of cavalry, against Muhammad and Medina. In this case, Muhammad and his followers reportedly dug a moat or trench to neutralize the Meccans' cavalry, forcing them to try to reduce Medina by siege. The so-called battle of the Trench (5/627) involved some skirmishing, but after several weeks the Meccan alliance once again began to unravel and Quraysh were forced to withdraw. In this case, too, Muhammad turned on his Jewish opponents in the aftermath of a major confrontation with Quraysh; this time the victims were the last large Jewish clan of Medina, Qurayza, who are said to have had treasonous contact with the Meccans during the siege of Medina. Their fortifications in the city were surrounded by Muhammad's followers, and when they surrendered, they agreed that a former ally of theirs in Muhammad's following should pass judgment on them. His judgment, however, was harsh: He ordered that the men should be executed and the women and children enslaved.

Muhammad now dispatched envoys to various tribes around Medina and further afield and organized several especially poorly understood campaigns to destinations north of Medina—to Dumat al-Jandal (again) and to the southern fringes of Syria, where his freedman Zayd ibn Haritha had gone on trade. Then, according to traditional sources, in 6/628, Muhammad and a large following marched unarmed toward Mecca with the avowed intention of doing the *'umra* or "lesser pilgrimage," which involved performing various rites at the Ka'ba; the fact that they set out without weapons was meant to confirm their peaceful intentions. Quraysh, however, were in no mood to allow Muhammad and his followers to come into their town unopposed, given the long hostilities between them and the fact that Muhammad was still blocking the passage of Meccan caravans. They therefore headed him off with a cordon of troops at a place called Hudaybiya, on the borders of the *haram* around Mecca. There, after lengthy negotiations, they concluded an agreement with Muhammad: He would return to Medina without doing the *'umra* and would end his blockade of Mecca in exchange for permission to perform the *'umra* unmolested in the following year. The two parties also agreed to a ten-year truce, during which neither side was to attack the other but each was free to make whatever contacts it wished.

The Hudaybiya agreement seems to mark a turning point in Muhammad's fortunes. Shortly after concluding it, Muhammad organized a large expeditionary force and marched with it on the Jewish oasis of Khaybar; this town had long been a key ally of Mecca in its struggle with Muhammad, but it was not explicitly protected by the agreement. Khaybar capitulated, but its Jewish residents were allowed to remain in order to cultivate the town's extensive groves of palm trees, from the annual crop of which Muhammad now took a share. Muhammad also launched, around this time, numerous raids on still-unsubdued nomadic tribes and sent several raids to the north. One of these, led (again) by Zayd ibn Haritha, penetrated into southern Syria but was repulsed by local Byzantine forces at Mu'ta, in what is today southern Jordan; Zayd was killed in this battle, but most of the force returned intact. A year after the Hudaybiya agreement, Muhammad and his followers made the *'umra* as planned. Around this time, those Believers who had many years before gone to Abyssinia during Muhammad's darkest days in Mecca finally returned to join Muhammad in Medina. Presumably their decision to return reflected Muhammad's and his community's increasingly secure position in Medina.

The Hudaybiya agreement with Quraysh had been for a term of ten years, but only two years later, in 8/630, Muhammad decided that by various actions Quraysh had violated the terms of the agreement. He therefore organized a large armed force (one report says it numbered ten thousand, including perhaps two thousand nomadic allies) and marched on Mecca. Quraysh capitulated without a fight and agreed to embrace Muhammad's message of monotheism; only a handful of Muhammad's bitterest opponents in Mecca were executed, and indeed many Meccan leaders were given important positions in Muhammad's entourage, a measure that dismayed some of his early supporters, both Emigrants and Helpers. Once inside Mecca, Muhammad set about removing from the confines of the Ka'ba shrine its pagan idols, purifying it for its future role as a focus of monotheist worship. In the view of Muslim tradition, the Ka'ba had originally been built by Abraham as a shrine to the one God, so Muhammad was by these actions merely rededicating it to its original monotheistic purpose.

The conquest (really occupation) of Mecca was perhaps the crowning event of Muhammad's political career. But, although his position was now incomparably stronger, he still faced some opposition. The tribe of Thaqif, which controlled the third major town of western Arabia, Ta'if, had long had close ties to Mecca and Quraysh and continued to reject Muhammad's advances. Moreover, Thaqif had as allies some powerful nomadic tribes in their vicinity, such as Hawazin, who were particularly threatening. Shortly after taking Mecca, therefore, Muhammad marched his forces against Thaqif and their Hawazin allies and defeated them at the battle of Hunayn, after which he surrounded Ta'if itself, which eventually capitulated.

Muhammad was now unquestionably the dominant political figure in western Arabia, and in the year or so after Mecca and Ta'if fell, he received delegations from numerous tribal groups in Arabia, both settled and nomadic, who hastened to tender their allegiance to him. He also organized at this time another major military expedition to the far north, this time directed against the town of Tabuk; its exact goals remain unclear, but it showed Muhammad's continued interest in the north. Muhammad astutely used these late campaigns as a way to secure the loyalty of those powerful leaders of Quraysh who had formerly been his opponents, such as their former leader Abu Sufyan, and his sons Mu'awiya and Yazid, by giving them important commands or extra shares of booty. Moreover, during these campaigns, he increasingly insisted that his able-bodied followers take active part in military service. At this time, too, Muhammad's growing political and military strength enabled him to dispense with the policy of making alliances with pagan tribes— something that had been necessary earlier in order to secure as many allies as possible in his struggle with Mecca. Now he announced a new policy of noncooperation with polytheists; they were henceforth to be attacked and forced to recognize God's oneness or to fight. (See Q. 9:1–16.)

At the end of 10/March 632, Muhammad is said to have performed the *hajj*, or major pilgrimage, to the environs of Mecca. Shortly after his return to Medina, he fell ill and, after several days, died at home, his head cradled in the lap of his favorite wife, 'A'isha (11/632). Following local custom, his body was interred beneath the floor of his house.

The Problem of Sources

This brief sketch of the events of Muhammad's life, although in many ways plausible (and probably in some respects accurate), is nevertheless vexing to the historian. The problem is that this detailed picture of Muhammad's career is drawn not from documents or even stories dating from Muhammad's time, but from literary sources that were compiled many years—sometimes centuries—

later. The fact that these sources are so much later, and shaped with very specific objectives in mind, means that they often do not tell us many things about which we would like to know more; for example, the position of women in society is often reported only incidentally. There is also reason to suspect that some—perhaps many—of the incidents related in these sources are not reliable accounts of things that actually happened but rather are legends created by later generations of Muslims to affirm Muhammad's status as prophet, to help establish precedents shaping the later Muslim community's ritual, social, or legal practices, or simply to fill out poorly known chapters in the life of their founder, about whom, understandably, later Muslims increasingly wished to know everything.

The vast ocean of traditional accounts from which the preceding brief sketch of Muhammad's life is distilled contains so many contradictions and so much dubious storytelling that many historians have become reluctant to accept any of it at face value. There are, for example, an abundance of miracle stories and other reports that seem obviously to belong to the realm of legend, such as an episode similar to the "feeding the multitudes" story in Christian legends about Jesus. The chronology of this traditional material about Muhammad, moreover, is not only vague and confused, but also bears telltale signs of having been shaped by a concern for numerological symbolism. For example, all the major events of Muhammad's life are said to have occurred on the same date and day of the week (Monday, 12 Rabi' al-awwal) in different years. Further, some episodes that are crucial to the traditional biography of Muhammad look suspiciously like efforts to create a historicizing gloss to particular verses of the Qur'an; some have suggested, for example, that the reports of the raid on Nakhla were generated as exegesis of Q. 2:217 (see "Text of Qur'an 2" Sidebar, p. 45). Other elements of his life story may have been generated to make his biography conform to contemporary expectations of what a true prophet would do (for instance, his orphanhood, paralleling that of Moses, or his rejection by and struggle against his own people, the tribe of Quraysh).

Even if we accept the basic outlines of Muhammad's life as portrayed in traditional accounts, the historian is faced with many stubborn questions that the sources leave unaddressed. (For example, why were the pagans of Medina so readily won over to Muhammad's message, while the Quraysh of Mecca resisted it so bitterly? What exactly was Muhammad's original status in Medina? What exactly was his relationship to the Jews of Medina?) Unfortunately, we have no original documents that might confirm unequivocally any of the traditional biography—no original copies of letters to or from or about Muhammad by his contemporaries, no inscriptions from his day written by members of his community, and so on.

These well-founded concerns about the limitations of the traditional Muslim accounts of Muhammad's life have caused some scholars to conclude that everything in these accounts is to be rejected. This, however, is surely going too far and in its way is just as uncritical an approach as unquestioning acceptance of everything in the traditional accounts. The truth must lie somewhere in between; and some recent work has begun to show that despite the vexing problems they pose, the traditional narratives do seem to contain some very early material about the life of Muhammad. A tolerably accurate and plausible account of the main events of Muhammad's life may someday be possible, when scholars learn more about how to sift the mass of traditional materials more effectively. However, such critical studies are just getting underway today, and for the present it remains prudent to utilize the traditional narratives sparingly and with caution.

Our situation as historians interested in Muhammad's life and the nature of his message is far from hopeless, however. A few seventh-century non-Muslim sources, from a slightly later time than that of

Muhammad himself but much earlier than any of the traditional Muslim compilations, provide testimony that—although not strictly documentary in character—appears to be essentially reliable. Although these sources are few and provide very limited information, they are nonetheless invaluable. For example, an early Syriac source by the Christian writer Thomas the Presbyter, dated to around 640—that is, just a few years after Muhammad's death—provides the earliest mention of Muhammad and informs us that his followers made a raid around Gaza. This, at least, enables the historian to feel more confident that Muhammad is not completely a fiction of later pious imagination, as some have implied; we know that someone named Muhammad did exist, and that he led some kind of movement. And this fact, in turn, gives us greater confidence that further information in the massive body of traditional Muslim materials may also be rooted in historical fact. The difficulty is in deciding what is, and what is not, factual. (See the "Text of Thomas the Presbyter" sidebar in Chapter 3.)

Moreover, the most important source of information about the early community of Believers is still to be discussed: the text of the Qur'an itself, Islam's holy book. For Believing Muslims, the Qur'an is, of course, a transcript of God's word as revealed to Muhammad. Each of its 114 separate, named *suras* (chapters), containing altogether thousands of *ayas* (verses—literally, "signs" of God's presence) is, for the Believer, an utterance of eternal value that exists outside the framework of normal, mundane, historical time. Traditional Muslim exegesis developed an elaborate chronology for the Qur'an, connecting the revelation of each verse to a particular episode in the life of Muhammad—the so-called "occasions of revelation" literature *(asbab al-nuzul)*. This literature, which was closely followed by traditional Western scholarship on the Qur'an, generally divided the text into verses considered, on grounds of both style and content, to hail from either the early Meccan, intermediate Meccan, late Meccan, or Medinese phases of Muhammad's career. Similarly, Muslim tradition preserves accounts of how the revelation came to take the form of a written book. According to this view, the various revelations that were first burned into the memory of their prophet were memorized by his followers; some passages were then written out by different people in the early community; finally, about twenty years after Muhammad's death, the scattered written and unwritten parts of the revelation were collected by an editorial committee and compiled in definitive written form.

The historian who questions the traditional narratives of Muhammad's life, however, is also likely to have difficulty accepting at face value this account of how the Qur'an text coalesced; but if we reject this account, we are left unsure of just what kind of text the Qur'an is and where it came from. Starting from this point, revisionist scholars using literary-critical approaches to the text have in recent years offered alternative theories on the origins and nature of the Qur'an as we now have it. One has suggested that the Qur'an originated as pre-Islamic strophic hymns of Arabian Christian communities, which Muhammad adapted to form the Qur'an. Equally radical is the "late origins" hypothesis first circulated the late 1970s. According to this view, the Qur'an, far from being a product of western Arabia in the early seventh century C.E., actually crystallized slowly within the Muslim community over a period of two hundred years or more and mostly outside of Arabia, perhaps mainly in Iraq. In the opinion of this theory's advocates, the traditional story of the Qur'an's origins as revelations to Muhammad is merely a pious back-projection made by Muslims of later times who wished to root their beliefs and the existence of their community in the religious experience of an earlier prophetic figure.

If true, the "late origins" hypothesis of the Qur'an, in particular, would have devastating implications for the historian interested in reconstructing Muhammad's life or the beliefs of the early community. But the "late origins" hypothesis fails to explain many features of the Qur'an text, analysis of which suggests that in fact the Qur'an

An Early Qur'an leaf, dated to the first century AH, from San'a', Yemen, covering Q. 7:37–44. Characteristic of its early date are the vertical strokes leaning to the right, the diacritical dots in a row, and many letterforms, which have more in common with monumental inscriptions than later cursive Arabic.

did coalesce very early in the history of Muhammad's community—within no more than three decades of Muhammad's death. For example, meticulous study of the text by generations of scholars has failed to turn up any plausible hint of anachronistic references to important events in the life of the later community, which would almost certainly be there had the text crystallized later than the early seventh century c.e. Moreover, some of the Qur'an's vocabulary suggests that the text, or significant parts of it, hailed from western Arabia. So we seem, after all, to be dealing with a Qur'an that is the product of the earliest stages in the life of the community in western Arabia.

This is not to say that we are all the way back to accepting the traditional view of the Qur'an's origins. Although the Qur'an itself claims to be in a "clear Arabic tongue," many passages in it remain far from clear, even in the most basic sense of knowing what the words might have meant in their original context, whatever it was. It may be that the Qur'an includes passages of older texts that have been revised and reused. The markedly different style and content of diverse parts of the Qur'an may be evidence that the text as we now have it is a composite of originally separate texts hailing from different communities of Believers in Arabia. Some recent studies suggest that the Qur'an text is not only aware of, but even in some ways reacting to, the theological debates of Syriac-speaking Christian communities of the Near East. Whether further work on the text will vindicate the close connection of particular passages in the Qur'an with specific episodes in Muhammad's life, as elaborated by both traditional Muslim and traditional Western scholarship, still remains to be seen. What we can say is that the Qur'an text is demonstrably early.

The Character of the Early Believers' Movement

The fact that the Qur'an text dates to the earliest phase of the movement inaugurated by Muhammad means that the historian can use it to gain some insight into the beliefs and values of this early community. Later literary sources may then be used, with caution, to elaborate on what these earliest beliefs may have been, but the problem of interpolation and idealization in those later sources makes even their "supporting" role often quite uncertain. It is best, therefore, to stick very closely to what the Qur'an itself says for information.

Basic Beliefs

What, then, does the Qur'an tell us about Muhammad and his early followers? To start, we notice that the Qur'an addresses overwhelmingly people whom it calls "Believers" *(mu'minun)*. In this, it differs from the traditional Muslim narratives and from modern scholarly practice, both of which routinely refer to Muhammad and his followers mainly as "Muslims" *(muslimun,* literally, "those who submit") and refer to his movement as "Islam." This later usage is, however, misleading when applied to the beginnings of the community as reflected in the Qur'an. It is of course true that the words *islam* and *muslim* are found in the Qur'an, and it is also true that these words are sometimes applied in the text to Muhammad and his followers. But those instances are dwarfed in number by cases in which Muhammad and his followers are referred to as *mu'minun,* "Believers"—which occurs almost a thousand times, compared with fewer than seventy-five instances of *muslim,* and so on. Later Muslim tradition, beginning about a century after Muhammad's time, came to emphasize the identity of Muhammad's followers as Muslims and attempted to neutralize the importance of the many passages in which they are called Believers by portraying the two terms as synonymous and interchangeable. But a number of Qur'anic passages make it clear that the words *mu'min* and *muslim,* although evidently related and sometimes applied to one and the same person, cannot be synonyms. For example, Q. 49:14 states, "The bedouins say: 'We Believe' *(aman-na).* Say [to them]: 'You do not Believe; but rather say, "we submit" *(aslam-na)*, for Belief has not yet entered your hearts.'" In this passage, Belief obviously means something different (and better) than "submission" *(islam)*; and so we cannot simply equate the Believer with the Muslim, though some Muslims may qualify as Believers. The Qur'an's frequent appeal to the Believers, then— usually in phrases such as "O you who Believe . . ."—forces us to conclude that Muhammad and his early followers thought of themselves above all as being a *community of Believers*, rather than one of Muslims, and referred to themselves as Believers. Moreover, the notion that they thought of themselves as Believers is corroborated by some very early documentary evidence dating from several decades after Muhammad's death. For this reason, I will break with standard scholarly practice and also refer, in these pages, to Muhammad and his early followers as "the community of Believers," or "the Believers' movement." (See "Ecumenism," later in this chapter, for a discussion of the exact early meaning of *muslim*.) For a short while, Muhammad may have called his movement "Hanifism" *(hanifiyya)*, presumably in reference to a vague pre-Islamic monotheism, but this usage does not seem to have become widespread.

If Muhammad and his followers thought of themselves first and foremost as Believers, in what did they believe? Above all, Believers were enjoined to recognize the oneness of God. (*Allah* is simply the Arabic word for "God.") The Qur'an tirelessly preaches the message of strict monotheism, exhorting its hearers to be ever mindful of God and obedient to His will. It rails against the sin of polytheism (*shirk*, literally "associating" something with God)—which, Muslim tradition tells us, was the dominant religious outlook in Mecca when Muhammad grew up there. From the Qur'an's or the Believers' perspective, failing to acknowledge the oneness of God, who created all things and gave us life, is the ultimate ingratitude and the essence of unbelief *(kufr)*. But the Qur'an's strict monotheism also condemns the Christian doctrine of the Trinity as being incompatible with the idea of God's absolute unity: "Those who say that God is the third of three, disbelieve; there is no god but the one God . . ." (Q. 5:73).

As we have seen, the idea of monotheism was already well established throughout the Near East, including in Arabia, in Muhammad's day, and it has been plausibly suggested that the Qur'an's frequent invective against "polytheists" may actually be directed at trinitarian Christians and anyone else whom Muhammad considered only lukewarm monotheists. Be that as it may, the Qur'an makes it clear that the most basic requirement for the Believers was uncompromising acknowledgement of God's oneness. And, as we shall see, it was from this most fundamental concept, the idea of God's essential unity, that most other elements of true Belief flowed.

Also important to the Believers was belief in the Last Day or Day of Judgment *(yawm al-din).* Just as God was the creator of the world and of everything in it, and the giver of life, so too will He decree when it will all end—the physical world as we know it, time, everything. The Qur'an provides considerable detail on the Last Day: how it will come on us suddenly and without warning; how just before it the natural world will be in upheaval—mountains flowing like water, the heavens torn open, stars falling; how the dead from all past ages will be brought to life and raised from their graves; how all mankind will be brought before God to face final Judgment; and how we will then all be taken either to a paradise full of delights and ease, or to a hell full of torment and suffering, for eternity. But the Qur'an does not merely describe the coming Judgment for us—above all, it warns us of its approach, enjoining us to prepare ourselves for it by believing truly in God and by living righteously.

From the Qur'an we can also deduce that the Believers accepted the ideas of revelation and prophecy. The Qur'an makes clear that God has revealed His eternal Word to mankind many times, through the intermediacy of a series of messengers (singular, *rasul*) or prophets (singular, *nabi*). (The technical distinction between *rasul* and *nabi* will be discussed more fully later in this chapter.) The Qur'an offers many stories about, and lessons drawn from, the lives of these messengers and prophets. These include many figures familiar from the Old and New Testament—Adam, Noah, Job, Moses, Abraham, Lot, Zachariah, Jesus, and others—as well as a few otherwise unknown Arabian prophets (Hud, Salih) and, of course, Muhammad himself, to whom the Qur'an was revealed. Indeed, the Qur'an, as the most recent revelation of God's word, obviously supercedes earlier revelations, which were said to have become garbled over time. And the Believers are repeatedly enjoined to refer matters "to God and His messenger" Muhammad. Part of this complex of ideas, too, is the notion of "the book," referring in some cases to the heavenly archetype of God's word, of which the Qur'an is merely an exact transcript, and in other cases apparently to the Qur'an itself or to other, earlier scriptures.

TEXT OF QUR'AN 7 (A'RAF/THE HEIGHTS): 11–18

We created you and gave you form, then we said to the angels: "Prostrate yourselves to Adam!" So they prostrated themselves, except for Iblis—he was not among those who prostrated./He [God] said, "What prevented you from prostrating yourself when I ordered you [to do so]?" He replied, "I am better than he; you created me of fire, but you created him of clay."/[God] said, "Then descend from it [the garden]; you are not entitled to be arrogant in it. Get out, you are surely among the humiliated."/He [Iblis] said, "Grant me a reprieve until the day they are resurrected."/[God] said, "You are reprieved."/[Iblis] said, "Indeed, I shall lie in wait for them on your straight path because you tempted me./Then I will come at them from before them and from behind them and from their right and their left; you will not find most of them grateful [to you]."/[God] said, "Get out of it, despised and banished! Verily, I will fill hell with all of those who follow you."

Believers are also enjoined to believe in God's angels—creatures that assist God in various ways, most importantly by carrying God's word to His prophets at the moment of revelation, by serving as "orderlies" during the Last Judgment, and in various ways intervening in mundane affairs when it is God's will that they do so. Satan (also called Iblis) is, in Qur'anic doctrine, merely a fallen angel who always accompanies man and tries to seduce him into sin (Q. 7: 11–22).

Piety and Ritual

Such, then, were the basic concepts that shaped the Believers' movement: one God, the Last Judgment, God's messengers, the book, and the angels. But the Qur'an makes it clear that to be a true Believer mere intellectual acceptance of these ideas was not sufficient; one also had to live piously. According to the Qur'an, our status as creatures of God demands pious obedience to His word; we should constantly remember God and humble ourselves before Him in prayer. But we should also behave humbly toward other people, who are equally God's creatures; the Qur'an's warnings against self-importance *(takabur)* and its injunctions to help the less fortunate are an important part of its vision of piety, one that projects a strongly egalitarian message that we see reflected in various rituals. Moreover, the Believers seem to have felt that they lived in a sinful age and feared that their salvation would be at stake unless they lived a more righteous life.

What, then, was the piety of the Believers' movement like? First and foremost, the Qur'an makes clear that Believers must engage in regular prayer. This includes both informal prayers requesting God's assistance or invoking His favor (called *duʿā'*), and the more formalized ritual prayer *(salat)*, performed at particular times of the day and in a particular way, and preferably in the company of other Believers who, whatever their social station, stood shoulder to shoulder

TEXT OF QUR'AN 11 (HUD/THE PROPHET HUD): 114

And perform ritual prayer at the two ends of the day, and part of the night; indeed, good deeds cancel evil deeds. That is a reminder for those who remember.

to submit themselves as equals before God. References to prayer, injunctions to perform it faithfully, and instructions on when and how to do it are so frequent in the Qur'an, that, as one observer has put it, "prayer is . . . in the Qur'anic vision of the world, the fundamental fabric of religious behaviour."

The Qur'an specifically enjoins prayer before dawn, before sunset, during the night, and during the day (see, for example, Q. 11:114, 17:78–79, 20:130, and 76:25–26). One reference to the "middle prayer" (Q. 2:238) suggests that three daily prayers may have been the standard pattern among the Believers at some point in Muhammad's life, but the Qur'an's references to times when prayer should be performed use varied vocabulary and are not clear in their temporal implications and may reflect different moments in an evolving situation. The systematization of ritual prayers into five clearly defined times—a systematization that occurred in the century after Muhammad's death—does not seem yet to have taken place (at least the Qur'an provides no compelling evidence for such systematization), but the early Believers were in general expected to remain mindful of God throughout the day. Regardless of how many prayers the early Believers performed daily, however, we can glean what it was like from the vocabulary the Qur'an uses in association with ritual prayer. It clearly involved standing, bowing, prostrating oneself, sitting, and the mention of God's name, although the exact mechanics and sequence of the ritual cannot be recovered from the Qur'an alone. Furthermore, the Qur'an refers to the Believers being called to ritual prayer beforehand and to the need for them to perform ablutions with water before praying. It is, then, absolutely clear that the Believers of Muhammad's day took part in regular ritual prayers that bore strong similarities to later "classical Islamic" prayer, even if the full details of earliest ritual practice remain unclear today.

Another practice that the Qur'an describes as vital for Believers is charity toward the less fortunate in life—another way of bringing home the idea that all humans are fundamentally equal and that whatever differences of fortune we may enjoy are only contingent. This is expressed unequivocally in many Qur'anic passages: ". . . but the righteous person is whoever Believes in God and the Last Day, in the angels and the book and the prophets; who gives [his] wealth, despite [his] love for it, to relatives, orphans, the destitute, the traveler, the beggar, and for [the manumission of?] slaves; and who performs the ritual prayer and pays the *zakat* . . ." (Q. 2:177).

Later Muslim tradition refers to such charity under the terms *zakat* or *sadaqa*, usually rendered "almsgiving"; these two terms are closely associated with prayer in numerous Qur'anic passages, and later Muslim tradition considers them, like prayer, to be one of the "pillars of the faith" that define a Believer. Recent research suggests, however, that the original Qur'anic meaning of *zakat* and *sadaqa* was not almsgiving, but rather a fine or payment made by someone who was guilty of some kind of sin, in exchange for which Muhammad would pray in order that they might be purified of their sin and that their other affairs might prosper. Indeed, even in the verse just cited, one notes that payment of *zakat* is mentioned *after* prayer, suggesting that it was something different than the giving of wealth to the poor (what we usually mean by almsgiving), which is treated in the verse *before* mention of prayer. This understanding of *zakat* or *sadaqa* as a payment for atonement or purification of sins is clearest in the following verses: "Others have confessed their sins . . . /Take from their property *sadaqa* to cleanse them, and purify [*tuzakki*] them thereby, and pray for them, indeed your prayer is a consolation to them. God is all-hearing, all-knowing" (Q. 9:102–103; the verb "to purify" is from the same Arabic root as *zakat*. The fact that Believers were sometimes required to make such purification payments, however, underscores how the community was, in principle, focused on maintaining its inner purity, on being as much as possible a community that lived strictly in righteousness, so as to set themselves apart from the sinful world around them and thus to attain salvation in the afterlife. As time went on, it seems that membership criteria became more relaxed, so that anyone who uttered the basic statement of faith would be included, but in doing so they at least theoretically made themselves subject to high standards of conduct.

The Believers were also required, if they were physically able, to fast during daytime hours in the ninth month of the Muslim calendar, Ramadan, and at other times as expiation for sins (Q. 2:183–185). Fasting, particularly at *'ashura'* (the tenth day of the first month), had of course long been practiced by Jews and Christians in the Near East; it may also have been current among adherents of pagan cults in Arabia and was a practice that continued well into Islamic times. It is not clear, however, in what measure this earlier fasting tradition contributed to the Believers' practices. However, in this season the Ramadan fast kept all Believers especially mindful of God, at least in theory, and was a way of binding the Believers together as a community through collective ritual activity. Eventually, the Ramadan fast came to be emphasized and the *'ashura'* fast was relegated to voluntary status.

The Qur'an also makes reference to pilgrimage rituals that the Believers are enjoined to perform. These include both the *'umra* or "lesser pilgrimage," performed about the Ka'ba in Mecca, and the *hajj* or "greater pilgrimage," performed on specified days in the month of Dhu l-hijja in 'Arafat and adjacent places a few miles from Mecca (Q. 2:196–200, 5:94–97.) Pilgrimage to the Ka'ba, including circumambulation and other rituals, had been practiced at the Ka'ba

> ### TEXT OF QUR'AN 2 (BAQARA/THE COW): 183–185
>
> O you who Believe, fasting is prescribed for you, as it was for those who came before you, that you should be God-fearing [184]. For a specified number of days. But whoever of you is sick, or traveling, [prescribed are] a number of other days. And upon those who are able to do it [but do not], redemption is feeding a poor person; but whoever does a good deed of his own accord, that is better for him, and that you fast is better for you, if you could know. [185] The month of Ramadan, in which the Qur'an was sent down as guidance to the people, and clear evidence of the guidance and the commandments: Whoever of you is present in the month shall fast for it, but whoever is sick or traveling [shall fast] a number of other days. God wishes to make it easy for you, he does not wish to make it difficult. So complete the number [of days] and magnify God because He guided you; perhaps you may be thankful.

in pre-Islamic times, but forms of pilgrimage were also a well-established practice in late antique Judaism and Christianity, and these may also have formed part of the background against which we should view the pilgrimage practices of the early Believers. Yet it seems likely that the pilgrimage was enjoined as a duty on the Believers only in the later years of Muhammad's career in Medina, for the simple reason that Muhammad and his followers in Medina did not have access to Mecca as long as the two towns were locked in open hostilities. It is noteworthy that the *suras* of the Qur'an that are generally dated to the Meccan phase of Muhammad's career make no mention of pilgrimage. We see Muhmmad forcing the issue of pilgrimage, however, in the Hudaybiya expedition of 6/628, when he and a large group of followers marched, en masse but unarmed, toward Mecca intending to perform the pilgrimage. The Believers were turned back by Quraysh but not before concluding an agreement that gave them permission to make a pilgrimage to Mecca in the following year. Of course, the pre-Islamic pilgrimage rites at the Ka'ba, which were pagan rituals, had to be reinterpreted in light of the Believers' monotheistic views. Muslim tradition claims that the Ka'ba rites were originally established by Abraham, the first monotheist, but subsequently became corrupted by pagan practices. The Believers' pilgrimage was thus portrayed as the restoration of an originally monotheistic practice. The story of Muhammad's occupation of Mecca in 8/630, as we have seen, relates how Muhammad purified the Ka'ba enclosure of the pagan idols that had been introduced into it.

The likelihood that the Believers saw themselves as living in a world beset with sin, from which they wished to differentiate themselves, also finds expression in other, more routine practices that are singled out in the Qur'an for emulation or prohibition. Believers are urged to dress modestly (Q. 24:30–31)—the implication that this was in contrast to those around them is obvious—and are forbidden from eating pork, carrion, and blood (Q. 2:173). They are instructed not to come to prayers while intoxicated (Q. 4:43). General moral guidelines are also frequently encountered. For example, Q. 60:12 prohibits, in a few lines, a whole series of gravely sinful practices that were apparently all too common: associating something with God (shirk), theft, adultery, infanticide, bearing false witness, and disobeying the prophet. Passages such as these suggest, again, that the Believers were concerned with what they saw as the rampant sinfulness of the world around them and wished to live by a higher standard in their own behavior.

The piety that is enjoined on Believers by the Qur'an, then, required them constantly to demonstrate their mindfulness of God: through regular prayer, the doing of good works, proper deportment, and so on. The Qur'an's emphasis on the importance of righteous

> ### TEXT OF QUR'AN 60 (MUMTAHANA/THE WOMAN EXAMINED): 12
>
> O prophet, when Believing women come to you, pledging that they will not associate anything with God, nor steal, nor commit adultery, nor kill their children, nor bring slanders they have fabricated out of thin air [lit. "between their hands and feet"], nor disobey you in any customary thing, then accept what they pledge and ask God to forgive them, for God is forgiving, merciful.

behavior is so great that we are fully justified in characterizing the Believers' movement as being not only a strictly monotheistic movement, but also a strictly pietistic one. In this respect, the Believers' movement can be seen as a continuation of the pietistic tendency found in Near Eastern religions in the late antique period. Although it makes sense to view the Believers' movement in this general context, it is of course true that the pietism of the Believers' movement, as we reconstruct it from the Qur'an, represents a unique manifestation of this broad trend toward piety, tailored to the Arabian cultural environment. Even though the Believers perceived the world around them to be full of iniquity, the pietism of their movement lacks, at least as a central element, the kind of ascetic orientation that was so prominent in the late antique Christian tradition, especially in Syria and Egypt. True, modesty and humility are enjoined as part of the Qur'an's egalitarian ethos, and wealth is occasionally deemed a snare for the unwary. One passage even hints that children and family may be distractions from the duty of devoting one's thoughts to God: "wealth and sons are the ornaments of the nearer life; but enduring works of righteousness are better before your Lord . . ." (Q. 18:46). But these sentiments are more than counterbalanced by many verses noting that the good things of this life are the result of God's grace

TEXT OF QUR'AN 16 (NAHL/THE BEE): 114–115

So eat of that which God has provided you with as lawful and good, and be thankful for God's bounty, if you serve Him [115]. He has forbidden to you only carrion, and blood, and flesh of the pig, and that which has been consecrated to other than God; but whoever is forced [to eat of these] unwillingly and without going to excess, indeed God is forgiving and merciful.

and are to be accepted as favors he bestows on the Believers: "O you who Believe, do not forbid the good things that God has allowed you, nor go to extremes, for God does not love those who go to extremes" (Q. 5:87). It seems, then, that the iniquity the Believers perceived around them was a purely human or social phenomenon, which in no way implied that the blessings of the natural world were anything other than that—God's blessings. Enjoyment of them, and of many of the joys of society as well, are permissible to Believers, as long as they are enjoyed in moderation—at least, they are not prohibited. Marriage and the raising of children are assumed to be the norm and are not generally presented as incompatible with a righteous life. In short, the Believers' piety is a piety that is meant to function in, and to be part of, the world and of everyday life—not divorced from it in ascetic denial, as in the late antique Christian tradition. In this respect, the Believers' piety resembled more closely the commonsense notions of righteousness that were found in late antique Judaism.

Ecumenism

The Qur'anic evidence suggests that the early Believers' movement was centered on the ideas of monotheism, preparing for the Last Day, belief in prophecy and revealed scripture, and observance of righteous behavior, including frequent prayer, expiation for sins committed, periodic fasting, and a charitable and humble demeanor toward others. All of these ideas and practices were quite well known in the Near East by the seventh century, although of course in the Qur'an they found a unique formulation (and one in a new literary idiom, Arabic). The earliest Believers thought of themselves as constituting a separate group or community of righteous, God-fearing monotheists, separate in their strict observance of righteousness from those around them—whether polytheists or imperfectly rigorous, or sinful, monotheists—who did not conform to their strict code.

On the other hand, there is no reason to think that the Believers viewed themselves as constituting a new or separate religious confession (for which the Qur'anic term seems to be *milla,* Q. 2:120). Indeed, some passages make it clear that Muhammad's message was the same as that brought by earlier apostles: "Say: I am no innovator among the apostles; and I do not know what will become of me or of you. I merely follow what is revealed to me; I am only a clear warner" (Q. 46:9). At this early stage in the history of the Believers' movement, then, it seems that Jews or Christians who were sufficiently pious could, if they wished, have participated in it because they recognized God's oneness already. Or, to put it the other way around, some of the early Believers were Christians or Jews—although surely not all were. The reason for this "confessionally open" or ecumenical quality was simply that the basic ideas of the Believers and their insistence on observance of strict piety were in no way antithetical to the beliefs and practices of some Christians and Jews. Indeed, the Qur'an itself sometimes notes a certain parallelism between the Believers and the established monotheistic faiths (often lumped together by the Qur'an in the term "people of the book," *ahl al-kitab;* Q. 48:29).

Closer examination of the Qur'an reveals a number of passages indicating that some Christians and Jews could belong to the Believers' movement—not simply by virtue of their being Christians or Jews, but because they were inclined to righteousness. For example, Q. 3:199 states, "There are among the people of the book those who Believe in God and what was sent down to you and was sent down to them . . ." Other verses, such as Q. 3:113–116, lay this out in greater detail. These passages and other like them suggest that some peoples of the book—Christians and Jews—were considered Believers. The line separating Believers from unbelievers did not, then, coincide simply with the boundaries of the peoples of the book. Rather, it cut across those communities, depending on their commitment to God and to observance of His law, so that some of them were to be considered Believers, while others were not.

Believers, then, whatever religious confession they may have belonged to—whether (non-trinitarian) Christians, Jews, or what we might call "Qur'anic monotheists," recent converts from paganism—were expected to live strictly by the law that God had revealed to their communities. Jews should obey the laws of the Torah; Christians those of the Gospels; and those who were not already members

---

TEXT OF QUR'AN 3 (AL 'IMRAN/THE FAMILY OF 'IMRAN): 113–116

. . . Among the people of the book are an upright company; they recite God's verses through the night while prostrating themselves. They Believe in God and the Last Day, and enjoin kindliness and forbid abominations, and hasten to do good things. These are among the righteous ones. For no good thing that they do will be passed over without thanks; for God knows the pious. But those who disbelieve, neither their wealth nor their children will be of any help to them against God. Those are the companions of hellfire; they shall be in it forever.

of one of the preexisting monotheist communities should obey the injunctions of the Qur'an. The general term for these new Qur'anic monotheists was *muslim*, but here we must pause for a moment to discuss in more detail the exact meaning of the words *muslim* and *islam* in the Qur'an.

The notion that the early community of Believers of Muhammad's day included pious Christians and Jews is, of course, very different from what the traditional Muslim sources of later times tell us. In later Islamic tradition, right down to the present, "Islam" refers to a particular religion, distinct from Christianity, Judaism, and others, and "Muslim" refers to an adherent of this religion. These terms are indeed derived from the Qur'an, but their meaning, as used by later tradition, has undergone a subtle change. When, for example, one reads the Qur'anic verse "Abraham was neither a Jew nor a Christian, rather he was a *muslim hanif* and not one of the *mushrikun*" (Q. 3:67; the Arabic text reads *hanifan musliman*), it becomes clear that *muslim* in the Qur'an must mean something other than what later (and present) usage means by "Muslim": for one thing, *muslim* in the sentence is used as an adjective modifying the noun *hanif* (the meaning of which itself remains in dispute—perhaps a pre-Islamic term for "monotheist"). The basic sense of *muslim* is "one who submits" to God or "one who obeys" God's injunctions and will for mankind, and of course also recognizes God's oneness. In other words, *muslim* in Qur'anic usage means, essentially, a committed monotheist, and *islam* means committed monotheism in the sense of submitting oneself to God's will. This is why Abraham can be considered, in this Qur'anic verse, a *hanif muslim*, a "committed, monotheistic *hanif*." As used in the Qur'an, then, *islam* and *muslim* do not yet have the sense of confessional distinctness we now associate with "Islam" and "Muslim"; they meant something broader and more inclusive and were sometimes even applied to some Christians and Jews, who were, after all, also monotheists (Q. 3:52, 3:83, and 29:46). But, we can readily

TEXT OF QUR'AN 29 ('ANKABUT/THE SPIDER): 46

Do not debate with the people of the book except by what is best (i.e., with courtesy?)—except those of them who do evil. Say, "We believe in what was revealed to us and revealed to you. Our God and your God is one, and to him we submit."

understand how these Qur'anic words, *islam* and *muslim*, could subsequently have acquired their more restrictive, confessional meanings as a new faith distinct from Christianity and Judaism. Those Believers who were Christians or Jews could always be identified as such, but a Believer who had formerly been a polytheist could no longer be called *mushrik*, so the only term that was applicable to her, once she had embraced monotheism and observed Qur'anic law, was *muslim*. And, with time, the term *muslim* came to be used exclusively for these "new monotheist" Believers who followed Qur'anic law.

Besides the Qur'an, there is additional evidence for the idea that some Jews, at least, were members of Muhammad's community. Although we have until now eschewed reliance on the traditional Muslim sources, which are later than the Qur'anic era, the agreement between Muhammad and the people of Yathrib described earlier, known as the *umma* document, seems to be of virtually documentary quality. Although preserved only in collections of later date, its text is so different in content and style from everything else in those collections, and so evidently archaic in character, that all students of early Islam, even the most skeptical, accept it as authentic and of virtually documentary value.

One passage in the *umma* document reads, "The Jews of the tribe of 'Awf are a people [*umma*] with the Believers; the Jews have their *din* [law?] and the *muslimun* have their *din*. [This applies to] their clients [*mawali*] and to themselves, excepting anyone who acts wrong-fully and acts treacherously, for he only slays himself and the people of his house" [Serjeant transl. Para C2a, with modifications]. In other words, this and many other passages in the *umma* document seem clearly to confirm the idea that some of Medina's Jews made an agreement with Muhammad in which they were recognized as being part of the *umma* or community of Believers. The term *muslim* in this passage also probably refers to those Believers who followed Qur'anic law (rather than the Jews, who as the document says, had their own law.)

The *umma* document raises many perplexing questions in view of the traditional sources' description of Muhammad's relations with the Jews of Medina. For example, whereas the traditional sources describe in great detail his conflicts with the three main Jewish clans of Medina—the Qaynuqa', Nadir, and Qurayza—none of these clans is even mentioned in the *umma* document. How are we to interpret their omission from the document? Is the *umma* document's silence on them evidence that the document was only drawn up late in Muhammad's life, after these three Jew-ish tribes had already been vanquished? Or were there once clauses (or other documents) that were simply lost or that were dropped as irrelevant after these tribes were no longer present in Medina? Or should we interpret this silence as evidence that the stories about Muhammad's clashes with the Jews of Medina are greatly exagger-ated (or perhaps invented completely) by later Muslim tradition— perhaps as part of the project of depicting Muhammad as a true prophet, which involved overcoming the stubborn resistance of those around him? These and many other questions remain to be resolved by future scholarship. We can note here, however, that later Muslim tradition mentions a number of Believers of Muham-mad's day who were of Jewish origin—that is, they are described as "converts" from Judaism to Islam. We may wish to ask whether in fact these figures were converts; might they have been simply Jews who, without renouncing their Judaism, joined the Believers' movement, and so were subsequently dubbed "converts" by later traditionalists for whom the categories of Believer and Jew had in the meantime become mutually exclusive?

Recognizing the confessionally ecumenical character of the early Believers' movement as one that was open to piety-minded and God-fearing monotheists, of whatever confession, requires us to revise our perceptions of what may have happened in various episodes during the life of Muhammad (to the extent that we wish to accept the reconstructions of his life as related by the traditional sources). For example, parts of the traditional story of Muhammad's life, involving his clashes with certain groups of Jews, have led some scholars to see Muhammad's preaching and movement as in some way specifically anti-Jewish. This is especially true of the story of the ugly fate of the clan of Qurayza, members of which were executed or enslaved following the battle of the Trench. But in view of the inclusion of some Jews in the Believers' movement, we must conclude that the clashes with other Jews or groups of Jews were the result of particular attitudes or political actions on their part, such as a refusal to accept Muhammad's leadership or prophecy. They cannot be taken as evidence of a general hostility to Judaism in the Believers' movement, any more than the execution or punishment of certain of Muhammad's persecutors from Quraysh should lead us to conclude that he was anti-Quraysh.

Muhammad's Status in the Community

Traditional narratives describe how Muhammad was invited to Yathrib/Medina to serve as arbiter of disputes between feuding tribes there, particularly the Aws and Khazraj and their Jewish allies. The selection as arbiter of an outsider—one not belonging to any of the feuding parties—who was recognized as being of upright character was not unusual in the Arabian context. The numerous

Qur'anic verses that enjoin hearers to "obey God and His apostle," or merely to obey the apostle, presumably reflect his role as arbiter. There is no reason to think that Yathrib's important Jewish tribes were at the start any less willing to accept him as arbiter, and as noted above, the Jews were included as part of the new, unified community in the *umma* document. Muhammad's role as political leader, then, probably posed little problem for Jews or Christians of Muhammad's day .

More difficult to assess, however, is the status of Muhammad himself in the religious ideology of the Believers' movement. The Believers, as we have seen, belonged to a strongly monotheistic, intensely pietistic, and ecumenical or confessionally open religious movement that enjoined people who were not already monotheists to recognize God's oneness and enjoined all monotheists to live in strict observance of the law that God had repeatedly revealed to mankind— whether in the form of the Torah, the Gospels, or the Qur'an. But what did the Believers perceive Muhammad's role to be, and in particular, how might this understanding have affected the willingness of Jews or Christians who heard Muhammad's message to join the Believers' movement?

Once again, our only sure source of evidence for approaching this question is the Qur'an, which offers many specific passages about Muhammad and his religious status. A number of different words are applied to Muhamamad in the Qur'an; he is called, above all, messenger or apostle *(rasul)*, that is, God's messenger, and prophet *(nabi)*. Whether these two terms are to be considered synonyms is not clear, but in at least one verse (Q: 33:40), where he is called "apostle of God and seal of the prophets," both terms are applied to him simultaneously. In Q. 7:157, they seem to be essentially interchangeable: ". . . Those who follow the messenger, the *ummi* prophet . . ." He is called the prophet who is foretold in the Torah and Gospels (Q. 7:94). He is also called a bearer of good tidings *(mubashshir)*, a warner *(nadhir)*—particularly a warner of the coming

Last Judgment—and occasionally, a witness *(shahid)* or inviter/ summoner *(da'i)*, one who invites others to believe. He is described frequently as the recipient of inspiration or revelation *(wahy)*, charged with bringing to those around him what was revealed to him. The process of inspiration or revelation itself is called "sending down" (usually *tanzil*) and is clearly identified as having divine origin (for example, see Q. 11:14). The substance of what was sent down is described variously as the Qur'an (Q. 6:19, 12:3, and 42:7), the book (29:45, 3:79, 6:89, 18:27, 35:31, and 57:26), wisdom (3:79, 6:89, 57:26, and 17:39), prophecy (3:79, 6:89, and 57:26), knowledge of hidden things (3:44, 12:102, and 11:49), and knowledge that God is one (Q. 11:14 and 18:110).

Muhammad thus claimed to be not only inspired in some way, but truly a prophet bringing a revealed scripture, just as earlier prophets had done. He was even called "seal of the prophets," that is, the final one in a long series of recipients of God's revelation. Those who followed Muhammad were expected to believe not only in God and the Last Day, but also in Muhammad's claim to prophecy and in the validity or authenticity of what was revealed to him (Q. 5:81). How contemporary Jews and Christians would have received the claim that Muhammad was a prophet bearing divine revelation is harder to assess.

As we have seen, the notion that prophecy was still alive in the world seems to have survived in various parts of the Near East in the centuries before the rise of Islam, although we still know far too little about it. Such ideas seem to have been widespread in Arabia; later Muslim tradition remembers a number of Arabian "false prophets" who emerged in widely scattered parts of the peninsula in Muhammad's time. The concept of prophecy that we find in the Qur'an, including the notions of a series of prophets and of a "seal of the prophets," is similar to that found in some Jewish-Christian sects of the early centuries C.E., from which it spread to other groups, such as the Manicheans. Muhammad's prophetic activity may thus have seemed quite unexceptional to people who shared such ongoing expectations of periodic outbursts of prophetic activity. Yet, certain aspects of his teaching would doubtless have been more difficult for Christians and Jews to accept. The small number of Qur'anic verses that explicitly attack the idea of the Trinity (as defaulting from strict monotheism) would have posed an insurmountable obstacle for a committed trinitarian Christian; and some Jews may have balked at the idea that Muhammad, whom they knew and could see and hear, was to be put on the same plane as their revered patriarchs of old—Abraham, Moses, David, and so on.

Yet, when considering this question we must remember that it is much easier for us, thinking about these events almost fourteen centuries later, to be aware of the full implications of such contradictions and tensions. We must remind ourselves that in Muhammad's day, most people who joined his Believers' movement were probably illiterate; and even if they could read, they did not have a copy of the Qur'an to examine, as those parts that were known in all likelihood were known mostly from recitation of memorized passages. They did not have the advantage that we have today, of being able to comb patiently through the Qur'an text in its entirety in search of passages that might be particularly problematic. Indeed, it is fair to assume that most of the early Believers probably knew only the most basic and general religious ideas we today can find articulated in some detail in the Qur'an. That God was one, that the Last Day was a fearful reality to come (and perhaps to come soon), that one should live righteously and with much prayer, and that Muhammad was the man who, as God's apostle or prophet, was guiding them in these beliefs—that was probably all that was known to most people of Muhammad's day, even to many dedicated participants in the Believers' movement itself. And these notions would have posed few problems for Christians or Jews.

Apocalypticism and Eschatological Orientation

Another feature of the early Believers' movement, and one central to its evident dynamism and ability to mobilize its participants, was its eschatological orientation. We have already seen that one of the central ideas that Believers held was the reality of the Last Judgment. Some passages in the Qur'an suggest that this was more than simply the idea that the Judgment (also called "the Last Day" or simply "the Hour") would happen in some indeterminate, distant future. Rather, certain passages suggest that the community of Believers expected the Last Day to begin soon—or, perhaps, believed that the "beginning of the End" was already upon them. This kind of apocalyptic outlook is typically associated with movements that perceive great sinfulness in the world and that draw a sharp division between good and evil—which, as we have seen, the Believers did. They commonly articulate these ideas, moreover, in what one scholar of apocalyptic thought has described as "easily visualized scenes and strongly-drawn characters," such as we find plentifully in the Qur'an.

The idea that the Last Day was near is mentioned explicitly in several verses: "People ask you about the Hour. Say: Knowledge of it is only with God, but what will make you realize that the Hour is near? (Q. 33:63); "Truly we have warned you of a punishment near, a day on which a man shall see what his hand has done before, and [on which] the unbeliever says, 'I wish I were dead!' " (Q. 78:40). Moreover, the incessant warnings to repent and be pious in preparation for the rigors of the Last Judgment, which are such a pronounced feature of many of the shorter chapters of the Qur'an, imply very strongly that the Hour is perceived to be nigh. But other passages state explicitly that, although near, the exact time of the Judgment is known only to God (Q. 7:187).

As for the nature of the Hour itself, the Qur'an, as noted previously, describes it in often terrifying detail. Its arrival will be signaled by numerous portents that display unequivocally the transcendent might of God and the transient quality of everything in His created world, the permanence of which we take for granted. So, on that day, when the trumpet is sounded, the stars will fall and grow dark, the heavens will be torn open, the mountains will simply vanish, flowing away like sand or water. The seas will boil and burst forth. There will be deafening noise as the physical world comes apart. People will be in complete confusion; no one will ask after his own loved ones, newborns will be neglected by their mothers, children will become grey-haired like the elderly. The graves of the deceased will be opened and the dead raised up, and they will march forth to face the Judgment of their Lord. The angels will come down from on high, bearing God's throne. Then the Judgment itself will begin; the righteous will feel no fear and their faces will shine with joy, but the wicked and unbelievers will feel complete terror and despair and will faint or be convulsed with weeping. Each person's deeds will be assessed and weighed in the balance, and each person rewarded or punished accordingly. The unbelievers will be rounded up and dragged through fire on their faces, on their way to the eternal torments of a fiery hell, while the righteous will go to a garden full of greenery, shade, rushing brooks, delicious food and drink, and beautiful companions.

The Qur'an's unmistakable emphasis on the Last Judgment—a concept that is closely intertwined with the notions of God's oneness and His role as creator of all things—reflects the Believers' conviction that the Hour was imminent, which was the motive force behind the Believers' intense focus on piety and living righteously. Convinced that the world around them was mired in sin and corruption, they felt an urgent need to ensure their own salvation by living in strict accordance with the revealed law, as the Judgment could dawn at any moment. Here one senses in the Qur'an a slight tension, however, between the idea of the individual's ultimate responsibility for his belief and piety, which is emphasized repeatedly, and the notion that the individual can best attain a righteous life in a community of other

Believers—that is, a hint that one's salvation was enhanced by being a communal enterprise. A few passages in the Qur'an suggest that, at the Last Judgment, religious communities may be judged collectively (Q. 16:84–89). Hence the individual's fate is partly decided by his membership in a Believing community or in a sinful one—such as the poor souls who on the Day of Judgment will be led down to hell by Pharaoh, the Qur'anic archetype of the sinful, oppressive leader (cf. Q. 11:98–99).

Some question whether the Believers really did focus on the coming End, pointing to the Qur'an's extensive passages that regulate such matters as inheritance, the punishment of torts, and the like. In their view, these passages seem to reflect a concern for the here and now, not for the afterlife. But the two sets of concerns are not mutually exclusive. Indeed, one who believes that the End is nigh and that one's salvation in the afterlife depends on the righteous conduct of his community would, for this very reason, pay meticulous attention to the details of social conduct in the community. The very prevalence of these "here and now" rulings in the Qur'an, in other words, may be merely another reflection of an end-time mentality among the early Believers.

For the early Believers, then, the terrifying expectation of a Judgment soon to come made them intent on constructing a community of the saved, dedicated to the rigorous observance of God's law as revealed to His prophets. It was a community that followed closely the leadership of the latest prophet, Muhammad; they believed that his guidance, more than any other thing, would ensure their individual and collective salvation when the End suddenly came.

But this is not all. We noted earlier that traditional Muslim exegesis of the Qur'an, and many contemporary studies of it as well, divide the Qur'an text broadly into "Meccan" and "Medinese" verses, according to when in Muhammad's life a particular verse is thought to have been revealed. If we choose to accept this division, an interesting fact emerges: The overwhelming majority of the intensely apocalyptic verses are clustered in Meccan verses. The Medinese verses, by comparison, seem much less explicitly absorbed with warning of the Last Judgment and do not indulge in such potent apocalyptic imagery as do the Meccan verses; on the other hand, the Medinese verses contain the majority of the Qur'an's "legal" material, regulations and rulings on social and personal issues presumably intended as guidelines for the Believers' new "community of the saved." Scholars sometimes suggest that this reflects the fact that, in Medina, the community had grown larger and hence needed social regulation, whereas in Mecca the religious message had been imperative. It seems just as likely, however, that the early Believers were convinced that, by establishing their community in Medina, they were ushering in the beginning of a new era of righteousness, and hence that they were actually witnessing the first events of the End itself. It is possible, then, to conjecture that they thought that the events leading to the Last Judgment were actually beginning to unfold before their very eyes. We have noted that some passages in the Qur'an express an apocalyptic eschatology and speak of the many portents that would herald its arrival; but other verses describe those telltale portents as already happening: "Are they waiting for anything but the Hour that will come to them suddenly? For its portents have already come . . ." (Q. 47:18); "The Hour has drawn nigh, the moon is split in two!" (Q. 54:1). Still other passages portray the Believers as already beginning to realize the events of the Judgment, which included, it seems, the vanquishing of sinful communities by the righteous and the transfer of sovereignty to the Believers. As Q. 10:13–14 states: "We destroyed generations before you when they acted oppressively while their apostles brought them proofs, yet they did not Believe. Thus do we repay a guilty people. Then we made you successors in the land after them, so we may see how you behave."

As a result of this process, the Believers would literally inherit the Earth from the sinful, just as the followers of earlier prophets had done: in Q. 14:13–14, for example, Moses is told how God will drive Pharaoh and the evildoers out of their lands and "settle you in the land after them." A Qur'anic passage that exegetes traditionally connect with the battle of the Trench, after which Muhammad's followers occupied the properties of the Qurayza Jews, provides an example contemporary with the prophet's time: "God repulsed those who had disbelieved in their rage; they attained no good. God was sufficient for the Believers in combat: God is strong and mighty./And those people of the book who had backed them [i.e., they backed the unbelievers], he brought them down from their fortresses, and cast terror in their hearts; some you kill, and some you take captive./And he made you inherit their land and homes and property, and land you have never trodden. God is powerful in all things" (Q. 33:25–27). The notion that God's reward and punishment affects not only one's fate in the afterlife but also one's fate here on Earth could suggest that this change of fortune for the Believers might be part of the dawning Judgment scenario.

For those Believers who fully accepted Muhammad's mission, this complex of ideas, which combined the displacement of unbelieving opponents from their property with God's plan for the End of Days, must have been a powerful motivator to engage in positive action—military if necessary—to vanquish unbelief in the world and to establish what they saw as a God-guided, righteous order on Earth. This brings us to the final feature of the early Believers' movement we wish to consider: its militancy.

Militancy

As the preceding remarks suggest, another characteristic of the early Believers' movement of which the Qur'an provides evidence was its militancy or activist orientation, for which the Qur'anic term is *jihad*. In the Qur'an, *jihad* seems to be a voluntary, individual commitment to work "in the cause of God," (literally, "in the path of

God," *fi sabil allah*), not yet the classic doctrine of religious warfare that would crystallize in later Islamic law (by the eighth century C.E.). It was not enough for the Believers to be merely pious in their own lives and complacent about the world; they were also to strive actively to confront, and if possible to root out, impiety in the world around them. Q. 4:95, for example, reads, "Those Believers who remain passive [literally, "who sit"], other than those who are injured, are not on the same plane with those who strive in the way of God with their property and their selves." This "striving" (*jihad*) sometimes meant working tirelessly to realize righteousness in his or her own life, but it also meant that the Believer should try to spread knowledge of what God has revealed (Q. 3:187), and should actively "command what is good and forbid what is evil, and Believe . . . in God" (Q. 3:110). Other Qur'anic verses, however, take a much more aggressive stance. Q. 9:73 commands the Believers to "strive against the unbelievers and hypocrites and to treat them roughly." In another, Muhammad is actually instructed to incite the Believers to fight against unbelief (Q. 8:65) and even to "make great slaughter in the earth" in the struggle against unbelievers (Q. 8:67). Nor are the prophet and the Believers to seek pardon for the *mushrikun*. Their sin of denying God's oneness was so abominable in God's sight that showing mercy to them was not possible: "It is not for the prophet and those who Believe to ask forgiveness for the *mushrikun*, even if they are close relatives . . ." (Q. 9:113).

It is a distinctive feature of Qur'anic discourse, however, that many of its most uncompromising indictments of unbelief and impious behavior are conjoined with mitigating clauses that temper their apparent harshness and provide an opening for a more flexible approach. For example, verses 5 and 6 of the Qur'an's ninth chapter, *Surat al-tawba*, which is generally one of the most uncompromising and militant in the whole Qur'an, begins with passages ordering the Believers to capture or kill unbelievers by every means, but it then pulls back rather abruptly and commands that unbelievers should be allowed to go unharmed if they repent or if they ask the Believers for protection. This use of "escape clauses" is characteristic of the Qur'an and seems to be its way of providing for the flexibility that is needed in practical situations in life. On the one hand, Believers should try to coerce unbelievers into believing when possible, but, on the other, one should not be fanatical and must make allowances for the realities of a given situation and for the behavior of the individual unbeliever. It seems to be advising its hearers that leniency may, in certain cases, be more effective than brute force and that a range of policies is most effective in pursuing the one goal of universal recognition of God.

The Qur'an thus displays a considerable variety of opinions on the question of activism or militancy, ranging from an almost pacifistic

---

TEXT OF QUR'AN 9 (TAWBA/REPENTANCE): 1–6

[1] A disavowal (bara'a) from God and His apostle [addressed] to those mushrikun with whom you had concluded an agreement. (2) Go about in the land for four months, but know that you do not weaken God, rather God disgraces the ungrateful (kafirun). (3) An announcement from God and His Apostle to the people on the day of the greater pilgrimage: God disavows the mushrikun, and his apostle [likewise], . . . (4) except those mushrikun with whom you concluded an agreement, and who have not failed you in anything and have not aided anyone against you; fulfill your agreement with them to this term: verily, God loves the [God-] fearing. (5) [But] when the sacred months are over, then kill the mushrikun wherever you find them. Seize them, besiege them, ambush them in every way—but if they repent, and do the prayer, and bring zakat, let them go their way. God is forgiving, merciful. (6) And if one of the mushrikun asks you for protection, grant him protection so that he may hear God's word, then deliver him to his refuge—that is because they are a people who do not know.

quietism, in which only verbal confrontation is allowed, through permission to fight in self-defense, to full authorization to take an aggressive stance in which unbelievers are not only to be resisted but actually sought out and forced to submit. Muslim tradition has construed this range as evidence of a smooth progression occurring over Muhammad's lifetime and corresponding to the gradually increasing strength and security of the Believers' community. Recent work, however, has shown that these different injunctions may reflect the divergent attitudes of different subgroups that coexisted simultaneously within the early community of Believers. Although, as noted above, the classic doctrine of *jihad* was not yet formulated, it also seems clear that by the end of Muhammad's life the dominant attitude in the community had become the legitimation of, and the exhortation to pursue, ideological war. Unbelievers were now to be sought out and fought in order to make them submit to the new religious ideology of the Believers' movement—even though the other, less aggressive, positions were still held by some. It is important to remind ourselves here, however, that the Qur'an speaks of fighting unbelievers, not Christians or Jews, who were recognized as monotheists—*ahl al-kitab*—and at least some of whom, as we have seen, were even numbered among the Believers.

By the end of Muhammad's life, then, the Believers were to be not merely a pietist movement with an emphasis on ethics and devotion to God, but a movement of militant piety, bent on aggressively searching out and destroying what they considered practices odious to God (especially polytheism) and intent on spreading rigorous observance of God's injunctions. Although the Qur'an never uses the phrase, this sounds like a program aimed at establishing "God's kingdom on Earth," that is, a political order (or at least a society) informed by the pious precepts enjoined in the Qur'an and one that should supplant the sinful political order of the Byzantines and the Sasanians. There are some grounds for believing that another expression of this activist orientation was the notion of *hijra*. In the traditional sources, *hijra* is interpreted mildly to mean "emigration" (used, as we have seen, particularly to refer to Muhammad's move from Mecca to Medina). But closer examination of the uses of the word *hijra* in the Qur'an (and, as we shall see, in some later sources as well) suggests that *hijra* had a broader range of meanings. For one thing, there is some evidence that *hijra* required leaving a nomadic life. In this sense, the Believers' movement was one based in towns and settlements, for it was only there that the full ritual demands of the faith could be properly observed. This may be why the Believers, when they spread outside of Arabia after the prophet's death, seem to have become known to the peoples they contacted as *muhajirun* (Syriac *mhaggraye*; Greek *agarenoi*). On another level, *hijra* meant taking refuge with someone in order to escape oppression—hence the traditional sources' references to some early Believers' *hijra* to Abyssinia. In a related sense, there are also Qur'anic references to those who "make *hijra* to God and His apostle" to escape from a sinful environment (Q. 4:100). But those passages that speak of "making *hijra* in the way of God" imply that *hijra* is roughly equivalent to *jihad*, "striving," which is also done "in the way of God," and several passages associate *hijra* with leaving home for the purpose of fighting (Q. 3:195, 22:58). Indeed, *hijra* in this larger sense may have served as the decisive marker of full membership into the community of Believers, much as baptism does for Christians: "Verily, those who have Believed and made *hijra* and strive [*yujahidun*] in God's way with their property and themselves, and those who gave asylum and aided [them]—those shall be mutual helpers of one another. But those who have Believed and [yet] have not made *hijra*, they have no share in the mutual assistance [of the others], until they make *hijra* . . ." (Q. 8:72).

Muhammad was an inspired visionary who lived in western Arabia in the early seventh century and who claimed to be a prophet receiving revelations from God. He inaugurated a pietistic religious movement that we can best call, following its adherents' own usage, the "Believers' movement." The testimony of the Qur'an reveals the basic tenet of this movement to have been insistence on the oneness of God and absolute rejection of polytheism, or even of a lukewarm commitment to monotheism. Because many, if not most, of the people of the Near East were already ostensibly monotheists, the original Believers' movement can best be characterized as a monotheistic reform movement, rather than as a new and distinct religious confession. Nevertheless, the Believers seem to have had a clear sense of being a unique community founded on observance of God's revelations and unified, perhaps, by the notion of *hijra*.

The Believers also were convinced of the imminence of the Last Judgment, and, feeling themselves surrounded by corruption and sin, they strove to form themselves into a righteous community so as to attain salvation on Judgment Day. Hence the movement was one of intense piety, demanding of all Believers strict observance of God's revealed law. As this movement was at the start not yet a "religion" in the sense of a distinct confession, members of established monotheistic faiths could join it without necessarily giving up their identities as Jews or Christians; "New monotheists" who had just given up paganism were expected to observe Qur'anic law, but Believing Jews could follow the injunctions of the Torah and Christians the injunctions of the Gospels. (As we have seen, some Christian groups especially engaged in stringent, even ascetic, religious observance on the eve of Islam.) Toward the end of Muhammad's life, the piety of the Believers' movement became increasingly militant, so that the Believers more and more interceded in the sinful world around them, engaging in *jihad* in an effort to establish a righteous order and to spread what they considered to be true Belief. This activist or militant quality eventually came to include confronting unbelievers militarily—fighting or striving "in the path of God" (*fi sabil allah*, as the Qur'an states)—in order to vanquish unbelief. The Believers may even have felt that they were witnessing, in the military successes that are traditionally reported to have come in Muhammad's last years, the beginnings of the great events leading up to the Last Day; for among these events would be their victory and the establishment of their hegemony, replacing the sinful polities around them. Thus they would inherit the Earth and establish in it a righteous, God-guided community that could lead humanity to salvation when the Judgment scenario reached its culmination. This is not entirely an unfamiliar program, for there is something in the Believers' aim of bringing all of mankind to salvation that is reminiscent of the Byzantines' objectives of bringing everyone in the world to what they considered the true faith; and, in both cases, this objective was to be achieved either by mission or, if necessary, by war.

Having examined what the early Believers' movement was, it is also important to consider here what it was not. It is often alleged—or assumed—that Muhammad and the Believers were motivated by a "nationalist" or nativist impetus as "Arabs," but this identity category did not yet exist, at least in a political sense, in Muhammad's day, so it is misleading to conceive of the Believers as constituting an "Arab movement." The Qur'an makes it clear that its message was directed to people who conceived of themselves as Believers, but being a Believer is not related to ethnicity. The term *a'rab* (usually meaning "nomads") is used only a few times in the Qur'an, and mostly seems to have pejorative overtones. The Qur'an does refer to itself a few times as an "Arabic Qur'an," but this seems to be a linguistic designation, perhaps an indication of a certain form of the spoken language we today call Arabic.

Nor was the Believers' movement primarily an effort to improve social conditions. It is true that the Qur'an often speaks of the need to have pity on the poor, widows, and orphans, among others, but these social actions are enjoined because compassion for others is one of the duties that come with true Belief in God and His oneness. The social dimensions of the message are undeniable and significant, but they are incidental to the central notions of the Qur'an, which are religious: Belief in the one God and righteous behavior as proof of obedience to God's will.

3

The Expansion of the Community of Believers

Following the death of Muhammad in 11/632, the Believers quickly (if, as we shall see, somewhat contentiously) resolved the question of leadership of the community and then embarked on a process of rapid political expansion, usually called the "Islamic conquests" or (less accurately) the "Arab conquests." This expansion lasted, with various interruptions, for roughly a century and carried the hegemony of the community of Believers as far as Spain and India—truly an astonishing feat. This chapter will attempt to explain how this expansion began, to establish the character of the expansion, and to trace the main developments that took place, especially in its crucial first three decades, until about the year 35/656. But first, we must once again consider for a moment the sources historians can use to reconstruct this period in the history of the community.

Sources

The Qur'an continues to be an important source for the history of the community in the years immediately after Muhammad's death, at least in an indirect way. Even if we consider the Qur'an to be a product entirely of Muhammad's lifetime, we can assume that its guiding ideals continued to shape the outlook and actions of the Believers in the first years following Muhammad's death. If we take the alternative view that the Qur'an text was still crystallizing during these first few decades after Muhammad's death, we may take the text to reflect more directly the differing attitudes of various groups within the community on crucial issues confronting the Believers at this time.

The Qur'an, however, ostensibly provides no direct information on the expansion movement as it played out after Muhammad's death. For this reason, the historian who wishes to examine the history of the early decades of the expansion must take into account the voluminous body of traditional narratives that the later Muslim community collected on this subject. These narratives are, like the narratives about the life of Muhammad, very problematic for the historian and must be used with great care. Like the narratives about Muhammad, the conquest narratives contain many interpolations of issues of concern only to the later community; in particular, they tend to portray events in an idealized way as evidence of God's favor for the Believers and probably overemphasize the amount of centralized control exercised by the leadership in Medina. But recent study of these traditional narrative sources suggests that we can indeed draw from them a basic skeleton of the course of historical events, both for the later years of Muhammad's career in Medina and for the expansion movement, even though their interpretation and evaluation of those events is sometimes strongly colored by later, rather than contemporary, concerns.

Furthermore, with the first decades of the expansion, we begin to encounter, for the first time in the history of the community of Believers, some truly documentary evidence about it. This comes in the form of the first known coins issued by the Believers and in contemporary inscriptions or papyri written by them, or about them. It is true that there are very few documentary sources for the early years of the expansion, but that simply makes their testimony all the more precious to us, for whatever we wish to say by way of reconstructing an historical picture of the Believers' movement must fit with the evidence these documents provide. They are to the historian of this period what the fleeting glimpses of a few fixed stars are to the navigator attempting to make his or her way under cloudy skies: without them, the navigator works mainly by guesswork.

Almost as important as the first true documents are some very early literary sources that describe the Believers but that were written by people who were not themselves members of the Believers' movement. Of particular importance are writings from various Near Eastern Christian communities—in Syriac, Greek, Armenian, and Coptic—and a few Jewish sources. As with the later Muslim sources, we must scrutinize and evaluate these non-Muslim literary sources very carefully to be sure we understand exactly when they were first written, how accurately they have been transmitted to us, and especially, what biases and preconceptions (contemporary or later) may have shaped their description of the Believers and their actions. Nonetheless, they provide us with a welcome alternative perspective which, taken in concert with other sources both literary and documentary, helps us to achieve a more historically grounded understanding of the period. We shall draw on some of these sources below, particularly when discussing the character of the expansion.

The Community in the Last Years of Muhammad's Life

The rapid expansion of the community of Believers after Muhammad's death has its roots in the events of the last years of his life. As we saw earlier, Muhammad and his followers began to meet with significant political success following his conclusion of the Hudaybiya agreement with Quraysh (6/628). It is reported that the terms of this agreement initially distressed some of Muhammad's more ardent followers. They were perhaps opposed to the very idea of making any kind of "deal" with the still-hostile Meccan *mushrikun*. They were offended particularly by the refusal of Quraysh to allow Muhammad to be called "Apostle of God" in the document or to allow the Believers to enter the sacred area of Mecca that year. Despite their misgivings, however, Muhammad and his followers were able, shortly thereafter, to conquer the major northern oasis of Khaybar, to launch numerous other raids to the north, and to bring many hitherto unaligned groups of pastoral nomads into alliance with Medina. All of these activities solidified Muhammad's military and political situation; in particular, the conquest of Khaybar, long an ally of Mecca against him, allowed Muhammad to make his final assault on Mecca without fear that Medina might be attacked by hostile forces coming from his rear. We noted earlier how the increasingly secure position of the community of Believers in Medina may have been the reason the emigrants to Abyssinia returned to the Hijaz at this time. Another reflection of Muhammad's improved position can be seen in the fact that a number of key members of Quraysh joined his movement in the years between the Hudaybiya agreement and the conquest of Mecca. Two who did were Khalid ibn al-Walid and ʿAmr ibn al-ʿAs. Khalid, a member of the powerful Quraysh clan of Makhzum, was an outstanding military commander. His skill had once worked against Muhammad at the battle of Uhud, but he would henceforth lead many campaigns for Muhammad and, after Muhammad's death, would play a major role in the expansion of the community of Believers. ʿAmr ibn al-ʿAs, having declared his allegiance to Muhammad, was sent to act as Muhammad's agent or governor in distant ʿUman, in eastern Arabia, and would also emerge in the years following Muhammad's death as an important political and military figure.

With the conquest of Mecca in 8/630, and that of the town of Taʾif shortly thereafter, Muhammad's growing power was so evident that many groups in Arabia sent representatives to him to tender their submission. This took place especially during the so-called "year of delegations," the penultimate year of Muhammad's life (9/April 630–April 631). As Muhammad's position solidified following the conquest of Mecca, he no longer needed to make alliances with pagan groups for reasons of political expediency, as he had during his precarious early years in Medina. The Qur'an (9:1–6) refers both to the existence of earlier treaties with "associators"/*mushrikun*, and to a change of policy that barred such alliances in the future; one phrase states, "when the sacred months are over, then kill the *mushrikun* wherever you find them." (See the Sidebar on page 84, "Text of Qur'an 9 (Tawba/Repentance): 1–6.") Henceforth, then, *mushrikun* were to be barred from participation in the community, which becomes now more integrally focused on establishing itself as a group separated by its belief and its righteousness from the sinful world around it. It existed now in a state of perpetual war with the *mushrikun*, who are to be pursued and forced to recognize God's oneness. The many tribal delegations who are said to have come to Muhammad during his last years became not simply allies of the new community of Believers, but—in order to be allies—full members of it, and thus on whom were incumbent the duties of prayer and of making tax payments (or purification payments, to atone for earlier sinfulness). Allies were now required to toe the line in ideological and financial terms, and payment of a tax by all members of the community would henceforth be an important token of their commitment to it.

In its early days, the community of Believers in Medina was still small; people still continued to belong to their traditional tribal and lineage groups but were now contracted to cooperate with one another in new ways. This must have created many tensions and rivalries that, for want of other institutions, Muhammad himself had to defuse personally. In doing so he relied on the backing of close personal supporters to do his bidding—in particular on Abu Bakr and

'Umar ibn al-Khattab, who seem to have been Muhammad's main advisers, and to whom Muhammad had tied himself by marrying their daughters 'A'isha and Hafsa. By the final years of Muhammad's life, however, the community of Believers had grown in size and complexity. It now embraced a large number of formerly independent settlements and towns, including Medina, Mecca, Ta'if, Khaybar, the villages of Wadi al-Qura, and many others. It also included numerous groups of pastoral nomads that lived in the vicinity of Medina and Mecca, such as Sulaym, Hawazin, Muzayna, and Khuza'a. Some of these settlements or groups were tribute-paying former monotheists whom Muhammad had subjected, such as the Jewish residents of Khaybar or Wadi al-Qura, and some lived far from Medina.

As the community grew in size and complexity, Muhammad increasingly found it necessary to delegate important tasks of governance to trusted subordinates, who carried out raiding parties against recalcitrant tribes, or destroyed the shrines of pagan idols, or served as the effective governors over various settlements and groups. Many of these subordinates were trusted early converts, Emigrants or Helpers who had shown their loyalty many times over. However, Muhammad did not spurn the services of former *mushrikun*, even those who had joined his movement quite late, particularly if they possessed skills that were needed to manage the growing community. The careers of the Meccans Khalid ibn al-Walid and 'Amr ibn al-'As, mentioned briefly above, are cases in point. Even more striking, Muhammad allowed a number of Qurayshites who only submitted at the last minute, on his occupation of Mecca, to hold important posts in his administration—indeed, he even made special bonus payments to some of them, presumably to bind them firmly to the community. However, this special treatment for some of his former enemies— referred to in the Qur'an as "those whose hearts are reconciled" *(al-mu'allafa qulubuhum)* (Q. 9:60)—distressed some of Muhammad's early followers. They disliked seeing the likes of Abu Sufyan—chief of the Umayya clan of Quraysh and longtime leader of Mecca's opposition to Muhammad—and his sons Yazid and Mu'awiya showered with favors and high positions, while they continued to serve in the rank and file of the movement. But this policy of "reconciling hearts" gave such people, who with their important contacts and managerial talents would have been dangerous opponents, a stake in the success of the Believers' movement and thus helped ensure their loyalty to it. By making such concessions, Muhammad seems to show a pragmatic outlook that enabled him, while still adhering to the basic ideals he advanced, to make his movement practical in the world. In the long term, Muhammad's policy contributed greatly to the success of the Believers' movement.

By the time of Muhammad's death, then, the community of Believers was expanding its control and influence rapidly from its original base in western Arabia. In some respects the exact extent of its control at this time remains unclear, but there can be no doubt that it was much larger than even a few years before. Outposts of Believers are reported in Yemen (in South Arabia), in 'Uman (in eastern Arabia), and throughout much of northern Arabia as well. Muhammad seems to have been particularly interested in expanding to the north; we have seen how, already in the years before the conquest of Mecca, he had dispatched a raid (or several raids?) to the distant oasis town of Dumat al-Jandal (modern al-Jawf), roughly 600 km (about 375 mi) north of Medina. After the occupation of Mecca, this northward outlook seems to have intensified even more, including at least two campaigns into the southern fringes of Byzantine territory in Syria (today's southern Jordan). What was behind this apparent concern for the north? It may be that geographical Syria, with its large cities and fertile farmland that were well known to Quraysh through their trading activities, appealed to some in Muhammad's retinue for commercial and other economic reasons. Some Qurayshites apparently owned property in Syria before Muhammad's prophetic activity began; a few cases we know include property owned by the Quraysh chief Abu Sufyan near Damascus and by 'Amr ibn al-'As in southern Palestine. Moreover, if the Believers thought that they were indeed destined to inherit the Earth, there could be no better place to begin than in fertile Syria.

Another possible reason for this attraction northward may inhere in the eschatological tone of the Believers' movement. Convinced that the Last Judgment was soon to come, some Believers may have felt an urgent need to try to secure control of the city of Jerusalem, which has been called "the apocalyptic city *par excellence.*" Many apocalyptic scenarios circulating among Jews and Christians in late antiquity described the Judgment as taking place in Jerusalem, and although this notion is not expressed in the Qur'an, it soon became part of Islamic eschatological views. The Believers may have felt that, because they were in the process of constructing the righteous "community of the saved," they should establish their presence in Jerusalem as soon as possible.

Succession to Muhammad and the *Ridda* Wars

The death of Muhammad in 11/632 posed a serious challenge to the Believers who were left behind. Some of his followers—including, reportedly, 'Umar—did not wish to believe that he was actually dead. (This reluctance may have been rooted in their conviction that the Last Judgment would come during Muhammad's lifetime.) Muhammad's leadership of the Believers had been intensely personal. Although he had come to rely on key supporters for advice and to carry out various tasks, there was no clear-cut "chain of command" that made it obvious who was to take charge on his demise. Moreover—although Muslim tradition is contradictory on this question—Muhammad seems to have made neither an unambiguous designation of a successor, nor suggested a way of choosing one, a matter on which the Qur'an also offers no unequivocal guidance. During his life, he had kept under control—sometimes only with difficulty—numerous rivalries and resentments among the Believers themselves; on his death, these rivalries quickly came to the surface again. The old hostility between the Medinese tribes of Aws and Khazraj, the not-always-so-friendly rivalry between the Emigrants and the Helpers, and the resentment felt by some of Muhammad's early supporters toward highly favored last-minute converts from Quraysh all threatened to tear apart the core of the Believers' movement, the community in Medina. At the same time, news of Muhammad's death emboldened tribal groups that were not entirely content with their situation under Muhammad and his tax collectors to consider trying to break away from Medina's control.

As a result of these tensions, Muhammad's death called into question the unity of the community even in Medina. There seem to have been proposals that the Medinese Believers should have a chief for themselves, while Quraysh (presumably including the Emigrants?) would have their own leader—in short, a proposal for the political fragmentation of the community of Believers, essentially along tribal lines. This immediate crisis of leadership seems to have been settled quickly: The traditional sources describe a tumultuous meeting of the Helpers held at a meeting place of the Banu Sa'ida, a clan of Khazraj, and, as a result, they decided that the community of Believers should remain united and that Muhammad's closest adviser, Abu Bakr, should serve as Muhammad's political successor but without any prophetic authority. It is difficult, however, to be sure of just what happened during this crucial episode, because the traditional sources provide many conflicting reports about it that cannot be reconciled. For example, some reports state that the prophet's cousin and son-in-law, 'Ali, refused to swear an oath of allegiance recognizing Abu Bakr's selection for as long as six months, whereas other reports deny this. Whatever happened behind the scenes, Abu Bakr emerged as the community's new leader.

Muhammad's political successors (with the possible exception of Abu Bakr) at first bore the title *amir al-mu'minin*, "commander of the

---

DAM INSCRIPTION IN AL-TA'IF

This dam belongs to the servant of God Muʿawiya, *amir al-muʾminin*. ʿAbdullah ibn Sakhr built it with God's leave in the year fifty-eight. O God, forgive the servant of God Muʿawiya, *amir al-muʾminin*, strengthen him and help him, and let the Believers profit by him. ʿAmr ibn Habbab wrote [this]. (Trans. Hoyland, *Seeing Islam*, 692, slightly modified.)

Believers," a title that is interesting for at least two reasons. First, it reveals that the members of Muhammad's religious movement continued to conceive of themselves in the first instance as *Believers*, as is evidenced in the Qurʾan. Second, the title suggests that the movement's leadership had a military character, as the word *amir*, "commander," "one who gives orders," is used in Arabic mainly in military contexts, rather than to describe other forms of social or group leadership. This is presumably a reflection of the movement's increasingly militant, even expansionist, quality. The title *amir al-muʾminin* was used by Abu Bakr's successors, and its use is confirmed by several very early documentary sources—inscriptions, coins, and papyri, some dating from the time of one of his successors, Muʿawiya (ruled 40–60/660–680). Later Islamic tradition (and most modern scholarship) generally refers to Abu Bakr and his successors as "caliphs" (Arabic sing. *khalifa*)—meaning "successors"—but there is no documentary attestation of this term before the end of the first century AH/seventh century C.E. For this reason, I shall continue to refer to the leaders of the community of Believers by the term they used for themselves—*amir al-muʾminin*.

On his selection as leader of the community, Abu Bakr first dispatched a campaign to the north, which Muhammad had organized just before his death but which had not yet departed. In doing so, Abu Bakr overruled the requests of several advisers, who argued that the forces were needed at home in Medina to defend the city against nearby nomadic tribes hoping to take advantage of the disarray caused by Muhammad's death. Fortunately for Medina, a few nearby tribes, such as the Aslam, remained loyal to Medina and thwarted such designs. This force departed, but its campaign seems to have been of brief duration; evidently it was directed against the Quda'a tribes who lived north of Medina and went perhaps as far as the Balqa' region (the district around Amman in modern Jordan). It returned intact after about two months.

It was not too soon, for by this time Abu Bakr and the Believers in Medina needed reinforcements. Numerous tribal groups had sent delegations to him reaffirming their support, but some, while expressing themselves willing to observe the Believers' religious ordinances, had refused to pay the *sadaqa* tax to the new leader and had withdrawn without an agreement. Moreover, various nomadic groups, even some near Medina, were organizing themselves to resist Medina, perhaps to attack the city itself. This opposition to the new regime in Medina is called by our sources *ridda*, "going back" or (in religiously colored terms) "apostasy."

After the forces who were sent north returned, Abu Bakr led a raid to break up a brewing coalition of clans of the Ghatafan and Kinana tribes near the village of al-Rabadha, about 200 km (124 mi) east of Medina. Then he organized several other forces under reliable commanders, most of them drawn from Quraysh. For example, Muhajir ibn Abi Umayya and Khalid ibn Asid were sent to Yemen to help the governor there cope with an uprising by a rebel named Aswad al-'Ansi, who had proclaimed himself a prophet. Three more commanders were sent to subdue (or to establish the Believers' control in) distant 'Uman and the Mahra country of southeastern Arabia. Another was sent on a similar mission to the Bakr tribes of northeastern Arabia—with some of whom, such as the tribe of Shayban, Abu Bakr may already have forged some kind of alliance.

The most celebrated campaigns of the *ridda*, however, were those of an army of Emigrants and Helpers led by Khalid ibn al-Walid. In a series of decisive battles, he defeated powerful groups in the region of northern Arabia called Najd, some of which were led by people claiming also to be prophets like Muhammad (considered, of course, "false prophets" by later Muslim tradition). The "false prophet" Talha ibn Khuwaylid of Asad, who had been active already in Muhammad's day and was joined by remnants of the Ghatafan, was defeated at the battle of Buzakha; the tribes of Tayyi', 'Amir, Sulaym, and Hawazin were likewise humbled. The tribe of Tamim and their "false prophetess" Sajah joined the most potent of all Medina's rivals, the "false prophet" Musaylima (Maslama) and his tribe, the Hanifa, which dominated the important eastern Arabian oasis of al-Yamama (al-Hajr, modern Riyadh). Khalid's successful campaigns in Najd convinced many local groups that had been temporizing to join his force as it made its way toward the showdown with Musaylima. During this clash at the battle of 'Aqraba' (known as the "garden of death" because of the great number of casualties on both sides), the Hanifa tribe was defeated and Musaylima killed.

As a result of these campaigns, which extended over the length and breadth of the Arabian peninsula and lasted for more than a year (11/March 632–March 633), the whole of Arabia was brought under the political control of Medina and the Believers' movement. One can suppose that the Believers' astonishing success in overcoming all resistance in Arabia must have been interpreted by many contemporaries as a sign that God was, indeed, on their side—which may have made some people more willing to accept their rule. The Believers' hegemony meant that anyone living under their purview, if not already a monotheist of some kind, had to become one by openly declaring God's oneness and agreeing to live by Qur'anic law. (Presumably, the numerous Jews and Christians of Arabia were allowed, as monotheists, to continue observing their own religious laws, although the sources tell us nothing about this question.) But in addition to recognizing God's oneness, these new Believers were also required to live righteously and to pay the tax (*sadaqa*) to Medina. Abu Bakr seems to have insisted especially on the latter provision, and it may be for this reason that he is known in the sources as "al-Siddiq." The traditional sources usually interpret this epithet to mean "the one who speaks the truth," but "the one who collects *sadaqa*" (that is, "the tax collector") seems just as likely.

On the completion of the *ridda* campaigns, the community comprised three strata. At the top was the old core of Muhammad's community of Believers—including the Emigrants, the Helpers, Quraysh, and Thaqif, the last representing the three main towns of the Hijaz, Mecca, Medina, and Taif—with Abu Bakr, and his closest advisers (mostly of Quraysh) in the leading positions. A second stratum consisted of the many individuals and tribes in Arabia who had tendered their submission to the new regime and supported it during the *ridda* (for example, previously unaffiliated tribesmen who had joined Khalid's forces during the *ridda* wars). They included such tribes as Aslam, Ghifar, Muzayna, Ashja', and Juhayna, and parts of Sulaym—all of them nomadic groups living near Medina—as well as parts of other tribes with partly nomadic populations: Tamim, Tayyi', Bajila, Sakun (a branch of Kinda), Bali, Shayban and other Bakr tribes, and many others. The bottom of the hierarchy was occupied by tribes and communities that had resisted Medina's expansion during the *ridda*—groups like the Hanifa tribe, as well as parts of Tamim, Tayyi', Asad, Kinda, and many others. These groups formed the subject population of Arabia in the years after the *ridda*, and from them were taken many captives who served the early Believers as slaves. Among the most famous of these captives was Khawla bint Ja'far, a woman of Hanifa who eventually became the concubine of 'Ali ibn Abi Talib. She bore him a son, Muhammad ibn al-Hanafiyya ("son of the Hanifite woman"), who later became politically prominent. She is exceptional in that, through the fame of her son, she emerges in the sources as an identifiable individual. Most such Arabian slaves remain lost in anonymous obscurity, but occasional reports in our sources—such as one describing the extensive estates in Yamama owned by the future *amir al-mu'minin*, Mu'awiya, that were worked by several thousand slaves (probably also of Hanifa)—suggest that enslavement of such "enemies of God" was not an unusual fate for defeated *ridda* opponents.

The completion of the *ridda* campaigns, then, marked the extension of Medina's control over all of Arabia. But it also represented something far more important—the integration of all Arabian tribal groups into the community of Believers, most of them (with the exception, perhaps, of Hanifa) in such a way that they could be called on to contribute to the further expansion of the Believers' movement. Powerful nomadic groups such as Tamim, Asad, and Shayban, and settled tribes of Yemen such as Bajila, Azd, and Madhhij, became key sources of military recruits on whom Abu Bakr and his ruling group could rely when organizing future campaigns. It was these tribes who would carry the urgent message of God's word and the need to live in righteous obedience to it to ever-wider horizons in the years ahead.

The *ridda* campaigns were also important to the fledgling state in Medina for another reason: They marked, and partly precipitated, the transition to a new level of military organization. In the days of Muhammad and before, military campaigns in Arabia, whatever their scale, can best be termed raids—operations of limited duration and always undertaken with very finite objectives, such as the capture of flocks from a certain tribe or the reduction of a particular settlement to tribute-paying status. Although such raids sometimes involved sizable coalitions or alliances of people from different tribal groups, they only lasted until their particular objective was attained (or until the raid was thwarted)—if that long. They had a tendency to fall apart if the campaign became prolonged; the dissolution of Quraysh's large coalitions against Muhammad at both Uhud and the Trench are good examples. The ephemeral quality of these pre-Islamic raiding parties is doubtless rooted in the fact that they lacked both ideological content and any organic structure.

The *ridda* campaigns launched by the Believers, by comparison, had a strong ideological component. The Believers participating in them were engaging in *jihad*, "striving" in the cause of God, and although they certainly had specific objectives when setting out, such campaigns had an open-ended quality that had been lacking in pre-Islamic Arabian raids. Now a victory would be followed not by an immediate return of the army homeward, but by the thought of moving on to the next objective in the campaign of spreading God's rule. In some cases the forces sent out by Abu Bakr were in the field for a year or even longer—something hitherto unknown in Arabia—and therefore cannot be viewed as simple raiding parties along traditional Arabian lines. Moreover, forces that engaged in a year of unbroken campaigning were no longer merely temporary assemblages of discrete tribal units that might come apart at any moment. Rather, they must be considered troops in a more tightly integrated military unit, whose long experience together in the field (as well as their mutual commitment to the community's religious ideology and mission) forged ties of camaraderie that could begin to transcend their purely tribal affiliations. The traditional sources unfortunately offer us only occasional glimpses of the details of this organizational transformation, but one dimension of it we can perhaps see. The long duration and the scope of the *ridda* campaigns would have required the reliable provisioning of troops. Traditional sources tell us how the early *amir al-mu'minin*s established a protected pasture *(hima)* at al-Rabadha, roughly 200 km (124 mi) east of Medina, where flocks of livestock could be maintained. We cannot be certain from such accounts, of course, that this was done in order to provision the Believers' armies with mounts and meat. However, archaeologists have discovered evidence of large-scale slaughtering of livestock, particularly camels, at al-Rabadha, in the form of massive deposits of camel bones that are archaeologically datable to the period of the earliest community of Believers. If this evidence holds up—it has never been fully published—it suggests that Abu Bakr and his first successors as *amir al-mu'minin* may indeed have organized a centralized system to supply basic provisions to their armies in the field.

It is apparent, then, that the *ridda* campaigns witnessed the evolution of the Believers' forces from simple raiding parties into true armies. It is probably no accident that most of the leaders of these *ridda* campaigns were men of Quraysh, whose long experience in the caravan trade provided them with the managerial skills required to help effect this transformation. The crystallization of these standing armies during the Arabian *ridda* wars provided the Believers with the forces that enabled them to expand outside Arabia.

The conclusion of the *ridda* campaigns brought the Believers to the frontiers of the Byzantine and Sasanian empires on the fringes of northern Arabia. The Believers crossed these unmarked frontiers, however, and began to raid and integrate the populations on the borders of the great empires themselves, many of whom already spoke Arabic. Both empires eventually sent armies to try to thwart this encroachment on their rich tax base. This direct political confrontation of the Believers with the two empires is traditionally taken as the beginning of a much larger process, usually called the "Islamic conquest," whereby the Believers expanded into areas outside Arabia. The first campaigns of this conquest were organized in the last months of Abu Bakr's rule (11–13/632–634) and were continued by his successors, 'Umar ibn al-Khattab (ruled 13–23/634–644) and 'Uthman ibn 'Affan (ruled 23–35/644–656). The traditional view of the conquest movement presented by later Muslim writers is that of a series of major military confrontations between armies of Arabian tribesmen organized by the *amir al-mu'minin* in Medina and the armies of the Byzantine and Sasanian empires trying to stop this encroachment on their territory. Although interrupted by periods of discord within the community of Believers known as the first and second civil wars, the conquest movement resumed after each of them and continued for more than a century. Eventually, the Believers conquered not only the areas immediately adjoining Arabia (that is, Syria, Iraq, Egypt), but also much more distant areas as well—North Africa and most of the Iberian peninsula in the west; Iran, the Caucasus, and the fringes of Central Asia and Afghanistan in the east; and even securing a foothold in the Indus valley (modern Pakistan) and elsewhere in South

Asia. Before examining a more detailed description of the course of the expansion movement, however, it is necessary to consider for a moment exactly what the nature of this expansion might have been.

The Character of the Believers' Early Expansion

As noted, the expansion of the community of Believers beyond Arabia into the wider Near East is traditionally viewed as a military conquest. However, this view is, in some ways, problematic. Traditional Muslim sources, to be sure, depict it as a frontal assault on the two great empires by armies of the Believers, involving major battles by thousands of troops, the siege of many cities, and the like. There is surely a significant element of truth in this traditional picture, for some aspects of it are confirmed by nearly contemporary literary accounts produced by various Near Eastern Christian writers. For example, Thomas the Presbyter, writing around 640 C.E., describes a battle between the "Romans" (that is, the Byzantine army) and the "nomads (Syriac *tayyaye*) of Muhammad" some 19 km (12 mi) east of Gaza, after which, he claims, 4,000 villagers of Palestine were killed—Christians, Jews, and Samaritans—and the whole region ravaged.

> ### TEXT OF THOMAS THE PRESBYTER
>
> In the year 945 [634 C.E.], indiction 7, on Friday 4 February at the ninth hour, there was a battle between the Romans and the nomads of Muhammad (*tayyaye d-Mhmt*) in Palestine twelve miles east of Gaza. The Romans fled, leaving behind the patriarch Bryrdn, whom the *tayyaye* killed. Some 4,000 poor villagers of Palestine were killed there, Christians, Jews and Samaritans. The *tayyaye* ravaged the whole region. (Trans. Hoyland, *Seeing Islam*, 120, slightly modified.)

Other contemporary sources provide similar kinds of details. The bishop of Jerusalem, Sophronius, in a homily of 637 or 638 C.E., describes raids by troops of "Saracens" (from a Greek word referring to Arabian nomads), outpourings of blood, churches pulled down or burned, villages burned, cities plundered, fields devastated, and opposing armies sent against them by the Byzantines. A Coptic homily of the 640s speaks of "the Saracens who are oppressors, who give themselves up to prostitution, massacre, and lead into captivity the sons of men, saying, 'We both fast and pray.'" Much later, Anastasius of Sinai (died ca. 700 C.E.) speaks of the defeat of the Byzantine army, referring to the "bloodshed at [the three battles of] Gabitha, Yarmuk, and Dathemon . . . after which occurred the capture and burning of the cities of Palestine, even Caesarea and Jerusalem. Then there was the destruction of Egypt, followed by the enslavement and fatal devastation of the Mediterranean lands and islands . . ." He also mentions the defeat of the Byzantine army and navy at the battle of Phoenix (ca. 31/651–652 or 34/654–655).

There thus seems to be nearly contemporary literary evidence that supports what we can call the "violent conquest model" of the early expansion of the Believers. The problem is that an increasing burden of archaeological evidence has turned up little or no trace of destructions, burnings, or other violence in most localities, particularly in geographical Syria, which is the area both most fully described by the literary sources and most thoroughly explored by archaeologists. Instead, the archaeological record suggests that the area underwent a gradual process of social and cultural transformation that did not involve a violent and sudden destruction of urban or rural life at all. In town after town, we find evidence of churches that are not destroyed—but, rather, continue in use for a century or more after the "conquest"—or evidence that new churches (with dated mosaic floors) were being constructed.

Moreover, the "violent conquest" model of the Believers' expansion into the Fertile Crescent is not convincing from a sociological

Mosaic floor from St. Menas Church, Rihab, Jordan. The Greek inscription from this floor reveals that it was built a few years after the arrival of the Believers, suggesting that the rhythms of local life were not at first markedly affected by the change of regime. It reads: "By grace of Jesus Christ, our God and Saviour, the Temple of Saint Menas was built, paved with mosaics and completed at the time of the metropolitan Theodore, most holy and honored by God, through offerings of Procopius, [son] of Martyrius and Comitissa, his consort, and of their sons, for the remission of sins and the repose of [their] parents. [It] was written in the month of March at the time of the eighth indiction of the year 529 [era of Bostra, ca. 635 C.E.]." (Text [slightly modified] from M. Piccirillo, *Mosaics of Jordan*, plate, p. 313.)

point of view. It is predicated on the mistaken notion that the "conquerors" came with the intention of imposing a new religion by force on local populations. However, in regions such as Syria, Iraq, Egypt, and Iran—which already had deeply entrenched religious traditions (Judaism, Christianity, Zoroastrianism) that were highly adept at waging religious polemic to defend themselves—this would surely have failed. For, if the Believers already embraced a clearly defined and distinct new creed and had tried to demand that local communities

observe it, those populations of the Fertile Crescent would have resisted their arrival stubbornly, in word and deed. But no significant
Christian or other polemics against the Believers' doctrines appear
for almost a century. The "violent conquest" model thus presents the
historian with the double problem of explaining, first, how the conquest could have succeeded in the face of certain opposition to it by
these articulate religious communities, and second, how the minute
number of conquerors could have maintained their hegemony over a
vastly more numerous hostile population. The "violent conquest
model" also makes it difficult to understand how the Believers could
have maintained their distinctive identity and avoided acculturation
or assimilation into this large conquered population, particularly
during the first few years when they had no local infrastructure of
their own on which to rely.

The difficulties posed by the "violent conquest" model of the Believers' expansion into the lands adjoining Arabia are thus significant. But, if we take into account the ecumenical or non-confessional
quality of the earliest community of Believers, as described in the
preceding chapter, another way of viewing the expansion suggests
itself, one that accords better with the lack of destruction found in
the archaeological record for this period. Although the expansion
unquestionably included some violent episodes, we can propose that
the arrival of the Arabian Believers in many localities in the Fertile
Crescent would not always, or even usually, have taken the form of
violent confrontation, because the overwhelming majority of these
communities consisted already of monotheists who were, for this
reason, eligible in principle for inclusion in the Believers' movement. The predominantly West-Arabian leaders of the Believers'
movement were not asking the people of Syria-Palestine, Egypt, and
Iraq to give up their ancestral religion to embrace another—that
surely would have led to violent confrontation. But they were imposing their political hegemony on the conquered populations, requir-
ing them to pay taxes, and asking them, at least initially, to affirm

their belief in one God and in the Last Day, and to affirm their commitment to living righteously and to avoid sin. They were, in short, establishing a new political order and perhaps advancing a program of monotheistic (and moral?) reform but not proposing religious revolution or demanding conversion to a new faith. Some localities in the Fertile Crescent may have refused to accept the Believers' terms, but the majority accepted; to the many Jewish, Samaritan, and monophysite Christian communities of Syria, Mesopotamia, and Egypt, in particular, the Believers' terms may have seemed very acceptable indeed, as they involved none of the pressure to change their core beliefs that they had long experienced at the hands of the "orthodox" Byzantine authorities. Indeed, even orthodox Christians could easily acquiesce in such terms; the payment of tribute or tax that was required by the Believers' regime was not materially different from what the Byzantines or Sasanians had formerly imposed on them. The near-contemporary reports of pillage and captives we noted above may refer only to those communities or individuals who actively rejected the Believers' call to monotheism and righteous living; some (such as Sophronius's description of depredations by "Saracens") may sometimes refer to nomadic raiders who had no connection with the Believers' movement at all but were only taking advantage of political instability in Byzantine Palestine in the 630s.

Whether Zoroastrian communities, found mainly in Iran and southern Iraq, were incorporated at the outset into the growing Believers' movement in some way is less clear. The dualistic theology and fire worship of Zoroastrians must have posed a significant obstacle to their inclusion in the Believers' movement at first. Later Muslim chronicles describe the destruction of Zoroastrian fire temples at the time of the conquest, but it is not clear how reliable such later reports are. Some Zoroastrian communities, like Jewish and Christian ones elsewhere, may have tendered their submission and may have been integrated in some way with the community of

Believers. On the other hand, some large provinces of Iran, especially in the north, were hardly penetrated by the Believers for a century or more; the Iranian noble families that traditionally controlled these areas evidently made terms with the Believers early in the conquest era, winning virtually complete autonomy in exchange for remission of tribute or tax payments to the *amir al-mu'minin* and his governors. Certainly Zoroastrians continued to exist in large numbers in northern and western Iran and elsewhere for centuries after the rise of Islam, and indeed, much of the canon of Zoroastrian religious texts was elaborated and written down during the Islamic period. Unfortunately, we have far fewer sources for the history of the Zoroastrian communities than we do for the Christians and Jews of geographical Syria and Egypt. We have almost nothing by way of archaeological exploration of predominantly Zoroastrian communities from the conquest era, and the non-Muslim literary sources that inform us about Zoroastrian communities are also much more limited and, in many cases, of later date.

Of course, one assumes that the Arabian Believers who came into the Fertile Crescent recognized Muhammad as having been their prophet. But it is not clear how Muhammad's claim to prophecy was at first received or understood by the Christians, Jews, or Samaritans of the area (or, for that matter, by those of Arabia, already incorporated during the *ridda* wars into the new polity). Christian literary sources from the early Islamic period that actually mention Muhammad (most do not) generally do not call him prophet, but rather refer to him with terms like "leader," "teacher and guide," or "king," or note that he was a merchant, or that he called people to the worship of one God. Only a century or more after Muhammad's death do we begin to find Christian sources noting that his followers call him prophet and apostle. Certainly in later times— from perhaps the early second century AH/eighth century C.E. or a little later, by which date Islam had begun to coalesce from the Believers' movement into a clearly defined and distinct religious confession—the recognition of Muhammad as prophet was the decisive marker that distinguished Muslims from Christians, Jews, and all others. By that time, to utter the "statement of faith" (*shahada*, literally, "bearing witness") "There is no god but God, Muhammad is the apostle of God" (*la ilaha illa llah, Muhammad rasul allah*) was decisively to declare oneself a Muslim. But here again the early evidence is suggestive; the earliest documentary attestations of the *shahada*, found on coins, papyri, and inscriptions dating before about 66/685, include only the first part of the later "double *shahada*": "There is no god but God" (sometimes with the addition, "who has no associate")—Muhammad is not yet mentioned. If this is not merely an accident of preservation, we may see in it yet another indication of the ecumenical or non-confessional character of the early community of Believers, for the statement "There is no god but God" would have been acceptable to all monotheists, including Christians and Jews. It is not unreasonable to propose, then, that many Christians and Jews of Syria, Iraq, and other areas, as monotheists, could have found a place in the expanding early community of Believers.

By incorporating such monotheist communities into their growing domains, the Believers worked toward their goal of establishing the hegemony of God's law over the whole world. The Qur'an, as we have seen, promised the Believers that they would "inherit the earth" (Q. 33:25–27), but this could be understood to imply not the dispossession of existing monotheist populations, but their inclusion within the Believers' movement in exchange for the payment of taxes. The status of these communities and of the people in them was, then, probably analogous to that of many Arabian tribes or communities who had joined the Believers during the *ridda* wars. An East Syriac Christian text written in northern Mesopotamia in 687 or 688 (*Ktaba d-rish melle* of John Bar Penkaye) notes that the Believers (referred to in the text as "the kingdom of the *tayyaye*" [nomads]) demanded tribute but allowed people to stay in whatever faith they wished. It also

Two early coins of the Believers' regime. The first coins issued by the
Believers were based on Sasanian or Byzantine coin types. The upper coin
resembles a typical Sasanian coin, with a portrait of Great King Khosro on
the obverse and a fire temple flanked by two attendants on the reverse. In the
obverse outer margin, however, the Arabic slogan *bism Allah* ("In the name
of God") has been added at about 4 o'clock. The Pahlavi writing in the fields
to either side of the bust of Khosro shows that the coin was issued by Ziyad
b. Abi Sufyan, Mu'awiya's governor in the east, from the mint in Kirman,
in the year 52 (672 C.E.). The lower coin, in bronze, is made in imitation of
Byzantine coinage. It was issued in Hims (ancient Emesa); it is undated but
generally considered to have been issued in 693–694 C.E. The obverse shows
the bust of an emperor, possibly Constans II, wearing a diadem and breast-
plate; to the left, in Greek, ΚΑΛΟΝ ("good"); to the right, in Arabic, *bi-hims*,
"[minted] in Hims." The reverse shows a large M, the mark on Byzantine
coins indicating its value (40 *nummia*); flanking the M are the Greek letters
Ε μισις ("of Emesa") and beneath it, in Arabic, the word *tayyib*, "good."

notes that among the Believers who engaged in widespread raiding parties in these years were many Christians. The Nestorian patriarch Isho'yahb III in Iraq, writing a letter to one of his bishops in 647 or 648 C.E., notes that the new rulers "not only do not fight Christianity, they even commend our religion, show honor to the priests and monasteries and saints of our Lord, and make gifts to the monasteries and churches."

We should also take note here of a comment made by the Armenian bishop Sebeos, writing in the 660s, whose chronicle provides one of the earliest extant descriptions of the Believers and their actions. Among other things, he notes that the Believers' first governor of Jerusalem was a Jew. Imputation of close ties to Judaism was a favorite polemical technique used by Christian authors of this period to discredit their opponents, so this claim needs to be handled with caution; but if true, it provides further evidence of the confessional, open character of the Believers' movement. It is usually claimed that, with the arrival of the "Muslims," Christians and Jews were either reduced to subject status as "protected peoples" *(ahl al-dhimma)*, who paid tax but formed a distinctly lower level in society, or converted to Islam and incorporated into the Arabian Muslims as clients *(mawali)*. But the passages from Bar Penkaye, Isho'yahb, and Sebeos noted above, and a few others like them, suggest that some Christians and Jews may have been fully integrated, as such, into the early community of Believers; conversion was not at issue, because as monotheists they did not need to "convert" to anything in order to become active participants in the community, even in areas outside Arabia.

The ecumenical quality of the early Believers' movement, then, may help to explain why evidence of widespread destruction of towns, churches, and so on, is largely lacking in the archaeological evidence of relatively well-explored areas, such as Syria-Palestine: Presumably, it is because most communities, which already consisted of monotheists, were not destroyed or even seriously disrupted but merely underwent a change of masters (and tax collectors). As we have seen, churches could still be—and, the archaeological record shows, were—built after the "conquest." Indeed, the Arabian Believers may even have shared places of worship with Christians when they first arrived in a new area. Later Muslim tradition contains a number of accounts describing how the newly arrived "Muslims" prayed in part of a church in certain localities (Jerusalem, Damascus, and Hims are mentioned) because they had no mosque of their own. But, it is possible that the first Arabian Believers to reach such places, having won the local Christians over to their cause, simply prayed at first in their churches, because as monotheists the Christians were considered to be Believers whose places of worship were suitable. Later Muslim traditions about shared churches may be a vestigial memory of that early arrangement. Such collective worship of Qur'anic and Christian Believers may also be reflected in later Muslim traditions that describe an early *qibla musharriqa* or "east-facing *qibla*" (direction of prayer) in Syria, perhaps an echo of an earlier stage in the Believers' movement, when they faced eastward like the Christians rather than southward, toward Mecca, in accordance with the later *qibla*. Some archaeological evidence seems to support the idea of joint places of worship as well; excavation at the Cathisma Church, a Byzantine-era construction between Bethlehem and Jerusalem, has revealed that in its final phase it was modified to accommodate the Believers by the addition of a *mihrab* or prayer niche on the south wall (facing Mecca), while the rest of the building continued to function as a church oriented in an easterly direction.

The early expansion of the Believers outside Arabia, then, must not be understood simplistically as a case of direct confrontation between different religions and subsequent conquest of one by another. It may be true that the Arabian Believers first arrived, in many areas, as organized military forces and that when the Byzantine or Sasanian regimes sent armies against them, pitched battles were fought;

both traditional Muslim narratives and the earliest non-Muslim (mostly Christian) records describe such clashes, and, as we shall see, sources are in general agreement also on the major battles that were fought. Such battles, however, usually take place in open country and leave no archaeological record.

We can also assume, however, that the first arrival of the Believers in many areas may have been accompanied by widespread—though probably short-lived and superficial—plundering and raiding, of a kind that would have been observed and reported by some early sources (such as the sermons and homilies of Sophronius in the 630s), but that would also leave little archaeological record because major towns were not involved. The reasons for this petty plundering are simple. Many of the Arabian tribesmen who had joined the Believers' movement during the *ridda* wars were probably very undisciplined. Most of these troops probably knew little more about the movement they had joined than that a prophet had promised them riches in this world and paradise in the next, in exchange for their willingness to engage in *jihad*, fighting in the way of God, to vanquish the evil empires of Byzantium and Persia. Of the Qur'an (which, if we choose to follow Muslim tradition on this point, was not yet authoritatively written down), they probably knew little more than the few phrases required for the performance of prayer with the other troops. Their knowledge of the doctrines of the movement, then, was probably limited to the idea that God was one, and enshrined mainly in enthusiastic slogans such as "God is Great!" (*allahu akbar*), which they used as a battle cry. It is hardly to be expected that such troops would take pains to inquire closely whether the isolated villagers and farmers they encountered were good monotheists and committed to a righteous life or not. It seems fair to assume that the widespread pillaging reported in so many of the near-contemporary sources was largely their doing, or that of brigands taking advantage of the collapse of local authority structures that a change of regime always involves.

TREATY TEXT—TIFLIS

This text is placed in the descriptions of the conquests of the Caucasus region in the chronicle of Tabari, under the year 22 (642–643 C.E.). While many of the purported treaty texts found in literary sources are suspect as later inventions, some features of this one suggest that it may be more authentic. The term jizya here seems to be used in the sense of "tribute," not "poll tax" as in later law; also, unlike some other treaty texts, this one does not speak of Muhammad specifically, but only of God and His prophets generally. Both of these features may indicate that the text is based on an actual early document of the Believers' movement.

In the name of God, the Compassionate, the Merciful. This is a document from Habib ibn Maslama to the people of Tiflis of the Georgians, in the land of Hurmuz, [guaranteeing] the security of their persons and their property and their monasteries and churches and prayers, on condition that they submit the *jizya* with humility, a full dinar on every household, and [on condition that they provide] to us their advice and their assistance against God's enemy and our enemy, and a night's hospitality to the traveler—with lawful food of the people of the book and their lawful drink—and guidance on the road without being harmed on it by one of you. If you submit [to God] and perform the prayer and pay *zakat*, then [you are] our brothers in religion [*din*] and our clients. Whosoever turns away from God and His prophets and His books and His party, we summon you to war without distinction; God does not love traitors. Witnessed by 'Abd al-Rahman ibn Khalid and al-Hajjaj and 'Iyad, and written by Rabah. God and the angels and those who believe have witnessed [it]; and God suffices as a witness." (al-Tabari, *Tarʾikh*, ed. de Goeje, i/2675.)

Larger towns and cities, on the other hand, not so easily threatened by ragged and undisciplined bands of recruits, seem in most cases quickly to have made terms with the Believers once the latter's large armed forces arrived. Muslim traditional sources provide texts of some of these treaties; they are probably later idealizations made with legal purposes in mind, but their existence points to a general awareness that these towns had, in fact, been absorbed peaceably into the Believers' domain in exchange for payment of tax. It was only those cities and towns that refused to make terms that would have been subjected to siege, and these were few—and hence only in such places, such as Caesarea in Palestine, are we likely to find some archaeological trace of the "conquest" in the form of destruction layers. But even in these cases we can expect the damage to have been limited, for the Believers' goal was not to destroy these towns, but rather to bring their monotheistic populations under the rule of God's law. It was not the monotheist population against whom the Believers were waging war, after all, but the Byzantine and Sasanian regimes, which they saw as tolerating (or even imposing) sinfulness. The subjection of towns, then, was followed by the establishment of what the Believers considered a righteous public order, probably arranged in many cases with the participation of some of the "conquered" people integrated into the Believers' movement, who worked in association with Believers of Arabian origin. These Arabian Believers, or at least the leading cadres of them, show up in near-contemporary sources as *muhajirun* (Syriac *mhaggraye*; Greek *agarenoi* or *magaritai*), "those who have made *hijra*." As we saw in the preceding chapter, however, *hijra* was itself a word that carried overtones of migration, of full membership in and commitment to the Believers' movement, and of "fighting in God's way."

The Course and Scope of the Early Expansion

As noted at the beginning of this chapter, the traditional Muslim sources describe the Believers' expansion into the lands surrounding Arabia in great detail. On the basis of these traditional accounts, which were compiled mostly in the second century AH/eighth century C.E. and later, it is possible to sketch the outlines of what happened, but in doing so we must be alert to several tendencies in these reports and try to compensate for them. The compilers of these later reports tended, first, to portray the early Believers' movement as already being "Islam," in the sense of a distinct religious confession separate from Christianity and Judaism, rather than as a monotheistic religious movement—that is, they tried to eliminate or reduce the perception of the early movement's ecumenical qualities. Second, they portrayed the expansion primarily as a series of conquests *(futuh),* indeed, as the conquest by "Muslims" of "non-Muslims." That is, they tended to focus on the military aspects of the expansion, emphasizing recruitment of soldiers, battles, the takeover of cities, and the conclusion of treaties. They paid much less attention to the way the early Believers integrated themselves into the fabric of local life in various localities and the nature of their relations with the "conquered" populations, including the degree to which local populations may have cooperated with the Believers or what kinds of concessions the Believers may have made to the "conquered" populations. Third, in describing the expansion as a conquest, they depicted it in terms that suggested that it was a process that succeeded with divine assistance, because the "conquerors" were so much fewer in number than the "conquered." Only with God's help, they suggest, could so few "Muslims" have come to dominate much larger populations of "non-Muslims" and rout their huge armies on the battlefield. In short, the later Muslim sources described the expansion in ways designed to legitimize retrospectively the Muslim hegemony of their own day over vast areas

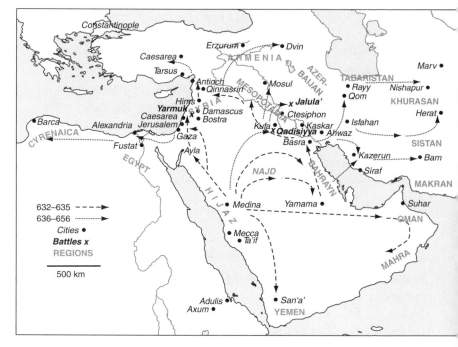

Map 4. Early campaigns of expansion (all features approximate)

and populations that were, when they wrote, still predominantly non-Muslim. They also emphasized the quasi-miraculous and divinely ordained character of the "conquests" and, consequently, of the political order that resulted from it.

As noted earlier, Muhammad and the early Believers showed a special interest in Syria. Muhammad, and then the first *amir al-mu'minin*, Abu Bakr, had made several efforts to pacify the tribes of the northern Hijaz who occupied the road to Syria and had dispatched at least two raids into Syria itself. On the completion of the *ridda* campaigns in late 12/autumn 633, Abu Bakr organized four separate armies and dispatched them to southern Syria. One force, commanded by 'Amr ibn al-'As, was dispatched to the Negev and southern Palestine (an area where, as we have seen, he owned property and which he presumably knew well). A second force, under Shurahbil ibn Hasana, was sent to what is today southern Jordan, but little is known of it. Two other armies, led by Yazid ibn Abi Sufyan and Abu 'Ubayda ibn al-Jarrah, were dispatched to the Balqa' region (the fertile area around Amman) and to the rich Jawlan (Golan) plateau east of the Sea of Galilee, respectively. These four armies together numbered an estimated twenty-four thousand troops and consisted mainly of commanders (*amirs*) from Quraysh and of townsmen and nomadic recruits from different parts of Yemen. Initially, these armies seem to have been concerned with winning over or neutralizing the rural populations, partly nomadic and partly settled, that occupied these regions; it is noteworthy that they were not sent in the first instance to more heavily settled areas such as the Galilee or against the major cities of Syria—Damascus, Tiberias, Jerusalem, Gaza, Caesarea, and so on. Muhammad's concern with ensuring control over nomadic groups as a basic strategy in building a secure base of power thus seems to have been continued by Abu Bakr at the beginning of the expansion into Syria. This process of assimilating the rural and pastoral populations on the fringes of Byzantine-controlled southern Syria lasted about six months (autumn 633–spring 634). The only clash with Byzantine forces of which we know in this early phase of operations took place at Dathin, near Gaza, where 'Amr ibn al-'As's troops defeated a Byzantine contingent (perhaps the Gaza garrison?) in late 12/February 634. As a result of this clash, 'Amr requested reinforcements.

Meanwhile, Abu Bakr was also dispatching commanders in other directions, specifically to northern Arabia and to Iraq, apparently with similar orders—to subdue or assimilate the rural (especially the nomadic) populations there. For example, Khalid ibn al-Walid, who had just completed his *ridda* campaigns through Najd and subdued the Hanifa tribe of Yamama at the battle of 'Aqraba' (near modern Riyadh), was ordered by Abu Bakr to proceed northward into southern

Iraq, probably in early 12/late spring or early summer 633. For almost the next year, Khalid and his core force of about one thousand
troops worked their way along the western fringes of the Euphrates,
making alliances with or subduing the numerous nomadic groups
they encountered and reducing or making treaties with the towns
and villages along the river. Many of the tribes Khalid and his forces
contacted during this campaign—Shayban, 'Ijl, Dhuhl, Namir ibn
al-Qasit, Tamim, and others—seem to have been divided among
themselves along lineage lines, or by religion, and Khalid exploited
these divisions effectively, using one section to help bring the re-
mainder to submission. Some of these groups, moreover, such as the
part of Shayban headed by Muthanna ibn Haritha, had been raiding
Sasanian territory before Khalid arrived. (We will meet Muthanna
again.) Khalid also relied heavily on local tribal recruits to swell his
forces and help subdue the numerous towns he encountered: Ubulla
(Apologos), Madhar, Kaskar, Hira, Anbar, and 'Ayn al-Tamr. In occupying these towns—often little more was involved than the impo-
sition of a tax payment and an agreement not to oppose the Believers—
Khalid's forces encountered and overcame Sasanian garrisons that
were stationed in each town. These were small outposts, maintained
by the Sasanians on their desert fringe to discourage raiding by nomadic tribes into the rich agricultural heartland of Iraq, the Sasanians' vital tax base. Their defeat by Khalid's forces was the first direct military confrontation the Believers had with the Sasanians, a
perhaps unintended consequence of the campaign's real goal, which
was to bring all the nomadic populations of the region under their
control.

In Syria, the Believers' forces had consolidated their position
among the nomadic populations there by early 13/spring of 634 and
were ready to begin their assault on the major cities of the region.
Abu Bakr ordered Khalid to march from Iraq to Syria with part of his
force to serve as reinforcements for the four armies there—and possibly because, as the ablest field commander, his tactical skills were

needed on the Syrian front. The exact course of events in Syria over the next two years is, unfortunately, impossible to reconstruct with confidence because the traditional Muslim sources provide conflicting reports that cannot be reconciled satisfactorily. We do know, however, that during this period the Believers occupied (sometimes after a siege) some of the major towns of central Syria—Bostra, Damascus, Fahl (Pella), Baysan (Beth Shaan), Ba'labakk, and Hims (Emesa). They also faced Byzantine armies sent to contain them, delivering major defeats to the Byzantine forces at Fahl, Ajnadayn (in central Palestine?) and, above all, at the decisive battle of the Yarmuk, which took place on the southern edge of the Jawlan plateau, where it drops off into the yawning Yarmuk canyon. It is unclear, however, whether these great battles preceded and opened the way for the occupation of the cities of Syria or whether the Byzantine armies were sent in response to the Believers' seizure of key cities and towns. An isolated Syriac fragment that may refer to the decisive battle at Yarmuk dates it precisely to August 20, 636, a date that agrees with the dating given by some (but not all) of the traditional Muslim sources on this event.

It is also unclear how the several armies originally sent to Syria by Abu Bakr operated in this phase. Most sources agree that Khalid received the submission of the city of Bostra, but on other points they provide divergent information. Were these forces now all under the command of Khalid ibn al-Walid, as some sources state, or were they still essentially autonomous forces that sometimes cooperated to confront major concentrations of Byzantine troops? And what was the exact nature of their activities? The situation is further confused by the fact that the first *amir al-mu'minin*, Abu Bakr, died in Medina in mid 13/summer 634, and his successor, 'Umar ibn al-Khattab (ruled 13–23/634–644), is said by some reports to have dismissed Khalid and appointed Abu 'Ubayda to supreme command.

None of these problems can be resolved satisfactorily on the basis of the traditional sources—and for this aspect of events we have no others. The sources do suggest, however, something about the makeup of the Believers' forces at Yarmuk and in Syria generally. Apparently they were composed primarily of Quraysh, nomadic tribes from the Hijaz (Sulaym, Kinana, and Bali) and large numbers of tribesmen from Yemen (Azd, Himyar, Hamdan, Madhhij, Khawlan, Khath'am, Kinda, Sakun, and Hadramawt). They seem to have been joined also by some of the local nomadic tribesmen (Judham and Lakhm), although others from these same tribes—often described as having been Christian tribesmen—allied themselves with the Byzantine forces at Yarmuk, as did the Byzantines' old allies in the region, the B. Ghassan. We can estimate the total size of the Believers' forces at Yarmuk at perhaps thirty thousand to forty thousand men.

By late 15/autumn 636, then, the Believers' armies had decisively destroyed the Byzantine military presence in Syria, defeating several large armies sent to contain them—including one commanded by the Emperor Heraclius's brother, Theodore. They had occupied several key towns as far north as Hims (Emesa), and were poised to occupy the rest of the region without major resistance. Over the next two years, Abu 'Ubayda dispatched several campaigns to northern Syria from his base at Hims (which was long to remain the Believers' main military base in Syria). The exact dates of these campaigns and the identities of their commanders are, as usual, confused in the sources, but by the end of 16/637 the Believers appear to have occupied Qinnasrin, Aleppo, Antioch, Manbij, and other towns of northern Syria. North of Antioch, around the Gulf of Alexandretta and the Cilician plain, the retreating Emperor Heraclius is said to have resorted to a "scorched earth" policy, removing garrisons and leveling fortifications in an attempt to deter the Believers from advancing further. (The mountainous districts of Lebanon and northern Syria were almost impenetrable and remained for decades untouched.) Farther south, most of Palestine seems to have been quickly occupied by forces under Shurahbil ibn Hasana and 'Amr ibn al-'As. Several well-fortified coastal towns held out longer because the Byzantines could supply them by sea, particularly Caesarea (which was besieged for several years before it fell) and Tripoli (which only fell after another decade).

Jerusalem deserves special notice because, as we have seen, it held unique religious significance and thus may have been one of the Believers' main objectives in invading Syria in the first place. As noted earlier, Jerusalem is reported by Muslim tradition to have been the place toward which Muhammad first instructed the Believers to pray. It seems unsurprising, then, that even after they came to face Mecca when praying, the early Believers continued to think of Jerusalem as a place of special sanctity—perhaps because of its significance in apocalyptic scenarios for the coming Last Judgment, key events of which, according to contemporary Jewish and Christian traditions, would take place in Jerusalem. The sources for the occupation of Jerusalem are very few and heavily overlaid with later legend, but it seems that the city capitulated to the Believers in 636, not long after the battle of Yarmuk, in the reign of the second *amir al-mu'minin*, 'Umar. The early Believers in Jerusalem are thought to have established their first place of worship in, or beside, the Church of the Holy Sepulchre, but all trace of this has vanished due to the subsequent destruction and rebuilding of the church by the Crusaders in the eleventh century. The Believers may have abandoned this first place of prayer some time after their arrival, however, for the European traveler Arculf, who visited sometime before 683 C.E., mentions nothing about the presence of Believers in or near the Church of the Holy Sepulchre. He does, however, describe a large, crude place of prayer atop the Temple Mount. This may have been a forerunner of the al-Aqsa Mosque.

More or less simultaneously with the Believers' defeat of Byzantine forces and occupation of Syria, they also embarked on a confrontation with the Sasanians and the conquest of Iraq. Once again, traditional Muslim sources are almost our only evidence for what happened, and once again they provide conflicting chronological information and many suspect accounts, but the general sequence of events in Iraq is clearer than in Syria.

Some time after the death of Abu Bakr in mid-13/late summer 634, the new *amir al-mu'minin*, 'Umar ibn al-Khattab, ordered a modest force from Medina to reinforce the small contingents that had remained in Iraq following Khalid ibn al-Walid's departure for Syria roughly six months earlier. This new force, numbering several thousand men, was placed under the command of Abu 'Ubayd al-Thaqafi, who hailed from the third town of the Hijaz, Ta'if. It had a core of soldiers from Medina (Helpers) and Abu 'Ubayd's tribe, the Thaqif, as well as members of nomadic tribes from the Hijaz, Najd, and northeastern Arabia, recruited *en route* to Iraq. This force joined the followers of Muthanna ibn Haritha (mostly local tribesmen) near Hira and proceeded to raid the fertile lowlands of Iraq, reducing many small Sasanian garrisons. But the Sasanians rallied and sent a sizable force that annihilated most of Abu 'Ubayd's army at the Battle of the Bridge, sometime in 13/634 or 14/635; Abu 'Ubayd himself, along with many of his troops, were killed.

In response to this debacle, 'Umar recruited additional troops from tribes (or parts of them) that had remained loyal to Medina during the *ridda* and dispatched them to bolster Muthanna, around whom the Believers' remaining forces in Iraq had rallied. These new reinforcements included more contingents from northeastern Arabia, as well as men from the tribes of the Sarat district, south of the Hijaz. Especially numerous were the Bajila, led by their chief Jarir ibn 'Abd Allah al-Bajali. These elements joined the Believers' surviving forces that were already on the fringes of Iraq—largely drawn from tribes that lived in the region anyway—and began to launch desultory raids on isolated Sasanian outposts; but it seems that Muthanna and Jarir fell into disagreement over who held supreme command in the area.

Meanwhile, 'Umar set about assembling another, larger, force to go to Iraq—partly in response to a Sasanian buildup and partly to settle the question of who was in charge there. This undertaking, according to all sources, began sometime after news reached him of the Believers' decisive victory at Yarmuk in Syria. 'Umar put this new force under the command of Sa'd ibn Abi Waqqas, a Meccan Emigrant and close early follower of Muhammad who had served both Abu Bakr and 'Umar as tribal governor in the Najd. Now he was sent with a core force numbering around four thousand troops, including sizable contingents from the Najd, and more troops from the Sarat region and the Yemen. After Sa'd's departure, additional "late arrivals" came into Medina who had been recruited from South Arabia, Najd, and the Hijaz. These were duly sent on to join Sa'd's army, also now augmented by tribesmen already in southern Iraq, and by the former Iraq forces that Khalid had taken with him to Syria, which now returned to Iraq. The total forces under Sa'd's command thus numbered around twelve thousand men. The striking thing here is the success with which the Believers were able to assemble fighting men drawn from many tribes and all corners of the Arabian peninsula, bringing them together to form a force of previously unknown size in Arabian terms.

It is noteworthy that this army, unlike its predecessor, seems to have included few men of Thaqif; but even more remarkable is that it included contingents from some tribes that had not been loyal to Medina during the *ridda*. Evidently, 'Umar decided that the need for fighting men was so acute that the old policy of relying only on *ridda* loyalists had to be abandoned. Indeed, some of the tribal contingents that formed part of Sa'd's force were led by chiefs who had backed the *ridda* rebellions of Talha ibn Khuwaylid in Najd, or of Aswad al-'Ansi in Yemen.

By the time Sa'd reached Iraq, Muthanna had died. Sa'd promptly married his widow, doubtless to solidify his ties with Muthanna's tribesmen of the Shayban, whose support—as locals—would be vital to the Believers' cause there. The Sasanian army, described by the traditional Muslim sources as being huge, now crossed the Euphrates and, under its general Rustam, advanced against Saʿd's forces, which took up a position southwest of Hira at a place called Qadisiyya. Descriptions of the battle of Qadisiyya itself are, although voluminous, hazy and often suspect, but the outcome was clear—a decisive defeat of the Sasanian army, including the death of Rustam himself. The shattered remnants of the Sasanian army retreated across the Euphrates in flight, pursued by Saʿd's forces into the agrarian heartland of Iraq, which was now occupied with only token resistance. The remaining Sasanian forces attempted to regroup around the Sasanian king Yazdagird III at the Sasanian capital, Ctesiphon (today a southern suburb of Baghdad), but Saʿd's army hemmed in Yazdagird and his forces there, giving the Believers a free hand to consolidate their grip on the rest of the country. Eventually Yazdagird and his forces abandoned Ctesiphon (after being trapped there for an uncertain length of time—some reports say a few months, others more than two years) and withdrew to the foothills of the Zagros mountains to the east to regroup. Here again, their efforts were in vain. Saʿd organized another army to confront them and decisively defeated them at Jalulaʾ (variously dated by our sources between 16/637 and 19/640). Saʿd established a garrison town, Kufa, adjacent to the old town of Hira that had been the seat of the Lakhmid allies of the Sasanians, and this became the center of the Believers' military operations from central Iraq.

Southern Iraq generally constituted a distinct front. The Sasanians made no major stand there, and a separate and much smaller force sent from Medina gradually wrested the area from the Sasanians' local garrisons, including the main towns of Ubulla, Maysan (Mesene), Abazqubadh, and others. The southern Iraqi garrison, Basra, was established near the old town of Ubulla. After the battle of Jalulaʾ in the Zagros, the Sasanians appear to have tried to regroup yet again in the city of Ahwaz in Khuzistan, but this was conquered by a force led by Abu Musa al-Ashʿari, which then systematically reduced several other towns of that district—Manadhir, Susa, Ramhormuz, and

Tustar. The forces in southern Iraq are not fully described in the sources, but their central component seems to have been men of Thaqif and Medinese Helpers and members of Hijazi nomadic groups, to which were probably added local tribesmen of 'Ijl, Dhuhl, and Tamim.

As a result of these campaigns, then, the whole of the rich Iraqi alluvium, including Khuzistan, passed under the Believers' control between roughly 13/634 and 21/642. Yazdagird and whatever troops remained loyal to him fled eastward through the Zagros into the Iranian plateau, never to return.

The Sasanian army regrouped yet again farther north, near Nihavand, around Sasanian Great King Yazdegird III. But troops from both Basra and Kufa routed this force also, killing their commander (ca. 22/642). Yazdegird fled to Khurasan in northeastern Iran where, some years later, the illustrious history of the Sasanians ended ignominiously when he was murdered by a brigand. Henceforth resistance to the Believers' expansion on the Iranian plateau was local and sporadic; the Sasanian state had been effectively destroyed.

The new encampment—soon city—of Basra played an important role in the conquest of the Iranian plateau. An early campaign had crossed the Persian Gulf to western Iran from eastern Arabia ("Bahrayn" in the sources) and occupied Fars province, but it was from Basra in southern Iraq that the main campaigns into the Iranian highlands were launched. As a result, in later years much of Iran was administered by the governor of Basra. Within a few years of its foundation, forces from Basra pushed farther into the central Zagros region, occupying the key towns—Isfahan, Qashan, Qom, and Qazvin. From these bases in western Iran, Basran troops in successive years campaigned into eastern Iran. Some forces headed eastward via Rayy (now in the south suburbs of Tehran) to Qumis, the Gorgan region, and Nishapur (by the early 30s/650s) in northeastern Iran. Other campaigns pushed from Isfahan eastward to Yazd and eventually to eastern Iran and Afghanistan; Herat was taken around

30/650–651, and from there campaigns entered Khurasan from the south (taking Marv, Sarakhs, and Tus) and pushed eastward nearly to the Oxus River, on the fringes of the Central Asian steppe. Many of these campaigns were led by, or dispatched by, 'Abdullah ibn 'Amir, governor of Basra for the third *amir al-mu'minin*, 'Uthman.

Meanwhile, another series of campaigns from Basra occupied the main cities of southern Iran during 'Uthman's reign—including Kazerun, Istakhr, Darabgird, and Bam. Further expeditions pushed eastward into mountainous Sijistan [Sistan], beginning a long struggle against the local rulers of Zabulistan (from the early 30s/650s onward). Campaigns were even sent into desolate Makran on Iran's southern coast. By the time the *amir al-mu'minin* 'Uthman was killed in 35/656, then, most of the Iranian plateau was under the political control of the Believers' movement—that is, most towns and rural districts had tendered their submission and agreed to pay tribute to Medina's agents. Only mountainous Tabaristan in the north, just south of the Caspian Sea, and the rugged southeastern part of Iran were still independent. It must be recognized, however, that in most areas and towns, especially those far from the key garrison towns, this control was nominal. The tiny number of Arabian Believers probably meant that they were seldom seen in many parts of the Iranian plateau; taxes (or better, occasional tribute) continued to be levied mainly by the local Iranian landed gentry (*dihqans*) who had simply switched their allegiance from the Sasanian great king, in distant Ctesiphon, to the *amir al-mu'minin* of the new state based in distant Arabia that had emerged out of the Believers' movement. No change in religious identity was apparently required for them to serve in this way; as much as a century and a half later, a Christian text describing Muslim tax collection (albeit in a different area, northern Mesopotamia) notes that the tax collector was a Zoroastrian.

Northern Mesopotamia (the Jazira) and Armenia to the north were conquered in the time of the *amir al-mu'minins* 'Umar (ruled

13–23/634–644) and 'Uthman (ruled 23–35/644–656) by forces coming from both Syria and Iraq. Mosul and other towns near the Euphrates were evidently conquered by forces from Kufa in 'Umar's time, and until the end of the seventh century C.E., Mosul remained an administrative dependency of Kufa, not an independent province with its own governor, even though it became an important military garrison for the new regime. The lion's share of the new state's expansion to the north, however, was undertaken by troops dispatched from Syria. Especially important on this front were the efforts of 'Iyad ibn Ghanm, who campaigned in Mesopotamia in the time of 'Umar, and of Habib ibn Maslama al-Fihri, who raided Armenia in the time of 'Uthman, penetrating as far as Erzurum and Dvin (near modern Yerevan). Neither the population of Armenia nor the Byzantine emperor (himself of Armenian descent) were ready to concede this important province, however, and for several decades it was wrested back and forth, with Byzantine counteroffensives being answered by renewed efforts by the Believers' movement to seize the region. This sustained pattern of on-again, off-again warfare also became the norm farther west, along the so-called *thughur* or border marches delimiting the frontier between the Believers' territory and the Byzantine empire in southern Anatolia. There the *amir al-mu'minins* launched annual summer campaigns (called *sa'ifa*) against Byzantine territory, with the main garrison at Hims serving as the rear staging-point and front-line outposts such as Massisa and Tarsus serving as the springboard for the annual incursions to the north. Eventually, these bases would be the starting-point for campaigns aiming to conquer Constantinople itself (674–678 and 717–718 C.E.).

Meanwhile, the Believers who had occupied Palestine and the rest of geographical Syria began to push westward into Egypt and, from there, into North Africa. The first step was the occupation of Egypt, the richest province of the Byzantine empire and a key source of grain for the Byzantine capital at Constantinople. Led by General

'Amr ibn al-'As, who evidently was familiar with Egypt from trading ventures earlier in his life, forces from Syria entered Egypt in 639. The reports about what happened in Egypt are confused; some relate a military defeat of Byzantine forces, others tell of a series of negotiations with Cyrus, the orthodox patriarch of Alexandria (who is sometimes called, for reasons not clear, "al-Muqawqis"). Tensions between the orthodox patriarch and hierarchy and the Coptic population, which was monophysite, may have been a factor. In any case, by 642 the Believers had occupied most of the country and surrounded Alexandria and were allowed to enter the city peaceably. The Byzantines sent a naval force which, with help from the local population, briefly reoccupied Alexandria in 645–646, but their restoration was soon reversed.

Although the Byzantines had always made their capital in Egypt at Alexandria, 'Amr established his main garrison at Fustat, adjacent to the former Byzantine stronghold of Babylon on the Nile (in the southern section of modern Cairo). Fustat became the Believers' main center and seat of government in Egypt and served as the base from which, for many decades to come, 'Amr and his successor as governor of Egypt, 'Abdullah ibn Abi Sarh, would launch raids and campaigns of conquest westward. They first raided Libya, seizing Barca and other towns in Cyrenaica. Over the next decade desultory raids were launched against the Byzantine province of Africa (*Ifriqiya*, as it became known in Arabic)—modern Tunisia—but a permanent presence was only established there in the 660s, after the conclusion of the first civil war.

In 23/644, the *amir al-mu'minin* 'Umar was killed in Medina—stabbed by a disgruntled slave. On his deathbed, he appointed six leading figures of Quraysh as a kind of selection committee, or *shura*, and instructed them to choose one of their number to be the next *amir al-mu'minin*. (Interestingly, he excluded any Helpers from this group.) All of the six had been early supporters of Muhammad, all were linked to him by kinship or by marriage, or both, and all were therefore deemed likely candidates for leadership of the Believers' movement. Among them were Muhammad's cousin 'Ali ibn Abi Talib, who had married the prophet's daughter Fatima, and the wealthy 'Uthman, the early follower from the powerful clan of Umayya to whom, as we have seen, Muhammad had also given two of his daughters, in succession, in marriage.

After several days of deliberation, the *shura* unanimously selected 'Uthman as the third *amir al-mu'minin* (ruled 23–35/644–656); he picked up where 'Umar had left off in supervising the expansion of the Believers, and many of the conquests in North Africa, eastern Iran, Armenia, and the north took place on his watch. Toward the end of his twelve-year rule, however, he came under increasing criticism from some Believers, which came to a head in a mutiny against him, resulting in his murder in 35/656. I will discuss these events, and the issues underlying them, in the next chapter.

Consolidation and Institutions of the Early Expansion Era

The expansion of the early community of Believers out of western Arabia to encompass vast new areas stretching from Egypt and North Africa to eastern Iran and Central Asia by the early 30s/650s involved far more than merely military operations, of course. The armies sent out by the successive commanders of the Believers represented only the leading edge of the community's expansion; once the Believers had established their control over an area, whether through military action or by persuading the locals to join them, those military forces tended to move on or, even if based there, were at least active elsewhere. What followed was a much more complex process of interaction between the small clusters of newly arrived Arabian Believers and the much larger local populations they now governed. Unfortunately, traditional sources, which provide such full (if sometimes contradictory) information on the expansion itself, are much less forthcoming on this complex process of social transformation that, ultimately, resulted in the gradual emergence of a new Islamic society in the Near East.

The Believers of Arabian origin who first settled in adjacent countries show up in the early non-Muslim sources under several designations, as we have seen. Sometimes they are referred to by words of general import used to designate nomadic peoples, such as the Greek *sarakenoi* (of uncertain etymology, anglicized as "Saracen") or the Syriac *tayyaye* ("bedouin, nomad"). But in other instances they are called, in Greek, *agarenoi* or *magaritai*, or in Syriac, *mhaggraye*— in both cases, words derived from the Arabic *muhajirun*, which seems, then, to have been a term the Believers who came to these regions applied to themselves. In the previous chapter, we discussed the concept of *hijra*, with its overtones of "emigration," "joining (or taking refuge with) a pious community," "fighting for the faith," and "adopting a settled (that is, non-nomadic) life." The fact that the new Arabian settlers called themselves *muhajirun* suggests that these values were at the outset an important part of the ethos of these new settlements.

We can assume—and, as we have seen, there is some evidence to support this assumption—that some local people joined, or were included in, the Believers' movement from the start and participated in the establishment of the new order. The new order required political obedience to the *amir al-mu'minin* or his representatives—the local commander or governor—and the payment of tax to the new regime. But the central concern of the new order was the observance of God's law (whether in the form of Qur'anic injunctions, or, for Jews or Christians, in the form of Jewish or Christian religious laws). This, the Believers knew, was urgently necessary to ensure their salvation when the Judgment came. This deep concern for the strict observance of God's law helps explain why the mere accusation that the governor 'Utba ibn Ghazwan had committed adultery was sufficient to warrant his dismissal; to engage in such behavior, in violation of a clear Qur'anic injunction (for example, Q. 24:2–3), was not just a personal matter of one's own private morality; it was a public threat to the very character of the new regime the Believers wished to establish.

The Believers inaugurated a number of distinctive institutions that were instrumental in establishing their rule, and the social order that came with it, on a firm and enduring basis. The most important institution of all was that of the *amir al-mu'minin* or "commander of the Believers." The creation of this office effectively institutionalized the notion that the whole community of Believers should be politically united, as it was agreed that it should have henceforth a single leader. It is worth considering for a moment, however, the degree of centralized control that the commanders of the Believers may have exercised. The traditional sources clearly exaggerate this; they not only depict the *amir al-mu'minin* as being responsible for the dispatch of armies under various commanders, but they sometimes suggest that virtually every decision those commanders made in the field, even on purely tactical matters, such as how to handle a besieged town, was referred back to the *amir al-mu'minin* for approval or consultation. Given the nature of communications of the time, this kind of detailed supervision by the *amir al-mu'minin* is not credible. On the other hand, we cannot really doubt that the expansion movement had a central mission, or that successive *amir al-mu'minin*s did, in fact, formulate policy and make decisions having broad strategic importance, even if many tactical matters were left to the autonomy of their generals in the field. The fact that the *amir al-mu'minin* sometimes coordinated the activities of military forces on different fronts suggests that even the earliest military phase of the expansion was undertaken with a goal to realizing certain definite objectives. Even more important as a measure of the degree of centralized control exercised by the *amir al-mu'minin* is the fact that they rotated or replaced generals, and later provincial governors, with some regularity. Moreover, the generals or governors who were removed from office almost always stepped down without resistance. Traditional sources provide us with regular listings of the generals or governors in charge of various provinces year by year, and such appointments are occasionally confirmed by coin evidence that proves without a doubt that a particular governor was in office at a particular time. The near-contemporary Armenian chronicler Sebeos also makes clear that governors consulted the *amir al-mu'minin* in Medina on important matters of policy. All of this establishes beyond serious doubt that some degree of centralization of authority and hierarchy of command existed within the Believers' new regime, even in its early years.

Another institution of great significance was the standing army, the first emergence of which, during the *ridda* wars, we have already seen. Closely associated with the army—indeed, in some ways inextricably bound up with the army's increasingly professional status—was an institution called the *diwan*. The *diwan* was originally created under the *amir al-mu'minin* 'Umar as a register of those Believers who were entitled to receive a share of the booty and tax revenues that were in his day beginning to flow into Medina. The recipients at first included some who were not in the army (notably Muhammad's widows), but the bulk of those on the first *diwan* were soldiers, who were entitled to a regular pay allotment—its level depending on how early they had joined up. As time went on, the *diwan* became almost exclusively a military payroll; eventually, the word *diwan* came to be applied to other branches of a fledgling bureaucratic system, with the meaning of "government department"; hence we begin to see references to a chancery (the *diwan al-rasa'il*) and a land-tax administration *(diwan al-kharaj)*. The *amir al-mu'minin*s also established something called the *barid*, or official courier system, through which they received reports from their governors and spies in the field.

Also closely associated with the rise of the army was yet another new institution: the special settlements the Believers established for themselves, often beside (or sometimes, it seems, within) existing towns or cities. These settlements were sometimes called, in Arabic, *amsar* (singular, *misr*), usually translated as "garrison towns." This translation is only partly accurate; the word *misr* does seem to be derived from an old South Arabic word meaning "expeditionary force," and the *amsar* were where the Believers' expeditionary forces outside Arabia were first encamped. But, although they may have begun as garrisons, the *amsar* became almost immediately much more than that. They were soon filled not only with soldiers but also with the soldiers' families, with other Believers from Arabia who were not soldiers, and probably with local people who had joined the Believers' movement. Fundamentally, these new settlements, set apart from the existing towns, were an expression of the Believers' concern for piety and righteous living—a concern that led them to isolate themselves from all of those in the surrounding society who, although monotheists, were not sufficiently stringent in their behavior or religious observances to be considered true Believers. This self-imposed isolation may help explain why the tiny number of Arabian Believers adhering to Qur'anic teachings did not vanish through acculturation into the much larger local populations.

Some of the *amsar* grew into great cities and eventually became the centers in which a new Islamic culture was elaborated and from which it radiated to surrounding areas—developments that only happened, however, many decades after they were first settled. Traditional sources mention the foundation of some of the *amsar*—in Iraq, Kufa (near Hira) and Basra (near Ubulla), and in Egypt Fustat ("Old Cairo"), for example. Curiously, we have no such references for new settlements near Damascus, Hims, Jerusalem, or other towns of Syria, suggesting that the Believers may have taken up residence inside existing quarters of these towns, which may have been partly abandoned by their Christian inhabitants. On the other hand, the best archaeological attestation of such a settlement comes from southern Syria—the excavated remains of Ayla (at modern Aqaba,

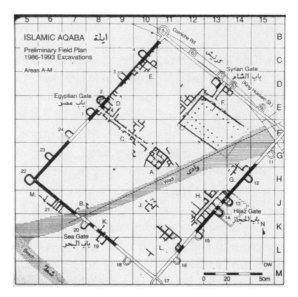

Plan and West Wall of Ayla (modern Aqaba, Jordan). This site, apparently founded at the time of the *amir al-mu'minin* 'Uthman (644–656), was clearly a planned settlement; excavation uncovered the city wall with regularly spaced defensive bastions and city gates in each direction.

Jordan), thought to date to the time of the third *amir al-mu'minin*, 'Uthman (ruled 23–35/644–656) and situated virtually at the gates of the existing Roman-Byzantine town, Aelana. The ruins of Ayla reveal that such settlements were carefully laid out according to an orthogonal plan, not haphazard camps or shantytowns. Ayla had a rectangular plan with four gates, one in the middle of each wall, and protruding towers spaced regularly along each outside wall, as well as a systematic street plan—a design adapted from Roman-Byzantine encampments familiar in the Levant. The one description of the layout of an early *misr* that is found in our traditional sources—which tells about the settlement of Kufa—speaks of the regular placement of streets around a rectangular central court or square, with specific tribes being assigned particular allotments along given streets (something we cannot know from Ayla's archaeological remains). It makes clear, however, that Kufa's original arrangement was overwhelmed by a huge influx of Believers coming from Arabia in the years after the conquest of Iraq, so that the original plan of the city had to be modified several times.

The language used in these new settlements was Arabic, regardless of where they were located. Arabic was, of course, the native language of the Arabian Believers, whether soldiers or not, who emigrated to the Fertile Crescent; it was also the language of the Qur'an and the language in which communal prayer was conducted. Moreover, some of the Believers of local origin probably spoke Arabic as well; for Arabic had spread in the centuries before Islam from the desert fringes into the settled farmland of southern Syria and southern Iraq, in particular, and even into the eastern desert of Egypt. Of course, most *amsar* were located in areas where other languages were current; some of the country population in Syria and Iraq spoke some form of Aramaic; the majority of the population around Fustat in Egypt spoke Coptic; and in the Syrian cities, where Arabian Believers seem to have occupied abandoned quarters in existing towns (as in Damascus or Hims) rather than building new settlements (as at Ayla), some of the urban population spoke Greek. In the Iranian plateau, early outposts such as Istakhr (north of Shiraz) or Marv were Arabic-speaking islands in a sea of peoples speaking various Iranian languages. The linguistic isolation of the Believers' early settlements, no less than what we might term their moral or pious separateness, helped the Believers maintain their sense of distinctness and avoid acculturation in the decades before they developed a clear-cut sense of themselves as constituting a separate monotheistic religious confession as Muslims and contributed in a fundamental way also to the eventual development of a vibrant new Islamic culture whose linguistic vehicle was Arabic.

The concerns of the Believers' regime in the newly acquired territories were manifold. They of course tried to maintain public order, in the settlement itself and in the surrounding countryside, not least because tax collection depended on it. The Believers' new settlements or colonies were headed by a governor who answered directly to the *amir al-mu'minin*. At first, these governors were usually the same commander who had led the Believers' military forces into an area, and the government of the settlements had a distinctly military flavor. With time, the governors' interests became less strictly military; in addition to administering the army, the governors also had to concern themselves with the collection of taxes, with keeping social order in accordance with God's law, and with dispensing justice within the community. Quite early, some of these functions were put in the hands of separate individuals, with a military governor (*amir*, "commander") serving in tandem with a financial governor or tax agent (*'amil*). Within the new *amsar*, the governors dispensed justice (Egyptian papyri show the governors doing this); enforced properly pious behavior and demeanor, including the conduct of regular prayers; and managed finances, including the distribution of stipends payable to soldiers and other recipients, and organizing and dispatching tax revenues, a share of which was sent to

Medina. In cases in which the settlement was the base of operations for military forces active in the field, the governor was also charged with distributing the booty brought in by those forces, including slaves and livestock as well as property of other kinds, a share of which was reserved for the *amir al-mu'minin* and had to be forwarded to Medina.

In the countryside, the governors were concerned above all with collecting taxes, which could be done only if calm reigned in the taxable districts. Papyri from Egypt show that local disputes were sometimes referred to the governor, but in many cases adjudication was left in the hands of subordinates such as the local village head-man. The evidence available suggests that during the early de-cades of the Believers' rule, the countryside was largely left to run itself, under the direction of village headmen or tribal chiefs, who organized periodic payment of taxes to the regime. There are a few murky references to Believers (especially well-connected chiefs of Quraysh) becoming wealthy because of their control over extensive country districts; many of these were probably lands abandoned by their erstwhile owners. It does not seem likely, however, that many Arabian Believers settled in the open countryside in these early years—more probably, those who had acquired rural properties re-mained clustered in the cities or smaller towns and simply har-vested wealth from their holdings as absentee landlords. It is also unclear to what degree rural populations and communities that had remained in place during the transition to the Believers' rule were moved about in the early years following the change of rulers. A few accounts describe the relocation of certain people to new places, usually to occupy or resettle a town that had resisted and been forcibly conquered. Tripoli in modern-day Lebanon, for ex-ample, which was besieged for years and resisted stubbornly, was finally evacuated by Byzantine ships, after which it was resettled with Jews—from where, we are not told—by 'Uthman's governor of Syria, Mu'awiya. This may mean that these Jews were considered especially likely to be loyal to the regime—or perhaps it merely reflects the *amir al-mu'minin's* unwillingness to have Christians repopulate a town from which the Byzantines had been expelled only with great difficulty.

We have reviewed the course of the Believers' expansion in the years following Muhammad's death and described some of the institutional and other innovations that accompanied this process. We have also considered the character of the expansion, arguing that the sources' emphasis on the military dimension of the expansion has obscured its nature as a monotheistic reform movement that many local communities may have seen little reason to oppose, because it was doctrinally not obnoxious to them. This may be why, to judge from the archaeological record, most localities came under the Believers' rule with little resistance. Military action must have been used by the Believers at times, perhaps mainly against Byzantine and Sasanian garrisons and standing armies. Most sources speak of major battles, sieges of entrenched garrisons, and some raiding and bloodshed at the time of the transition, but, whatever its extent, this seems to have ended quickly; the Christian author Bar Penkaye, writing in 681 or 682, can describe the era of Mu'awiya (ruled 41–60/661–680)—barely twenty years after the Believers came to power in Syria and Iraq—as one of justice, peace, prosperity, and religious tolerance.

The architects of the expansion—the early *amir al-mu'minins*—and the Believers generally seem in this period to have had as their objective the establishment of a new and righteous public order that conformed to the dictates of God's law as they understood it—particularly in its Qur'anic form. Their desire to establish a righteous, God-guided kingdom can be seen, perhaps, as a revolt against what they viewed as the pervasive corruption and sinfulness of the Byzantine and Sasanian empires, reflected in their adherence to what the

Believers considered erroneous doctrines (such as, in the Byzantine case, the idea of the Trinity). On the other hand, the Believers' ambition to establish the rule of God's law throughout the world—by conquest if necessary—can be seen as a continuation of, or analogy to, the ideologies of world conquest that, as we have seen, were part of both the Byzantine and Sasanian imperial traditions.

There were also, of course, powerful material incentives at work during the Believers' expansion; hopes for material gain may have drawn some people into the movement, and material benefits doubtless helped solidify many individuals' adhesion to the movement. But these material factors are not in themselves sufficient to explain the expansion. For one thing, such material incentives always existed but only contributed to a sudden expansion movement when placed in the context of the organizing ideology provided by the Believers' movement. Indeed, the material incentives for expansion were inextricably tied to the ideological underpinnings of the Believers' movement, so that the two dimensions were complementary, not contradictory. The Believers were motivated by religious commitment but saw the material benefits that came with their expansion as the natural consequence—or, rather, the divinely ordained consequence—of their success in creating a righteous new order. In their view, the influx of wealth that followed their conquests and expansion was nothing less than God's grace to them for having adopted His cause.

The Believers' ambition to establish the writ of God's word as widely as possible was apparently given special urgency by their conviction that the Last Judgment was imminent. This mood of apocalyptic expectation—in which, presumably, they followed the lead of the prophet Muhammad himself—made it important to get on with the business of creating a righteous order so that, when the End came, those who could be counted among the Believers would attain paradise. This may also explain the early Believers' desire to extend their domains to Jerusalem, which many apocalyptic scenarios depicted as the place where the events of the Last Judgment would be played out. They may also have believed that the *amir al-mu'minin*, as leader of this new community dedicated to the realization of God's word, would fulfill the role of that expected "last emperor" who would, on the Last Day, hand earthly power over to God.

4

❧❧❧

The Struggle for
Leadership of the Community,
34–73/655–692

In the generation after Muhammad's death in 632 C.E. (that is, from about 31/650 until 73/692), the community of Believers was torn apart internally by a bitter dispute over the question of leadership. This dispute manifested itself particularly in two periods of open strife among the Arabian leadership of the Believers' movement, which we can call the First and Second Civil wars (35–40/656–661 and 60–73/680–692, respectively). Because many of the key participants in these events were actually related to one another by blood or marriage, the Civil Wars—particularly the First—have something of the quality of an extended and very bitter family quarrel. The loss of unity manifested in the Civil Wars has made them very painful events for many Muslims up to the present. For many contemporaries, it was simply heartbreaking that the companions of Muhammad, who had worked shoulder to shoulder for over two decades— and with resounding success—to spread God's word and to establish the rule of God's law on Earth, should now come to blows. Later Muslim tradition, reflecting this discomfiture, referred to these events as *fitan* (singular, *fitna*), a Qur'anic word meaning "seduction" or "temptation"—in this case, implying the temptation to pursue personal power and worldly advantage at the expense of communal or spiritual interests. It is not clear when this term is first used, but it may go back to the Civil Wars themselves.

Background of the First Civil War

As we have seen, on the death of Muhammad in 11/632, the Believers in Medina agreed to recognize Abu Bakr as their political leader. This act not only secured the succession but also institutionalized the notion that the Believers should remain a single, united community. We also noted that Abu Bakr was succeeded by 'Umar ibn al-Khattab (ruled 13–23/634–644) and then by 'Uthman ibn 'Affan (ruled 23–35/644–656) and how under these leaders the first great wave of expansion of the Believers' movement took place. There can be little doubt that these first leaders of the community were recognized by the Believers because, at the time they were selected, they embodied in important ways the central values to which the Believers were dedicated. The Believers at this time were still very much united in their goals and outlook, and all three men chosen to lead them had been close associates of Muhammad from early in his career. Those who held the position of leadership bore the title *amir al-mu'minin*, "commander of the Believers," a title about which I shall have more to say presently.

We should not allow the apparent smoothness of succession to mislead us into thinking that the question of leadership was simple or clear-cut, even in those early days. For one thing, the Qur'an seems supremely unconcerned with the question of temporal leadership. It offers no explicit guidance whatsoever on how succession is to be arranged or even on the requirements for leadership of the community. Nor, apparently, had Muhammad clearly designated anyone to succeed him. It was therefore not a straightforward matter for the early Believers to decide what leadership of the community meant, let alone who should exercise it or how the selection should be made, and in fact each of the three commanders of the Believers was chosen in a different manner. As we have seen, Abu Bakr was acclaimed leader at a meeting involving many Medinese Helpers and some Meccan Emigrants. 'Umar was appointed by Abu Bakr on his deathbed to be his successor. 'Umar, on the eve of his own death, named six leading contenders for leadership of the community and instructed them to meet as a council *(shura)* and come to unanimous agreement on which one of them should be his successor. (To provide the conferees with an incentive to avoid deadlock, he also left instructions that if they had not reached unanimity within a few days, those in the minority should be killed.) Numerous reports also suggest that some people may have refused to recognize one or another of the new commanders of the Believers for a time after their selection. Many of these reports involve the prophet's cousin and son-in-law 'Ali ibn Abi Talib, although it is not clear how many of them are later inventions designed to bolster the claim of 'Ali's descendants. There are reports involving other persons as well.

The fact that Abu Bakr, 'Umar, and 'Uthman each received broad support on their accessions, however, enables us to deduce a few things about what the early Believers seem generally to have been concerned with in choosing their leaders. All three had been close associates of Muhammad during his lifetime, and their dedication to the Believers' movement was beyond any doubt. Although they were all from the tribe of Quraysh and were Meccan Emigrants (like most of Muhammad's earliest followers), each was from a different clan of Quraysh, and none was from the prophet's clan of Hashim. Their broad acceptability to the early community suggests that the Believers generally did not yet see narrow genealogical or lineage criteria, beyond their membership in Quraysh, as a decisive factor in choosing their leaders—in striking contrast to the social traditions of Arabia. Rather, their close association with Muhammad and their reputation for piety and upright behavior seem to have been the paramount concerns in their selection.

The Believers' more or less consistent support of Abu Bakr, 'Umar, and, during the first years of his reign, 'Uthman, was doubtless facilitated by the fact that during these roughly twenty years the Believers' movement was enjoying phenomenal worldly success, probably beyond anyone's wildest dreams. As we have seen, during this time they vanquished their opponents in Arabia and expanded their presence in new areas at a pace that must have suggested to many that God was, in fact, on their side, and that their goal of establishing a public order based on their understanding of God's word was, in fact, in accord with God's will. The glow of such success, which had brought to them resources, lands, and slaves, probably made it easier for many to ignore whatever irritations or complaints they may have had—to dwell on which, in the context of such God-granted success, might have seemed not only petty but even positively blasphemous. But conditions appear to have changed during the reign of 'Uthman, and dissatisfaction with 'Uthman's leadership of the community became increasingly acute, starting sometime around 30/650–51—that is, about twenty years after Muhammad's death.

A number of practical factors can be proposed to explain this increasing tension among the Believers. By the early 30s/650s, the Believers had to go farther afield from their *amsar* to wage raids and campaigns of conquest, and the areas to be raided or conquered were less developed, more rural, and hence less rich in booty than the rich lands of Syria, Iraq, and Egypt that had been conquered earlier. There were also more migrants coming to the *amsar* as *muhajirun* among whom stipends had to be divided. There are hints in the sources that the governors tried to reduce or eliminate stipends altogether, and this doubtless led to some grumbling.

Another sore point involved the disposition of the conquered lands. Almost immediately after the conquests, there had emerged a

---

TEXT OF QUR'AN 8 (ANFAL/SPOILS): 41

Know that whatever you take as booty, one-fifth is for God and His apostle and the close kinsmen and orphans and poor and the *ibn al-sabil*. . . ." (The last term, usually translated "wayfarer," is interpreted by some as poor Believers or poor *muhajirun*. The implication is that the four-fifths not reserved for God and His apostle—or later, for the state—should fall to the conquerors as booty.)

---

dispute between the soldiers who had participated in the campaigns and the *amir al-mu'minin*, 'Umar, over this issue. The soldiers wished to see all conquered lands divided among themselves, with only the traditional one-fifth reserved for the *amir al-mu'minin*; they pointed to Qur'an 8:41 and to the prophet's division of the lands of Khaybar as warrant for their claim. 'Umar (and later 'Uthman), on the other hand, argued that conquered lands whose inhabitants were still in occupation—which in most districts were the majority—were different from the regular soldiers' booty of war and became collective property of the whole community; the inhabitants of the land should remain on them and pay taxes for the benefit of all of the Believers. Only abandoned lands, in their view, were booty to be divided among the soldiers. The picture is not clear, however; many places reached *ad hoc* agreements with the conquerors, and sources provide very contradictory and confusing accounts of how landholding and taxation actually developed.

In addition to the tension over distribution of lands, moreover, there was resentment among many of the soldiers who had actually effected the conquests (or, as time went on, those soldiers' sons), because some well-connected individuals from the tribe of Quraysh, such as Talha ibn 'Ubaydallah and Zubayr ibn al-'Awwam, increasingly emerged as large landowners of great wealth. But this came about through caliphal grants or through various real estate transactions (including trades for properties in Arabia), not because they had participated in the conquest, which is what irked the soldiers. One of 'Uthman's governors in Iraq, Sa'id ibn al-'As, enraged the soldiers in an address by referring to Iraq as "a garden for Quraysh"; his arrogant remark sparked a mutiny—led by a hero of the conquests there, Malik al-Ashtar al-Nakha'i—that eventually caused Sa'id to be ejected from the town by the Kufans.

A further practical problem that faced the *amir al-mu'minin*, particularly by 'Uthman's time, was that of management of what was becoming a far-flung empire. As the areas controlled by the Believers grew, the proper supervision of distant military commanders, governors, sub-governors, tax agents, and the sometimes turbulent *amsar* themselves, with their mixed tribal populations, became ever more challenging. Moreover, this was happening at a time when the core of the Believers' movement, those from Mecca and Medina, was changing; as the years passed, more and more of the Believers who had actually known the prophet died off, and many others were becoming too old to be active as military commanders or governors. 'Uthman and his main subordinates increasingly had to look to a younger generation of Believers to hold important posts; yet the qualifications and commitment of many of these younger Believers were less obvious to those around them. Indeed, one of the charges raised against 'Uthman was that of using "youths" in important posts.

In addition to these practical concerns, there were probably other factors related to social and economic realities that generated tension among the Believers, but of which little record has survived. These may have included social disagreements among tribesmen of various tribes now living in close proximity in the *amsar*. The earlier settlers of the *amsar* saw themselves being swamped by increasingly large waves of newer immigrants from Arabia, including both new fighters and families of those already there. In addition, there was competition among individual leaders or tribal groups for influence with the local commander or governor, disputes over pay and benefits received from (or demands of military service to) the state, and squabbles stemming from the tribesmen's differing access to private economic activities such as pastoralism, commerce, or artisanship.

Also very important was a growing sense among the Medinese Helpers and some other Arabian Believers, especially those early converts of humble origins, that the affairs (and financial benefits) of the new state were being increasingly dominated by powerful members of Quraysh. Abu Bakr had followed closely the policy inaugurated by Muhammad himself in his last years of providing important posts to some of those Meccans who had earlier been among his bitterest opponents—the policy of "conciliation of hearts" that had so incensed some of his earliest followers. Abu Bakr's appointment of Khalid ibn al-Walid, 'Amr ibn al-'As, and Yazid ibn Abi Sufyan, all of whom had joined the Believers' movement late in Muhammad's life, can be seen in this light. On his accession, 'Umar moderated this policy, and relied more heavily for important appointments on those who had been early adherents of the prophet; he dismissed some, like Khalid ibn al-Walid, whom he considered to be too concerned with worldly affairs. Yet his policy was hardly consistent in this regard; he retained 'Amr ibn al-'As, widely known for his worldly orientation, as governor of Egypt after 'Amr conquered it.

As important as these practical issues may have been, however, there is good reason to think that the internal tensions that afflicted the community of Believers in the 30s/650s also revolved around the question of piety and how it related to leadership of the community. Competition over land, pay, status, and influence were important not only in their own right, but especially because the Believers saw in them indications that some of their leaders were not acting in accordance with the high principles of piety (including equitable treatment of all Believers) that were a central concern of the Believers' movement. Differences in status or influence or wealth were irksome, but people had long been familiar with such things; what was intolerable to many Believers seems to have been the thought that their leaders should be lax in trying to eliminate such inequities, or worse still, should be actively engaged in favoritism, giving some Believers an advantage over others. This concern came to a head during the time of the third *amir al-mu'minin*, 'Uthman—resulting, as we shall see, in his murder.

A number of 'Uthman's policies seem to have aroused sharp opposition. One charge raised against him was that of favoring members of his own family, the Umayyads, for important (and probably lucrative) positions such as key governorships. For example, he removed two governors in Iraq who were well-known companions of the prophet and heroes of the conquest, Sa'd ibn Abi Waqqas and Abu Musa al-Ash'ari, and replaced them with his half-brother Walid ibn 'Uqba and another relative, 'Abd Allah ibn 'Amir ibn Kurayz (who was also granted by 'Uthman large date plantations in the vicinity). When Walid ibn 'Uqba was forced to resign in disgrace (for drunkenness), 'Uthman replaced him with another Umayyad, his second cousin Sa'id ibn al-'As. He also took the governorship of Egypt out of the hands of the redoubtable 'Amr ibn al-'As, who had conquered it and then managed its affairs and who was very popular with his troops, and replaced him with 'Abd Allah ibn Abi Sarh, a foster brother and close ally of 'Uthman and his family. The new governor may have been under orders to tighten central control over Egypt's finances, which would have compounded his unpopularity, as revenues formerly retained in the province were forwarded to Medina. In Syria, 'Uthman placed the governorship in the hands of his younger kinsman Mu'awiya ibn Abi Sufyan; he had, admittedly, been first appointed by 'Umar, but 'Uthman increased his power by giving him control over the main garrison at Hims as well as over Damascus. 'Uthman's detractors took these signs of family favoritism as a moral failing on his part. It has been suggested that 'Uthman was, as *amir al-mu'minin*, merely trying to ensure firm control over the increasingly complex affairs of the empire by relying on individuals over whom, as a relative, he had strong personal influence. It is impossible to know which of these motivations was uppermost in 'Uthman's mind, but it is worth noting that 'Uthman distributed many estates from the conquered lands, not only to his Umayyad kinsmen, but also to important leaders from many groups, including some of the leaders of the conquests, such as Jarir ibn 'Abd Allah and Sa'd ibn Abi Waqqas. 'Uthman was not deaf to complaints of impiety, and he was able to dismiss relatives who were suspected of misdeeds; as we have seen, his half-brother Walid ibn 'Uqba was dismissed as governor of Kufa (and flogged) for drinking wine, which sowed deep enmity between 'Uthman and Walid's family, notwithstanding their close family ties.

'Uthman was also criticized for matters that had nothing to do with worldly gain, however, and those allegations highlight the fact that he was faulted above all for his perceived moral failings—his lack of piety—when, as *amir al-mu'minin*, he was expected by the Believers to be a paragon of piety. A few accounts in the traditional sources describe minor alterations in the pilgrimage ritual made by 'Uthman. Despite their apparent insignificance and despite the fact that the Qur'an is vague on how to do the pilgrimage (as it is on details of most rituals), these alterations seem to have caused consternation among some people, perhaps because the pilgrimage rituals had been affirmed by the prophet himself. Among the most important of 'Uthman's "innovations," however, may have been his decision to codify the Qur'an text.

The stories about this are many and confused; some scholars argue that the Qur'an text as we have it was already codified at the time of Muhammad's death, but many reports tell of people collecting parts of the revelation that survived the prophet only in people's memories or in scattered, partial written copies. One stream of tradition holds that 'Uthman asked a team of companions led by Zayd ibn Thabit to collect and compare all available copies of the Qur'an and to prepare a single, unified text. This aroused opposition not perhaps because of the procedure itself, but because once the new Qur'anic "vulgate" was established, 'Uthman had copies sent to the main *amsar* with orders that they be used there in place of regional versions that were considered authentic by their followers and that these earlier copies be burned. Despite this, several of the earlier versions of the Qur'an survived—for example, those associated with the early Qur'an reciters Ibn Mas'ud (died 33/653) in Kufa, Ubayy ibn Ka'b (died 29/649 or 34/654) in Syria, and Abu Musa al-Ash'ari (died 42/662) in Basra, among others, whose copies (or memories) could not be blotted out. There were also copies of parts or all of the Qur'an in the hands of some of the prophet's widows and of Abu Bakr, 'Umar, 'Ali, and other companions. Ibn Mas'ud is said to have refused to destroy his copy when 'Uthman's vulgate arrived in Kufa, but in any case the readings of companions who had been teaching those around them how to recite the text could easily have survived in their memories and been copied down again later, even if the original variant codices were destroyed. (Vestiges of these codices seem to survive in compilations of recognized Qur'anic variant readings that form part of the science of Qur'anic recitation.)

All of these factors, then, contributed to the rising tide of criticism against 'Uthman's conduct as *amir al-mu'minin*. Open opposition to his rule seems to have broken out first in the *amsar* of Fustat in Egypt and Kufa and Basra in Iraq. Groups of dissidents from these towns then marched to Medina to confront 'Uthman himself. The traditional Muslim sources provide us with lengthy reports about the events of the mutiny and those that followed, which we call the First Civil War; our sources refer to these events as the first *fitna*, using a pejorative Qur'anic word meaning "temptation, seduction" (by the lure of worldly advantage). The goal of all these reports is either to demonstrate 'Uthman's guilt or to exculpate him (or, similarly, to provide moral judgments on other participants in the events). Hence it is difficult, if not impossible, to reach a clear verdict today on the relative responsibility of different actors through the thicket of charges and countercharges these reports provide. We can discern quite clearly, however, the basic course of events, the individuals and groups involved, and the main issues at stake because most sources regardless of tendency agree.

This much seems clear in evaluation of 'Uthman's role in these events: Whether or not he engaged in controversial innovation or was guilty of moral failings, real or perceived, he seems to have lacked the decisiveness of character needed to deal effectively with the problems with which, as *amir al-mu'minin*, he was confronted. His prior history showed no outstanding activity, military or otherwise, except for his early decision to follow Muhammad and his generous support of the Believers' movement from his own personal fortune. Perhaps he was too inclined to leave important decisions to others, including his own relatives, whose good judgment he trusted; perhaps his trust was sometimes misplaced; perhaps he failed to anticipate or even to recognize the depth and character of discontent and tension within the community he led. In any case, the mutiny against him inaugurated a sequence of events that saw the Arabian Believers—hitherto the core of the Believers' movement—fragmented in a bitter battle for leadership.

The Course of the First Civil War (35–40/656–661)

Although critics of 'Uthman's regime were active in several centers, including Kufa (where they had, as we have seen, driven out his governor Sa'id ibn al-'As) and Basra, it was a group of agitators from the garrison of Fustat in Egypt who played the leading role in the unfolding of events that led to the First Civil War. After raising demands against 'Uthman's governor of Egypt, 'Abd Allah ibn Abi Sarh, these agitators made their way toward Medina to confront 'Uthman himself, arriving in late 35/May 656. There they were

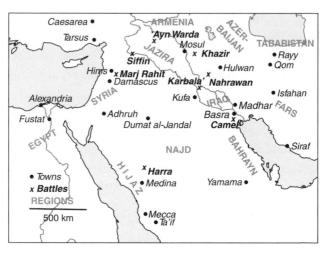

Map 5. The civil wars

joined by groups of insurgents from Kufa and Basra; this joining of forces suggests that there may have been some coordination of activities even before they marched on Medina. For several weeks 'Uthman (or his supporters) and his opponents engaged in negotiations to deal with the insurgents' grievances, but as time went on his critics grew bolder and his supporters seemed to dwindle in number. Eventually, the aged *amir al-mu'minin*, besieged in his house in Medina, was attacked and killed (end 35/June 656).

The fact that the *amir al-mu'minin* could be murdered in his own home by a group of provincial malcontents demonstrates that 'Uthman had lost the effective support of those longtime Believers in Medina who, under other circumstances, could surely have defended him and dispersed the rebels. Evidently the native Medinese Helpers, who were distressed at the degree to which they saw themselves increasingly sidelined in the distribution of influential positions and valuable properties by powerful men of Quraysh, were no longer inclined to rescue 'Uthman. As for 'Uthman's Quraysh kinsmen, many seem to have made only halfhearted efforts to defend him—either because he had antagonized them by his policies or because they had concluded that his cause was hopelessly compromised—and some may even have encouraged the dissidents. These included the ambitious Talha, the aggrieved 'Amr and Walid, and many others. The prophet's esteemed widow 'A'isha, "mother of the Believers," still only in her early forties, may or may not have incited the rebels by letter, but her decision to leave Medina on pilgrimage just when the mutiny was coming to a head makes it clear that she had no desire to exert her considerable influence among the Believers to calm the rising tide of opposition to 'Uthman, even in dire circumstances. 'Ali ibn Abi Talib, who perhaps had more influence than anyone with the population of Medina, must have been torn, as he believed himself to be more entitled to the office 'Uthman held; at any rate, he was not able to prevent 'Uthman's death, and sources disagree on how hard he tried. It is difficult to avoid the impression that by the time of the mutiny, many leading members of the community in Medina were already anticipating 'Uthman's abdication or removal from office and were maneuvering to secure what they thought would be the best outcome for themselves. It may be that some of these figures miscalculated matters and encouraged the mutiny in the hope that it would merely force 'Uthman to change his policies, only to see events get out of hand.

The immediate beneficiary of 'Uthman's death was 'Ali ibn Abi Talib, the prophet's cousin and husband of his daugher Fatima. He seems to have had the strong support of the Medinese Helpers and of some of the mutineers, particularly those from Kufa; they constituted the *shi'at 'Ali*, the "party of 'Ali" (for now merely his political bloc, but eventually to become the nucleus of the Shi'a, who held—and still hold—'Ali and all his descendants in special reverence). The day following 'Uthman's murder, 'Ali received the oath of allegiance as *amir al-mu'minin* in the mosque of Medina. He had very little support from other members of Quraysh, however, some of whom aspired to the leadership themselves. Leading figures from Quraysh simply left Medina quickly without swearing allegiance to 'Ali—or withdrew after they had given it and then repudiated it—to gather in Mecca, their hometown. 'A'isha, shocked to learn of the accession of 'Ali (whom she is said to have detested because he had questioned her virtue many years earlier), remained in Mecca after her pilgrimage and gathered her close relatives Talha and Zubayr, whose claims she supported, around her. The Umayyads who happened to be in Medina at the time of 'Uthman's death—notably Marwan, at this time the Umayyad clan's patriarch—also left and gathered in Mecca.

From Medina, 'Ali quickly named new governors for various provinces, intending to replace nearly all those who had served 'Uthman, some of whom had been unpopular. Mecca and Syria, however, rejected 'Ali's claims to lead the community. In Syria, 'Uthman's kinsman Mu'awiya, the longtime governor, argued that 'Ali could not claim to rule until he had brought to justice 'Uthman's killers, who were now in his entourage.

In Mecca, 'A'isha rallied most of Quraysh opposed to 'Ali and they now called for vengeance for the slain 'Uthman, despite the fact that they had done so little to save him. They also called for the convening of a *shura* or council to decide the question of who should lead the community. Not only Talha and Zubayr, but also 'Uthman's grown sons and many other powerful members of Quraysh joined the opposition, including 'Uthman's former governors of Yemen, who came with much wealth. Deciding that they should go to Basra to gather forces there before attacking 'Ali, they set out in 36/October 656. Arriving in Basra, they skirmished with 'Ali's governor and his troops and eventually took control of the city.

'Ali set out to confront them. He sent his son Hasan, along with the leader of the Kufan mutineers against 'Uthman, Malik "al-Ashtar" al-Nakha'i, ahead to Kufa to secure it from 'Ali's governor,

Abu Musa, who though pious was only lukewarm in his support of 'Ali. There Hasan quickly raised an army of Kufans to join 'Ali, who arrived and made camp east of the city. When 'Ali's force was ready, he marched on Basra. Both 'Ali's army and that of his Meccan opponents were multi-tribal, and most tribes had members in both armies, some backing 'Ali, some backing 'A'isha and her followers. This created hesitation in the hearts of many of the soldiers; moreover, there were in each army people who thought it was wrong for Believers to fight other Believers openly and who therefore withdrew and refused to back either side. The actual battle (called the Battle of the Camel because the epicenter of the fighting was around the camel carrying 'A'isha's litter) took place not far from Basra, and it cost many lives on both sides. But 'Ali's forces carried the day, and both Talha and Zubayr were killed. 'Ali promptly took control of Basra (which remained, however, a strong center for pro-'Uthman sentiment for many years); he also sent 'A'isha back to Medina with strict instructions that she stay out of politics thereafter. A number of prominent Meccans in 'A'isha's army evaded capture; some of them eventually made their way to join the Umayyad Mu'awiya, who had remained in Syria. 'Ali eventually went back to Kufa, which became his main base of activity.

'Ali's choice of governors to replace those of 'Uthman gives us some idea of the goals of his regime. Where 'Uthman had relied heavily on his own Umayyad kinsmen, 'Ali relied on the Medinese Helpers (whom he sent as governors to Medina, Egypt, Kufa, and Basra before the Battle of the Camel) and members of his clan of Hashim (selected as governors for Yemen, Basra after the Battle of the Camel, and Mecca). (The main exceptions were two members of other Quraysh clans who were very loyal to 'Ali; Muhammad ibn Abi Bakr was sent as a replacement to Egypt, and another Qurayshite was made governor in eastern Arabia). One surmises that his intent was to place the Believers' movement and the new state once again in the hands of those who, in his view, were most likely to lead it in the spirit of the prophet and his insistence on strict piety. It was intended to be a decisive departure from the leadership and policies of ʿUthman, roundly criticized for his impiety, who had relied on kinsmen from that clan of Quraysh—the Umayyads—who had long resisted Muhammad's message and whose commitment to it ʿAli (and the Helpers) still considered suspect.

ʿAli now had control, more or less, of the Hijaz, Iraq, and Egypt (although in the latter there was a strong faction that called for revenge for the slain ʿUthman and held aloof from ʿAli's governor). He now turned his attention to the sullen opposition of Muʿawiya, who for almost twenty years had been governor of Syria and who had not yet tendered his recognition of ʿAli as *amir al-muʾminin*. ʿAli's envoys invited Muʿawiya to obedience, but Muʿawiya knew that recognizing ʿAli would mean his own dismissal as governor of Syria. From Muʿawiya's point of view, furthermore, ʿAli's acclamation as *amir al-muʾminin* by the Medinan mob that had murdered his kinsman ʿUthman was invalid. Whereas ʿAli might accuse Muʿawiya of being a lukewarm Believer, slow to join the movement and a participant in the worldly minded regime of ʿUthman, Muʿawiya could point out that ʿAli's supporters included the mutineers themselves, whom ʿAli had never punished even though they were guilty of the unpardonable sin of killing a fellow Believer. It is not surprising that a number of prominent early Believers, such as the leader of the conquest of Iraq, Saʿd ibn Abi Waqqas, decided that they could back neither party in clear conscience and so withdrew in self-imposed isolation for the duration of the First Civil War.

Muʿawiya's political position was strengthened in late 36/early 657 by his conclusion of an alliance with ʿAmr ibn al-ʿAs. The two were not natural allies; ʿAmr had borne a grudge against the Umayyads ever since ʿUthman had removed him from the governorship of Egypt, and there was some suspicion that the Egyptian mutineers had been instigated in part by ʿAmr. Yet ʿAmr also knew that ʿAli, whose policies revealed a strong preference for Medinese Helpers and Hashimites, would never agree to make him part of his administration. His one hope of regaining his governorship of Egypt was to ally himself with Muʿawiya, which he now did, in exchange for assurances that he would again govern it. Fortunately for Muʿawiya, the divisions among the Arabian Believers in Egypt—the soldiers—meant that ʿAli's governors there had their hands full and were in no position to threaten Muʿawiya's Syrian base, at least for the time being. ʿAmr's job was to make sure it never happened.

At the end of 36/May 657, ʿAli assembled his army in Kufa and marched out to confront Muʿawiya and to force his submission. In Syria, meanwhile, Muʿawiya likewise gathered his troops and moved toward the Euphrates to block ʿAli's advance. Neither leader had the unwavering support of the people they ruled, as many on both sides thought it wrong that Believers should march against one another in open warfare. The two armies drew near each other in June, near the town of Siffin on the Euphrates, between Raqqa and Aleppo. A long period of desultory skirmishing and fruitless negotiation ensued between the two leaders. A pitched battle finally occurred in Safar in 37/late July 657 and lasted several days, with heavy casualties. Finally, Muʿawiya's forces appeared one morning with copies of the Qurʾan hoisted on their lances, a gesture taken by many in ʿAli's army as an appeal to stop fighting and let the dispute be settled by the principles of their holy book—which, whatever their disagreements, was the thing that united the two sides. The fighting stopped at once; in ʿAli's camp, some of those who had been lukewarm supporters of the idea of marching against Muʿawiya in the first place now pressed ʿAli to negotiate, while others insisted that he press the offensive, feeling themselves on the verge of victory. Those in favor of negotiation prevailed. ʿAli reluctantly agreed to submit the dispute to arbitration, to take place at a neutral venue in a few months' time, and equally reluctantly accepted his supporters' demand that he appoint as his negotiator Abu Musa al-Ashʿari, his erstwhile governor of Kufa. ʿAli's followers were evidently impressed by Abu Musa's piety, but ʿAli doubtless would have preferred someone who, unlike Abu Musa, backed him unequivocally. Mu'awiya appointed 'Amr ibn al-'As as his negotiator.

The divisions among 'Ali's supporters grew more acute as he marched his army back to Iraq. Although the majority still agreed with his decision to submit the rivalry over leadership to arbitration, a sizable minority grew increasingly vocal in their rejection of the idea of arbitration. Perhaps fearing that they might be called to account for their role in 'Uthman's murder, this minority now argued that 'Ali, by agreeing to arbitration, had taken the decision out of God's hands—that is, out of the hands of the soldiers who battled "in God's way"—and put it into the hands of mere men, the arbitrators. This, they held, was a grave sin, and they called on 'Ali to repent for it, and to express their view they began to circulate the slogan, "No judgment but God's!" These ultra-pious Believers were dedicated to strictly righteous behavior in accordance with the Qur'an and demanded such righteousness, especially from their leaders. In their view, by agreeing to arbitration, 'Ali and his followers had not only squandered any claim to lead but had actually left the faith itself and had to be fought as unbelievers. After a time they withdrew from 'Ali's army and encamped at a place called Nahrawan, some distance from Kufa. They came to be called Kharijites (Arabic *khawarij*, "those who go out"), although the exact significance of their name remains unclear. Perhaps they were so designated because they "went out" from 'Ali's camp or because by breaking solidarity with 'Ali they were felt to have left the community of Believers; or perhaps their name is a more positive reference to "coming forth in the way of God" (for example, Q. 60:1).

The arbitrators convened, probably in Dumat al-Jandal in northern Arabia between Syria and Iraq in late 37/spring 658. The details of their discussions are obscure, but they seem to have tried to settle the question of leadership of the community of Believers by referring to the Qur'an. As a first step, they agreed that 'Uthman had been unjustly murdered, but they were unable to reach further agreement and broke up, calling for the convocation of another *shura* of leading Believers to decide who should be *amir al-mu'minin*. Whether or not this decision was the result of a ruse by Mu'awiya's negotiator, 'Amr, as claimed by pro-'Alid sources, is hard to ascertain. But whatever its authority, announcement of this decision had major consequences. Mu'awiya and his followers now found themselves vindicated in their insistence on seeking vengeance for 'Uthman's murder, in particular against 'Ali and his followers, who included the murderers. Furthermore, Mu'awiya was some time thereafter acclaimed in Syria as *amir al-mu'minin*. The position of 'Ali as *amir al-mu'minin*, on the other hand, was undermined by the arbitrators' announcement, and 'Ali promptly denounced it and called on his supporters in Kufa to prepare to march, once again, against Mu'awiya in Syria.

Before doing so, however, 'Ali had to deal with the Kharijites gathered at Nahrawan. These self-righteous pietists, having withdrawn from 'Ali's forces in protest over his actions and policies, now considered anyone who recognized 'Ali's leadership to be similarly guilty of sin and, for this reason, eligible to be killed as an apostate, an ex-Believer. A number of people in the vicinity of Kufa had been done in by them, and 'Ali's soldiers were unwilling to embark on a new campaign against Mu'awiya, leaving their families unprotected in Kufa, unless the Kharijites were either won over or eliminated. 'Ali made a number of efforts to secure the Kharijites' allegiance once again, all of which were rebuffed by the Kharijite leaders—although a large number of individuals did accept his offers of immunity and withdrew quietly from the Kharijite ranks. Filled with pious zeal and convinced that 'Ali and his men were now apostates, the remaining Kharijites felt that they had no choice but to fight them until they vanquished the "unbelievers" or met their fate as martyrs in what they considered to be God's way. They attacked 'Ali's larger forces and were cut down almost to a man (end 37/May 658).

The Kharijites are commonly described as the "first sect" in Islam, as if they were an offshoot or aberration from the original principles espoused by the Believers of Muhammad's day. But in fact, the intense piety and militancy of these early Kharijites represented the survival in its purest form of the original pietistic impetus of the Believers' movement. They can therefore be considered the best representatives in the generations following the death of the prophet of the original principles of the Believers' movement of Muhammad's day—although they may have followed an extreme form of these principles, because the prophet himself seems to have been more flexible and practical than they in his dealings with his opponents. It is possible—although the evidence is scant—that the intensity of their commitment was rooted in a conviction that the Believers were the vanguards establishing God's kingdom on Earth in preparation for the Last Judgment that was soon to dawn (or that was, through their actions, already dawning).

The massacre at Nahrawan was a pyrrhic victory for 'Ali. He had secured his home base, Kufa, but the slaughter of something like fifteen hundred Kharijites, among whom were a large number of early Believers well known for their exemplary piety, undermined 'Ali's moral claim to lead the community. Moreover, after the battle, 'Ali's Kufan forces made clear their reluctance to embark on a new campaign against Mu'awiya, whose forces (as they knew from Siffin) included many tribesmen from their own tribes. 'Ali was forced to remain in Kufa and consider his options.

These options became increasingly limited. Mu'awiya's position, already buoyed by the declaration of the arbiters at Dumat al-Jandal and the Syrians' recognition of him as *amir al-mu'minin*, was further strengthened by developments in Egypt. There, as we have seen, 'Ali's governor Muhammad ibn Abi Bakr faced a determined (and, it seems, growing) body of troops who remained incensed at the murder of 'Uthman and were therefore reluctant to recognize 'Ali's leadership. Learning that 'Ali was preoccupied with the Kharijites,

Muʿawiya dispatched ʿAmr ibn al-ʿAs with a strong detachment of troops to Egypt. These joined forces with the Egyptians already opposed to ʿAli and destroyed Muhammad ibn Abi Bakr's army. ʿAli's governor was caught and killed shortly thereafter. By early 38/August 658, Egypt was once again firmly in the hands of ʿAmr ibn al-ʿAs, its former conqueror, and solidly in Muʿawiya's camp.

ʿAli's cause also began to show signs of unraveling closer to home. A near-mutiny in Basra was quelled but revealed the erosion of his support even in Iraq; and a temporary, but sharp, quarrel with his cousin ʿAbd Allah ibn al-ʿAbbas, whose backing was important to him and whom he could hardly afford to alienate, revealed (as had numerous other episodes) ʿAli's tendency to antagonize people and to misjudge situations. This quality had probably been a major reason for his failure to win recognition (even from his Quraysh kinsmen) commensurate with his ambition and early role in the community of Believers.

The arbitrators apparently now met for a second time in the month of Shaʿban 38/January 659, this time at Muʿawiya's behest, at Adhruh (today in southern Jordan). But inasmuch as ʿAli had dismissed his arbitrator, Abu Musa al-Ashʿari, after the first round, this meeting was really a public-relations ploy by Muʿawiya. In the meeting, Muʿawiya's negotiator, ʿAmr ibn al-ʿAs, tricked the pious Abu Musa into declaring that he considered ʿAli deposed as *amir al-muʾminin* by pretending that they were in agreement that both contenders should be dismissed; but once Abu Musa had made his statement, ʿAmr stood up and declared his recognition of Muʿawiya for the position. Whatever propaganda advantage Muʿawiya may have gained from this episode, however, does not seem to have translated into any immediate advantage on the ground.

Muʿawiya now took the initiative in his struggle with ʿAli. He began sending periodic raiding parties from Syria to the Euphrates region and into northern Arabia, hoping to win over groups under ʿAli's control, or those who remained neutral (38/659). ʿAli also sent a few raids into the Euphrates region but seems to have been preoccupied in the period 38–40/659–661 with his confrontation with the Khari-jites. Many of the latter who had gathered at Nahrawan had dispersed before the battle, and numerous groups of them continued to disrupt southern and central Iraq. Driven now not only by their pious scruples but also by the desire to avenge their many kinsmen and fellow Kharijites who had fallen at Nahrawan, they demanded that people reject ʿAli as impious, sometimes killing as apostates anyone who refused to join them. ʿAli was able to suppress these uprisings, but his killing of yet more Kharijites only deepened the hostility of those who remained.

Muʿawiya now dispatched a force to Arabia under his general Busr ibn Abi Artat, which marched through the Hijaz and into Yemen and Hadramawt. Whether or not the many reports of atrocities committed by Busr during this campaign are to be believed, or whether they are to be ascribed to anti-Muʿawiya propaganda, remains unclear; likewise, it is not clear whether ʿAli took any significant measures to counter this advance. But the campaign resulted in the expulsion of ʿAli's governors and brought all the major towns of these regions—not only the symbolically all-important holy cities of Mecca and Medina, but also Taʾif, Tabala, Najran, Sanʿaʾ, and others—under Muʿawiya's control.

ʿAli's position was now dire; his control was limited to Iraq, and even there he was plagued by the continuing opposition of the surviving Kharijites and lukewarm support of many others. As he was attempting (yet again) to rally his forces for a campaign against Syria, however, he was struck down in the mosque of Kufa by a Kharijite assassin (Ramadan 40/January 661). ʿAli paid the ultimate price for his long, unhappy relations with these ultra-pious erstwhile supporters.

Upon ʿAli's death, his followers in Kufa recognized his son Hasan ibn ʿAli as their leader and *amir al-muʾminin*. Hasan had none of his father's ambition, however, sitting passively in Kufa awaiting developments, rather than marching against Muʿawiya. He entered into desultory correspondence with Muʿawiya, who meanwhile gathered a large army of his own. Mu'awiya soon enough marched with his army down the Euphrates and secured Hasan's agreement to abdicate; Hasan agreed to recognize Mu'awiya as *amir al-mu'minin*, in exchange for a lifetime pension that allowed him the leisure to pursue his many love affairs, and he never played a role in politics again. Mu'awiya was duly recognized by the Kufans in Rabi' II 41/August 661. Except for a few bands of Kharijite holdouts, the Believers once more were united under a single *amir al-mu'minin*.

The First Civil War had involved economic and other practical issues but was fundamentally a debate over the nature of future leadership in the community of Believers, particularly its relationship to issues of piety and morality. In the bitter struggles that took place after 'Uthman's death, each claimant or group based its claim on a different set of criteria for what constituted appropriate leadership for the Believers.

The most central criterion, to which all groups and contenders made frequent appeal in some way, was that of piety, reflecting the central thrust of the original Believers' movement itself. The most unalloyed expression of this was found among the Kharijites, for whom piety was not merely an important criterion; it was the only criterion that mattered. In their view, only the most pious Believer was entitled to lead, and they rejected decisively all considerations of kinship, ethnicity, or social status. Any leader who was, in their eyes, adjudged as sinful had either to do penance or to be removed from office, for to follow a sinful leader was itself a sin that disqualified one from membership in the community of true Believers and endangered one's future in the afterlife.

Other groups tended to combine concern for piety with other criteria. Many pious Believers linked it with the notion of "precedence" *(sabiqa)*—that is, they felt that the community could best be led by men who had been among Muhammad's first and most loyal backers, because these would understand better than anyone else how to lead the community in accordance with Muhammad's ideals. Prominent early Emigrants, such as Talha ibn ʿUbayd Allah, Zubayr ibn al-ʿAwwam, ʿAbd al-Rahman ibn ʿAwf, and ʿAmmar ibn Yasir adhered to this view, as did many Medinese Helpers, and all of the first four commanders of the Believers—Abu Bakr, ʿUmar, ʿUthman, and ʿAli—had impressive credentials in this regard. It was a claim that was directed especially against those who had opposed the prophet, or had joined him only late in his career, such as many of the Umayyads.

A third criterion for leadership that emerged at an early date was that of kinship to the prophet. ʿAli, as the prophet's cousin and son-in-law, is presented by later tradition as having raised this claim most forcefully, even though he was no more closely related than other cousins of the prophet, such as ʿAbd Allah ibn al-ʿAbbas. On the other hand, ʿAli's close kinship with Muhammad obviously did not persuade most of the community to favor him over his three predecessors, so other considerations must have been uppermost in their minds. Moreover, in several places the Qurʾan emphasizes that ties to other Believers outweigh even the closest ties of kinship (for example, Q. 9:23).

Finally, there were those who asserted a claim to leadership based on effectiveness in practical matters, service to the Believers' move-

---

TEXT OF QURʾAN 9 (TAWBA/REPENTANCE): 23–24

O you who Believe! Do not take your parents and siblings as friends if they prefer disbelief (*kufr*) to Belief. Whosoever of you draws close to them, these are the oppressors. Say: if your parents and children and siblings and spouses and tribe and your wealth that you earned and the trade whose sluggishness you fear are dearer to you than God and His Apostle and striving (*jihad*) in His way [that is, for His cause], then wait until God brings His Decision. For God does not guide sinful peoples.

ment, and recognition by members of the community. Many disparaged (and still disparage) this claim as merely a cover for the seizure of power by those who lacked "real" qualifications of the three kinds enumerated above, such as ʿAmr ibn al-ʿAs or Muʿawiya ibn Abi Sufyan, who had been slow to embrace the Believers' movement and were sometimes less than models of piety. But they had in their favor the strong argument that in his final years Muhammad himself had pursued the policy of "conciliation of hearts," by which he gave even some of his bitterest former opponents important positions. This policy, which was also followed by Abu Bakr, was based on recognition of the fact that the Believers' movement, if it was to succeed in the world, needed to be in the hands of decisive men having the practical capacity to lead. Someone suggested to ʿUmar, on his deathbed, that he appoint as his successor his son ʿAbd Allah, who was highly esteemed for his piety, but ʿUmar replied, "How can I appoint someone who can't even divorce his own wife?" In making this statement, he was presumably voicing not merely his own judgment on his son's character but also the sentiment of many who knew that force of personality was a crucial ingredient in successful leadership.

The fact that piety was such a central feature of the early Believers' movement helps explain why the First Civil War was such a traumatic event for the Believers—as it was happening, in the decades after it, and for Muslims ever since. The Believers had faced other setbacks with relative equanimity—serious military defeats by armies of impious states, for example—but had responded to these setbacks with alacrity and increased vigor and confidence, even though such setbacks *could* have been viewed by them as a sign that they no longer enjoyed God's full favor. They do not seem to have done so partly, perhaps, because the Qurʾan itself makes clear that the righteous would have to fight unbelief and unbelievers, and hence some setbacks would be inevitable and simply spurred the Believers to greater efforts. But the First Civil War was different. It not only split the community of Believers; it divided its members on precisely that issue around which their communal identity was focused, the question of piety or morality. They were in open disagreement over whether 'Uthman had acted justly or not; and after his assassination, they were in even sharper disagreement over whether the mutineers and other main actors had acted morally. Moreover, regardless of what stand one took on the mutiny, it meant that the very leaders of the community—the persons who should, by all tokens, be most morally distinguished—had been called into doubt regarding their morality, because one could hardly claim that both 'Uthman and 'Ali were sinless. Only much later, after the passage of a generation or more had made the community numb to the pain of the events of the First Civil War and keenly aware of the danger of fragmenting the community that lay in any attempt to insist that one side or the other was at fault, did the community come to consider both 'Uthman and 'Ali (along with Abu Bakr and 'Umar) *rashidun*, "rightly guided ones," whose leadership was to be acknowledged as valid by everyone.

Between Civil Wars (40–60/661–680)

Mu'awiya's final emergence as the sole *amir al-mu'minin* in 40/661— called the "year of coming together" (*'am al-jama'a*) by Muslim tradition—ushered in two decades of relative calm. During this period the Believers once again turned their attention to implementing the movement's goal of spreading God's rule and ensuring a righteous order in areas they controlled.

Mu'awiya appointed as governor men whose loyalty to him and capacity to manage the affairs of their sometimes turbulent provinces were unquestionable. Many were Umayyads, such as his second cousin Marwan ibn al-Hakam and Sa'id ibn al-'As, rivals whom he played against one another in serving as governor of Medina, or

'Abd Allah ibn 'Amir, a distant relation who was his first governor of Basra. Other governors were not Umayyads but were selected for special reasons. He entrusted Mecca to the distinguished Khalid ibn al-'As, of the Makhzum clan of Quraysh, who had served as 'Umar's governor there and was well liked in the city. Egypt was, naturally, in the hands of 'Amr ibn al-'As (of the Sahm clan of Quraysh), who with Mu'awiya's consent appointed his younger nephew 'Uqba ibn Nafi' (of the Fihr clan of Quraysh) to invade and govern North Africa. Mughira ibn Shu'ba, a man of Thaqif (the tribe of Ta'if) was appointed governor of Kufa; an early follower (and bodyguard) of the prophet, he was in some ways an unsavory character, but Mu'awiya doubtless valued his ability, toughness, and reliable support. The most interesting of Mu'awiya's appointments, however, was Ziyad ibn Abihi ("Ziyad, son of his father"), a man of dubious paternity but undeniable executive and financial skill, who had been raised among the Thaqif tribe of Ta'if. He had been a stalwart supporter of 'Ali during the civil war, and though relatively young had been appointed by 'Ali as his governor of Fars province because of his brilliant ability. After 'Ali's death, Ziyad remained in Fars and in control of the provincial treasury and for some time held aloof from Mu'awiya. Mu'awiya finally won him over by recognizing him as his own half-brother (that is, as the son of his own father, Abu Sufyan, now safely in the grave and unable to object). This generous gesture paid handsome dividends for Mu'awiya, who appointed Ziyad—henceforth known as Ziyad ibn Abi Sufyan—to the governorship of Basra, replacing Ibn 'Amir in 45/665; later Ziyad was appointed governor of Kufa as well, so that he ruled the entire eastern portion of the empire. He did so with great effectiveness, and Mu'awiya never regretted his decision.

Mu'awiya's key governors supervised a resumption of the conquests into new areas. By this time the institutions of the Believers' regime had matured into something that had the unmistakable features of a state—not only a standing army, but also a network of tax collectors and a rudimentary chancery and bureaucracy. For this reason, the character of the conquests after 660 differed also in some measure from the earliest conquests of the 630s and 640s. Above all, those early conquests had been driven by the Believers' burning desire to supplant what they saw as the worldly, sinful regimes of Byzantium and Sasanian Iran and to erect in their stead a new, righteous order dedicated to the observance of God's law. The initial conquests had a centralized impetus but had nonetheless been carried out *ad hoc*, in response to the unpredictable developments on various fronts; and we might say that the embryonic regime in Medina that provided such centralized direction as existed was dwarfed by the military forces that were at its service. By Muʿawiya's day and thereafter, on the other hand, the conquests gradually became more institutionalized and routinized. The standing armies now operated from a number of well-established, fixed bases—the *amsar*, particularly Hims, Fustat, Kufa, and Basra—to which soldiers returned at the conclusion of a season's campaigning; and campaigns were for the most part undertaken on a regular basis and for a predetermined duration (often six or twelve months). Moreover, although the idea of spreading God's rule—waging "*jihad* on God's behalf" (*jihad fi sabil allah*)—and of establishing the Believers' righteous regime remained important, the new campaigns were also driven by the practical needs of the state for a steady flow of booty and captives to meet the payroll of soldiers' stipends and pensions. In short, by Muʿawiya's time the conquests had become less an expression of a charismatic moral-religious imperative, as they had been in the early years of the Believers' movement, and more an institutionalized state policy. This transformation coincided with the gradual disappearance from the scene of the last companions who had actually known the prophet.

An important front of new expansion during this period was in North Africa. Under ʿUmar and ʿUthman, the Believers' armies had established themselves as far west as Tripolitania in Libya, but despite some notable victories farther west they had only launched ephemeral raids into the Byzantine *Provincia Africa* (roughly modern Tunisia). During Mu'awiya's time, armies penetrated farther west and established a new *misr* at Qayrawan (50/670), which became in subsequent years not only the main military staging point for invasions into the western Maghrib but also an important economic and cultural center. There was at first a period of peaceful coexistence with the settled Christian Berbers of the Awraba tribe in the Aures mountains led by their chief Kusayla (or Kasila), and it seems possible that they joined the Believers' movement. But a little later still, with the re-appointment of 'Uqba ibn Nafi' (in 62/681, just after Mu'awiya's death) there seems to have been a change of policy, which resulted in warfare between the Berbers and the Arabian Believers. This did not go well at first—'Ubqa ibn Nafi' was killed near Biskra, and the Believers were almost forced to abandon their new *misr* at Qayrawan, but eventually Kusayla was defeated. Resistance to the Believers' expansion by the Berber population would continue for many years, but the establishment of Qayrawan did much to consolidate the Believers' presence in the eastern Maghrib; soon regular raids in this area became an important source of booty, particularly of slaves, for the Umayyad rulers.

Another wave of expansion, meanwhile, was also being undertaken in the east, dependent administratively on Basra and Kufa. 'Abd Allah ibn 'Amir dispatched troops to Sistan and reconquered Zaranj and then Kabul, but resistance tightened up thereafter. His successor in Basra, Ziyad, neglected barren Sistan and concentrated instead on expanding into the richer areas in and adjacent to Khurasan. He sent several campaigns to advance eastward from the *misr* at Marv against the Hephthalites or White Huns (a nomadic people who lived along the Oxus river), and eventually sent fifty thousand men from Basra to be stationed permanently in Marv to strengthen the garrison there. Ziyad's action must also be seen in the context of his concern for stabilizing Basra and strengthening his control over it and Kufa; Basra in particular had become crowded with new immigrants from Arabia, so the transfer of many fighting men helped reduce crowding and concomitant tensions in the town. Besides suppressing numerous Kharijite risings, he also took measures in both Kufa and Basra to rationalize (and perhaps to reduce?) soldiers' pay, and to reorganize the settlements in order to improve his ability to administer the towns. After Ziyad's death in 53/673, his son and eventual successor as governor of Basra, 'Ubayd Allah ibn Ziyad, pursued similar policies.

A final area of expansion during Mu'awiya's reign was to the north, against the Byzantine Empire. Besides the regular—almost annual—summer campaign into Anatolia, Mu'awiya sent troops at least twice in efforts to seize the Byzantine capital, Constantinople. The first (49/669) returned quickly, but the second, which was coordinated with a naval assault, besieged the city for three years (54–57/674–677) before finally giving up. On the maritime front, Arwad (off the Syrian coast) and Rhodes were occupied at this time (53/673), and Crete was raided.

Yet under the surface of relative calm that prevailed during Mu'awiya's reign, the fundamental disagreements among the Believers—especially among those of the west Arabian ruling elite—remained unresolved. Sometimes they came to the surface, as for example in the brief confrontation between Mu'awiya's governors in Kufa and a group of malcontents led by Hujr ibn 'Adi al-Kindi. Hujr and his companions, erstwhile supporters of 'Ali, increasingly objected to the practice of Mu'awiya's governors, Mughira and Ziyad, of praying for forgiveness for 'Uthman and cursing 'Ali during mosque services. (This policy of cursing one's opponent—called *sabb*—had apparently been started by 'Ali during the civil war, but Mu'awiya and his backers proved only too glad to respond in kind.) Hujr and his group heckled the governors and pelted them with pebbles to express their displeasure; they were eventually hunted down and sent off to Mu'awiya in Syria, where Hujr and a few others were executed. Although a relatively minor episode, it reveals that the issues of the First Civil War—especially the question of 'Uthman's piety and whether his murder had been justified and the legitimacy of 'Ali's claim to lead the community—were still unresolved and lay dormant.

Hujr's rising also may have been related to other, more mundane, issues. An account related by the ninth-century Byzantine chronicler Theophanes notes that Mu'awiya reduced the stipends of soldiers in Iraq and increased them in Syria. Although unsupported by other sources, this report is suggestive and plausible. Perhaps this policy, if in fact it was a policy, was simply Mu'awiya's attempt to reward the Syrian troops who had remained loyal to him during the civil war and to punish the soldiery of Iraq who had backed 'Ali. Or perhaps Mu'awiya (who, as we have seen, launched at least two attempts to seize Constantinople from the Byzantines) thought that the central challenge the Believers faced, now that the Sasanian dynasty had fallen, was the contest with Byzantium and so adopted a policy on stipends to emphasize the importance of the Byzantine front and to reward the soldiers who fought on it. In any case, such a policy—reducing the stipends of Iraq's soldiery—could easily have helped push soldiers discontented for other reasons over the line to outright rebellion.

Mu'awiya's reign also masked other tensions. He had apparently acquired large estates in Medina and elsewhere, sometimes by methods that left the previous owners feeling plundered and resentful. These he seems to have worked as investments; one report relates that he held properties in Yamama that were worked by four thousand slaves, and several dams bearing inscriptions mentioning him, still visible today in Medina and Ta'if, represent vestiges of his efforts to develop his holdings. It seems likely that many in the community were envious and resentful, particularly Quraysh or Medinese whose parents had been close followers of the prophet and who therefore thought that they should be prime beneficiaries of the Believers' regime but who realized that they were being left behind.

It is worth reiterating at this point that the early Believers' movement had an ecumenical quality that allowed it to accommodate within itself, in addition to those Arabians who followed Qur'anic law, many Jews and especially (it seems) Christians who shared a commitment to righteous living. It is generally assumed that the tax administration in Mu'awiya's time was manned largely by Syrian Christian or (in Egypt) Coptic scribes and in Iraq by Zoroastrian scribes of Aramaean or Persian stock. Mu'awiya's chief financial administrator was a Syrian Christian, Sergius (in Arabic, Sarjun) ibn Mansur. (His son John—John of Damascus—would serve later Umayyads in the same capacity before being recognized as a saint of the Byzantine church.) Christians seem to have participated even in the Believers' military operations. Mu'awiya himself had, from his earliest days in Syria, established close ties with the powerful Kalb tribe that dominated the Syrian steppe, a tribe that had long been monophysite Christian. To cement the alliance, he married May-sun, the Christian daughter of the chief of the Kalb, Malik ibn Bah-dal, and Kalbite troops formed an important contingent in his military, receiving a large stipend for their services. As we shall see, some of the troops in the Umayyads' Syrian army, even during the Second Civil War, were still Christian. The north Mesopotamian monk John bar Penkaye, who wrote about 67/687, chronicles the beginning of Muhammad's teaching and the Believers' movement and how they made raids each year; he notes that among the Believers were "Christians, not a few," of various denominations.

The relative "openness" of the early Believers' movement to participation by Christians (and, perhaps, Jews and Zoroastrians?) thus seems to have continued beyond the middle of the seventh century. Mu'awiya still chose to style himself *amir al-mu'minin*, "commander of the Believers," as a number of contemporary inscriptions show, and some papyrus documents into the middle of the first century

AH/seventh century C.E. refer to the "jurisdiction (or maybe the era) of the Believers" (*qada* *al-mu'minin*). There is, as yet, no documentary indication that the ruling elite, or people in general, were giving up this broader identity as Believers in favor of a more narrowly defined identity as "Muslims," distinct from other righteous monotheists. That shift, as we shall see, would not take place until after the Second Civil War.

The Second Civil War (60–73/680–692)

Although Mu'awiya had emerged in 40/661 as the victor of the First Civil War, the basic questions over leadership that had been at issue during the war had never really been settled; they had rather been made temporarily moot by the fact that the logical claimants for leadership at that time had been reduced to one. But on Mu'awiya's death in Rajab 60/April 680, the latent tensions dividing the ruling elite among the Believers quickly bubbled to the surface. Hoping to secure a smooth succession, Mu'awiya in his last years had issued a decree naming his son Yazid ibn Mu'awiya heir apparent. Yazid was not an unlikely candidate; he had led one of Mu'awiya's campaigns against Constantinople and was the son of Mu'awiya's Kalbite wife Maysun, so he was well liked on both counts by the Syrian army. Consequently, there were few objections to Mu'awiya's designation of him as heir apparent, except from several members of the Arabian elite, some of whom aspired to lead the community themselves. Significantly, all of them were of Quraysh, and all but one was the son of an earlier *amir al-mu'minin*, or of someone who had claimed that office during the First Civil War: 'Abd Allah ibn al-Zubayr, Husayn ibn 'Ali, 'Abd al-Rahman ibn Abi Bakr, 'Abd Allah ibn 'Umar, and 'Abd Allah ibn al-'Abbas. After Mu'awiya's death, the last three recognized Yazid as *amir al-mu'minin*; presumably their opposition had been mainly to Mu'awiya's efforts to get the oath of allegiance to Yazid sworn in advance, and not to Yazid himself. But Husayn ibn ʿAli and ʿAbd Allah ibn al-Zubayr refused to recognize Yazid. Slipping away from Medina to avoid the Umayyad governor there, they sought sanctuary in the sacrosanct confines of the *haram* of Mecca.

In Kufa, the many people who had formerly supported ʿAli took hope on Muʿawiya's death and wrote to ʿAli's younger son Husayn in Mecca, inviting him to come to Kufa, where, they assured him, he would find strong support in making a bid to become *amir al-muʾminin*. (As we saw earlier, his older brother Hasan had abdicated in favor of Muʿawiya and withdrawn from politics at the end of the First Civil War.) We can at this point begin to refer to the people who were loyal to ʿAli and his descendants as "Shiʿites" or "the Shiʿa," even though at this early state the "party of ʿAli" (Arabic, *shiʿat ʿAli*) had not yet developed the full range of theological doctrines found in later Shiʿism.

To prepare the way for a bid to be *amir al-muʾminin*, Husayn sent to Kufa his cousin Muslim ibn ʿAqil ibn Abi Talib, who was warmly received by the Shiʿites there; he lodged at the house of one of Kufa's Shiʿite leaders, a man named Mukhtar ibn Abi ʿUbayd. But the Umayyad governor, ʿUbayd Allah ibn Ziyad, got wind of their plans and was able to track down Muslim, who was executed for conspiring against the regime.

Husayn, however, had set out for Kufa with a small group of his family before word of Muslim's demise reached him. Outside Kufa, his little group was intercepted by ʿUbayd Allah's troops, who had been sent to look for him. Negotiations carried out over several weeks were fruitless; Husayn refused to recognize Yazid as *amir al-muʾminin*, nor would he withdraw, and ʿUbayd Allah would not let him enter the city. Finally, a battle was fought at Karbalaʾ, 75 km (46.6 mi) northeast of Kufa, where Husayn and virtually all of his following were cut down (Muharram 10, 61/October 10, 680).

POEM OF ʿALI IBN AL-HUSAYN IBN ʿALI IBN ABI TALIB

Said to be the first member of al-Husayn's family killed at Karbala? These verses were supposedly declaimed by him as he strode into battle against the Umayyad forces, units of which were led by Shabath ibn Ribʿi al-Riyahi and Shamir ibn Dhi l-Jawshan (hemistich 3). The last line is a reference to the Umayyad governor, ʿUbayd Allah ibn Ziyad, whose father had been recognized by the caliph Muʿawiya as his half-brother. The poem captures some of the central ideas that would be developed by the Shiʿa, notably the ʿAlids' legiti-macy rooted in closeness to the prophet and the idea that the righteous should wage struggle against tyrants, even in the face of hopeless odds. Whether or not the poem is authentic, it shows that these ideas were in circulation by the time of the relatively early author, Abu Mikhnaf (died 157/773–774).

I am ʿAli son of Husayn son of ʿAli;
    We and the household of God are closer to the prophet
Than Shabath and Shamir the vile.
    I strike you with the sword until it bends,
The blows of a Hashimite youth, an ʿAlid,
    And today I will not stop defending my father.
By God, the son of the bastard shall not rule over us!

[Abu Mikhnaf, *Maqtal al-Husayn ibn ʿAli*, ed. Kamil Sulayman al-Juburi (n.p.: Dar al-mahajja al-bayda', 2000), 139.]

The snuffing out of this little insurrection had been an easy task for ʿUbayd Allah's much larger force but was to have momentous and enduring consequences. Although in the short term it had re-moved one of Yazid's rivals from the field, the killing of Husayn—ʿAli's son and the prophet Muhammad's grandson, in whose veins the blood of the prophet flowed—as well as much of his family, shocked many Believers and contributed to the impression that Yazid was impious. The Shiʿites of Kufa who had invited Husayn to rebel were now full of remorse for having failed to support him but for the moment could do little. After the death of Husayn, ʿUbayd Allah expelled the Shiʿite leader Mukhtar, who made his way to Mecca to explore the possibility of joining forces with ʿAbd Allah ibn al-Zubayr in resisting Yazid's rule. The aristocratic and dour Ibn al-Zubayr, however, never one to warm to the idea of cooperating with anyone who might rival his own claims, rebuffed Mukhtar's advances, and Mukhtar withdrew to his hometown, Taʾif, for a time.

Yazid's efforts to win support in the Hijaz met with no success. He invited a delegation of prominent Medinese to Damascus to try to win them over, but many still nursed feelings of having been injured by Muʿawiya's policies. Added to this, their reports of Yazid's less-than-abstemious lifestyle at court generated further outrage, not sympathy, among the Medinese, who were shocked that one so lacking in piety could claim to lead the Believers. The Medinese also resented the Umayyads for another reason; after the First Civil War, Muʿawiya had confiscated estates in the town from the Medinese, who had generally backed ʿAli, reducing some Medinese virtually to the status of serfs. In 63/682–683, therefore, the Medinese repudiated Yazid's claim to leadership and expelled Yazid's governor, who had chided the Medinese for interfering with the Umayyads' reaping of profits from the land.

In Mecca, Ibn al-Zubayr also repudiated Yazid in an insulting sermon in which he referred to his reputed fondness for unusual animals and dissolute living: "Yazid of liquors, Yazid of whoring, Yazid of panthers, Yazid of apes, Yazid of dogs, Yazid of wine-swoons, Yazid of barren deserts" (the rhyming qualities of the original are, of course, lacking in the translation). Ibn al-Zubayr then defeated an armed force (led by his own brother ʿAmr, who was captured and killed with exquisite deliberation) that had been sent by Yazid to arrest him. With the Hijaz now in open revolt, Yazid organized a large Syrian army and dispatched it to the Holy Cities. Prominent in this force were tribesmen of Kalb and of the still largely Christian tribe of Taghlib, some of whom reportedly marched with a cross and a banner of their patron, St. Sergius. The Medinese now expelled all members of the Umayyad family and their supporters from Medina—said to be one thousand strong. Yazid's army marched south into the Hijaz and took up a position in the basalt lava field *(harra)* east of Medina. After a few days of fruitless efforts to persuade the insurgents to recognize Yazid, battle was joined. The Medinese (descendants of the Helpers and many non-Umayyad Quraysh who had long lived in Medina) seemed to be on the verge of victory, but the Syrians turned the tide. Many Medinese were killed, including many Quraysh, and Medina was subjected to three days of pillage. The so-called "Battle of the Harra" (end 63/August 683) may even have resulted in the enslavement of some Medinese. Then the defeated Medinese were forced to swear allegiance to Yazid as *amir al-mu'minin*.

Yazid's army now continued its march south toward Mecca to bring to heel 'Abd Allah ibn al-Zubayr, whom Yazid had from the start seen as his most serious rival. Mecca was besieged for several weeks (early 64/September 683); during the siege there was desultory skirmishing, and at one point the Ka'ba (that is, the hangings on it) were set afire and burned. But in the midst of the siege, word arrived that Yazid had unexpectedly died in Syria (Rabi' I 64/November 683). Learning this, the commander of the Syrian forces, who had never been very keen on the attack on Mecca or on Ibn al-Zubayr, broke off the siege and began negotiations with Ibn al-Zubayr, in which he invited him to march with him back to Syria to accept the post of *amir al-mu'minin*. Ibn al-Zubayr, however, refused to leave Mecca. The Syrian forces withdrew and headed north to Damascus.

With the death of Yazid, the fortunes of Ibn al-Zubayr seemed to improve greatly, while that of the Umayyads suffered a serious blow. Ibn al-Zubayr declared himself commander of the Believers in 64/683. In Syria, some recognized Yazid's young son Mu'awiya (II) as *amir al-mu'minin*, but outside Syria and even within it many people looked to other possibilities; we have seen that the commander of Yazid's army was disposed to recognize Ibn al-Zubayr, as were some members of the Umayyad family. Ibn al-Zubayr, already recognized as *amir al-mu'minin* in Mecca and Medina, sent a governor to Egypt and, after a period of confusion in Iraq, managed to bring it, too, within his sphere, sending his brother Mus'ab there as governor. Backers of Ibn al-Zubayr again expelled the Umayyads and their supporters from Medina.

Meanwhile, Mu'awiya II died after only a few months, leaving the Umayyads in total disarray. Those groups that had been tightly allied to the Umayyad dynasty and therefore had the most to lose if the office of *amir al-mu'minin* were to be held by someone else, naturally were the most eager to find an Umayyad claimant. These included especially the chiefs of the powerful Kalb tribe of central Syria, which had been allied to Mu'awiya I and Yazid by marriage; 'Ubayd Allah ibn Ziyad, whose service as governor of Iraq for Mu'awiya and Yazid made him eager to see a continuance of Umayyad rule there; and Sarjun ibn Mansur, the Christian chief administrator for Mu'awiya and Yazid. But some erstwhile supporters of the Umayyads, led by Dahhak ibn Qays (of the Fihr clan of Quraysh) and supported by the Qays tribes of northern Syria, backed Ibn al-Zubayr, who was now recognized over the whole empire with the sole exception of Damascus and its environs. Ibn al-Zubayr duly appointed Dahhak his governor of Damascus, *in absentia*. Even the head of the Umayyad family, the aged Marwan, appears to have been on the verge of recognizing Ibn al-Zubayr (according to some reports, he actually did so). But eventually he was persuaded by 'Ubayd Allah ibn Ziyad and Hassan ibn Malik ibn Bahdal, chief of the Kalb tribe, to claim the leadership for himself. The Umayyad family met at Jabiya, in the Jawlan plateau southwest of Damascus, where Marwan was recognized by them as *amir al-mu'minin*; and, after gathering his loyal supporters (particularly the leaders of Kalb and of the Judham tribe of Palestine), Marwan confronted Dahhak and those who backed Ibn al-Zubayr at Marj Rahit, northwest of Damascus. In the battle, Dahhak was killed and his backers, particularly those of the Qays tribes, were utterly routed, with heavy loss of life (Muharram 65/August 684). This battle reinforced the close tie between the Umayyads and the Kalb tribe and stabilized Marwan's position in Syria, but it sowed intense animosity between Kalb and its allies on the one hand and Qays on the other that would continue to fester for more than a century, bedeviling later Umayyad attempts to build a unified Syrian army. Marwan quickly moved to consolidate his power in Syria and Palestine (not least against the claims of rival Umayyad clan leaders) and then seized Egypt from Ibn al-Zubayr's governor by the middle of 65/early 685. When he died a few months later, Marwan was able to hand over to his son and successor, the vigorous 'Abd al-Malik, a secure base on which to restore Umayyad power.

In Iraq, meanwhile, Ibn al-Zubayr's grip was being shaken by developments among the Shi'a of Kufa. Mukhtar ibn Abi 'Ubayd, who as we have seen had been expelled from Kufa by Yazid's governor 'Ubayd Allah ibn Ziyad after the battle of Karbala', returned in Ramadan 64/May 684 after more than three years in Mecca and al-Ta'if. During that time, he had tried repeatedly to interest 'Abd Allah ibn al-Zubayr in an anti-Umayyad alliance, but the proud Ibn al-Zubayr would have none of it. Mukhtar began building a populist movement among the Shi'ites of Kufa, calling for the establishment of just rule and succor for the downtrodden. He also called people to recognize Muhammad ibn al-Hanafiyya, son of 'Ali ibn Abi Talib by Khawla, a captive of the Hanifa tribe taken during the *ridda*, as *amir al-mu'minin*; Mukhtar asserted that Muhammad ibn al-Hanifiyya was the rightful claimant not only because of his 'Alid ancestry but also because he was the eschatological redeemer *(mahdi)* whose arrival would vanquish evil and (finally) establish a just regime on Earth. (This is the first recorded instance in which the concept of the *mahdi* is evoked among the Believers.) Mukhtar's movement won broad support in Kufa not only among the Shi'a but also among Kufa's many *mawali*—former captives and their descendants. It also appealed to a number of the common fighting men, who resented the dominant elite of the city (regardless of whether the latter supported the Umayyads or Ibn al-Zubayr). Mukhtar tried to win over the tribal notables of Kufa also, whose support he deemed indispensable, but there was always an implicit conflict between their interests and the populist, "leveler" nature of Mukhtar's ideology; one source reports that the notables complained to Mukhtar, "You have taken aim at our *mawali*, who are booty which God bestowed upon us, and this whole country likewise; we freed [that is, conquered] them hoping for the reward and recompense (of God) in that, and for thanks; we are not pleased that you should make them partners in our spoils."

With tensions running high, word arrived in Kufa in late 66/early summer 686 that 'Ubayd Allah ibn Ziyad, the former Umayyad governor who had dispatched the forces that had killed Husayn at Karbala', was marching from northern Syria toward Iraq with a Syrian army. Almost two years earlier, a group of Kufans called the "Penitents" *(tawwabun),* who regretted their failure to support Husayn at Karbala', had marched out to face the same 'Ubayd Allah as he marched an army toward Iraq. They met him at 'Ayn Warda on the border between northern Syria and Iraq and were cut down (Jumada I 65/January 685), but following it, 'Ubayd Allah had become bogged down trying to subdue the Jazira region. Now, eighteen months later, he was ready and had begun his march toward Iraq. Mukhtar quickly organized a force, commanded by the brilliant Ibrahim ibn al-Ashtar, and sent it northward to block 'Ubayd Allah's advance.

Ibn al-Zubayr's governor in Kufa, and the tribal notables who backed him, immediately took advantage of the absence of most of Mukhtar's forces to organize an attack on Mukhtar, whom they hoped to get rid of once and for all. But Mukhtar was able to recall Ibrahim, who returned with his men only a few days after his departure. In the struggle that followed (end 66/July 686), Mukhtar's forces went into battle shouting the slogans "Vengeance for Husayn!" and "O Victorious One, kill!" (the latter a reference to a messianic redeemer), and those notables who had, under the Umayyads, had any part in supporting the campaign against Husayn were killed. When the failure of their rebellion became obvious to the notables, nearly ten thousand of them fled from Kufa to take refuge in Basra with Mus'ab ibn al-Zubayr, and Mukhtar's followers razed the houses of those who had fled. Muhktar exacted an oath of allegiance from the people of Kufa, promising to avenge the "people of the house" (*ahl al-bayt*, used in reference to the prophet's family—here meaning especially 'Ali and his descendants)—and appointed governors over Kufa's dependencies in the east, a vast area that included Armenia, Azerbaijan, Mosul, Hulwan, and the rest of central and northern Iraq.

With Kufa more securely under control, Mukhtar again dispatched forces under Ibrahim ibn al-Ashtar to deal with the approaching Umayyad army. Ibrahim's men, flush from their recent victory in Kufa, were eager to avenge the deaths of both Husayn and the Penitents, and blocked 'Ubayd Allah's passage in northern Iraq, near the Zab river. Again the tide went in their favor; at the battle of Khazir, near Mosul, 'Ubayd Allah's force was crushed (partly because Qays contingents in the Umayyad force, still smarting from their defeat at Marj Rahit two years earlier, deserted), and 'Ubayd Allah himself and a number of other important Umayyad commanders were slain (Muharram 67/August 686). This gave Mukhtar control of northern Iraq as well as Kufa and was a serious setback for 'Abd al-Malik's plan to reconquer the empire.

The revenge of the expelled Kufan notables was not long in coming; encouraged by them, Mus'ab ibn al-Zubayr began planning his effort to reclaim Kufa. By the middle of 67/early 687, they were ready and marched on Kufa. Mukhtar's forces were defeated in a first clash at Madhar and were pushed back to Harura' and eventually to Kufa itself, which was put to siege. When Mus'ab and his Kufan supporters finally took the city in Ramadan 67/April 687, Mukhtar was killed, along with six thousand of his supporters.

The elimination of Mukhtar and his movement put Iraq once more in the control of Ibn al-Zubayr, but his regime thereafter was hardly calm; the Zubayrids faced numerous Kharijite rebellions in Iraq, Fars, and especially in eastern Arabia, where a massive rebellion among the Hanifa tribe of the Yamama region of eastern Arabia, led by the Kharijite Najda ibn 'Amir, removed a large piece of territory from the Zubayrid realm. In 68/June 688 no fewer than four different leaders headed pilgrimage caravans to Mecca, representing those recognizing Ibn al-Zubayr, the Umayyad 'Abd al-Malik, the Kharijite leader Najda, and the 'Alid Ibn al-Hanifiyya.

Meanwhile, in Syria 'Abd al-Malik had to deal with a variety of threats to his power before he could think about launching another offensive against Ibn al-Zubayr to recover from the setback suffered by his forces at the Battle of the Khazir River. In early 67/summer 686, he had to suppress an uprising led by a leader of the Judham tribe in Palestine who had declared his support for Ibn al-Zubayr. He also had to deal with the northern front, where the Byzantine emperor had organized—and backed with money and troops—the invasion of the Syrian coastal regions as far south as Lebanon by a warlike mountain people from the Amanus, the Mardaites. Only by concluding a costly and humiliating treaty with the Byzantine emperor was 'Abd al-Malik able to secure the Mardaites' withdrawal. Thus it was in 69/689 that he left Damascus on a first campaign to try to dislodge Mus'ab ibn al-Zubayr from Iraq, but in his absence his distant cousin and rival 'Amr ibn Sa'id ibn al-'As seized Damascus and advanced his own claim to lead the Umayyad dynasty. 'Abd al-Malik had to cancel his

Two coins of rivals to the Umayyads. The upper coin, issued by a governor of ʿAbdullah ibn al-Zubayr, was minted in Darabjird, in Fars in western Iran, in the year 53 (of the Sasanian "Yazdegird era"), corresponding to 683–684 C.E. The name legend by the bust, in Pahlavi, reads ABDULA AMIR I-WRUISHNIKAN, "ʿAbdullah, *amir al-muʾminin*." The lower image shows a coin issued in Ardashir Khurra (in western Iran) in AH 75, corresponding to 694–695 C.E., by the Kharijite rebel Qatari ibn al-Fujaʾa, whose name appears in the name legend along with AMIR I-WRUISHNI-KAN, Pahlavi for *amir al-muʾminin*. The reverse shows a fire altar. In the obverse margin, the Kharijite slogan *la hukma illa lillah*, "There is no judgment except to God."

campaign and return to put down this rebellion and, eventually, execute ʿAmr. He also needed to quell the stubborn opposition to the Umayyads among the Qaysi tribesmen of Qarqisiya᾽ along the Euphrates (71–72/summer 691).

It was only in 72/late 691, therefore, that ʿAbd al-Malik was ready to embark on a definitive campaign against Ibn al-Zubayr᾽s position in Iraq. After making contact with the many groups and leaders in Iraq who had been alienated by Musʿab ibn al-Zubayr᾽s government there, ʿAbd al-Malik advanced. He met Musʿab᾽s army at Dayr al-Jathliq on the middle Tigris (somewhat north of modern Baghdad) and defeated it easily, as many of Musʿab᾽s troops melted away or refused to fight for him. In the end Musʿab was captured and executed (mid-72/end 691). ʿAbd al-Malik entered Kufa and was recognized there as *amir al-muʾminin*.

ʿAbd al-Malik then sent his loyal commander Hajjaj ibn Yusuf—soon to be his governor in Iraq—with a force of two thousand Syrians against Ibn al-Zubayr in Mecca. This small force was augmented in the following weeks by others and was joined by another that ʿAbd al-Malik had earlier dispatched to the northern Hijaz to guard Syria against any attempt by Ibn al-Zubayr to invade it. Hajjaj encamped first in Ta᾽if (his hometown) to collect his forces before closing in on Mecca. Toward the end of 72/March 692, the city was blockaded and a siege begun; after six months, during which many of Ibn al-Zubayr᾽s forces deserted because of the hopelessness of the situation or were lured away by promises of amnesty, ʿAbd Allah ibn al-Zubayr was decisively defeated and killed in a battle outside the city (Jumada I, 73/September 692). ʿAbd al-Malik was finally recognized in all the *amsar* and their dependencies as *amir al-muʾminin*. After twelve years of strife, the Second Civil War was finally over, and Umayyad rule had been restored.

Reflections on the Civil Wars

Several noteworthy points emerge from the accounts of the civil wars. First, in both civil wars, but particularly in the first, one is struck by how tightly the dispute is concentrated on the issue of who could best claim to rule the community of Believers. Moreover, it seems that most people saw the leadership as belonging properly within a small group—basically Quraysh. (The Kharijites were the main exception to this view.) This gives the civil wars, particularly the first, the quality of an extremely bitter family feud, as most of the principals in the civil wars were related to one another, often quite closely, by ties of blood or marriage, or at least knew one another personally.

Second, the civil wars were striking for the savagery with which they were carried out. There are many episodes in which our sources describe captives being executed in cold blood, in which sons are executed before their fathers, or men killed by, or at the order of, their relatives ('Amr ibn al-Zubayr by his brother 'Abd Allah; 'Amr ibn Sa'id by 'Abd al-Malik), in which the vanquished were massacred in large numbers (Nahrawan, Khazir, Mukhtar's followers in Kufa, Battle of the Harra). This may have something to do with the crude temper of the age and with the brutal manners of many participants, who were rough and unrefined bedouins or peasants. But it surely also owed much to the ideological character of many of the conflicts within the civil wars. This led people to demonize their opponents as the very embodiment of evil and also made them keenly aware that a defeated enemy who had not fully repented was, for ideological reasons, always a threat to rebel again, so it was safer to eliminate him. Moreover, the intensely ideological character of the early Believers' movement made the elimination of such "allies of the devil" morally acceptable, even praiseworthy, in peoples' minds. The Penitents who met their deaths at 'Ayn Warda were doubtless convinced of 'Ubayd Allah ibn Ziyad's status as a representative of the devil;

Kharijite groups executed as apostates anyone whose observance of proper Belief did not conform to their own stringent requirements; the Kufan notables who slaughtered Mukhtar's *mawali* supporters saw them as interlopers who had unjustly usurped their God-given property rights. But old-fashioned revenge played a large part in many bloody events as well—whether it was the Umayyads taking revenge on the Medinese at the Battle of the Harra for their expulsion from the city and for the murder of 'Uthman, or Mukhtar's followers exacting vengeance from the Kufan notables and on 'Ubayd Allah's troops for the murder of Husayn.

Third, with the Second Civil War in particular, we are palpably moving into a new phase in the history of the community of Believers. The era of the companions of the prophet is rapidly drawing to a close, and the *dramatis personae* are now members of a younger generation who had no memory of the prophet or of the struggles that shaped his life. One senses an attenuation of the intensely charismatic quality of the early movement, with its clear-sighted concern for piety and observing God's will; the commitment to piety is still there, but it has become more routinized and less personal and is tempered among many Believers with more practical and this-worldly concerns. The conquests by now apparently had become less a matter of the personal zeal of individual Believers driven by visions of an impending Last Judgment and more a lucrative form of state policy intended to keep revenues and plunder flowing into the treasury.

Fourth, we see in the civil wars—and particularly in the second—the emergence of those fissures that have, ever since, divided the once-united community of Believers. 'Ali's claims to be *amir al-mu'minin* during the First Civil War become gradually transformed into the beginnings of a true sectarian movement, Shi'ism, that held the family of 'Ali in special reverence; it received its defining event in the massacre of 'Ali's son Husayn at Karbala' in the Second Civil War, an event that came to be commemorated by later Shi'ite groups, right down to today, and that gave Shiʿism its special identity focused on the idea of martyrdom as a means of advancing the cause of the downtrodden. It would be a century and more before Shiʿism would fully refine many of its central concepts, such as the notion of the *imamate* or ideal, God-guided leader of the community, but the later movement has its roots in the First and Second Civil wars. These events thus became the starting point for the construction of two different narratives of legitimation in the Islamic community— one Shiʿite, focusing on the family of ʿAli, and the other (eventually called Sunni) focusing on the sequence of actual power-holders, including the Umayyads. We have also seen how a third group, the ultra-pious Kharijites, emerged during the First Civil War; although constituting only a small minority of Muslims today, they were quite significant in the first several centuries of Islam.

Fifth, the events of the long, intermittent conflict suggest decisively that the Hijaz, despite being the home of the holy cities of Mecca and Medina, the cradle and spiritual focus of the early Believers' movement, was not an effective base from which to project power on an imperial scale—and the community of Believers, with its far-flung *amsar* dominating most of the Near East, had by the time of the civil wars ascended to a truly imperial scale. More effective as bases of power were those areas that had a solid tax base (especially Egypt and Iraq) and a fairly sizable, stable population. The Hijaz offered neither of these and increasingly became a political backwater (or, at least, a side channel) in the history of the community of Believers.

Economic and other practical issues surely contributed a great deal to these conflicts—indeed, it was the fact that so much was at stake economically that made the struggle worth embarking on for many participants. The accounts of Mukhtar's revolt reveal clearly that Kufa was torn by serious social and economic tensions, pitting the descendants of the first conquerors, who formed a kind of Arabian aristocracy, against the descendants of former captives (*mawali*); at

times there was added a heavy overtone of social distance separating
those whose native language was Arabic from those whose mother
tongue was something else. Social and economic tensions of this
kind probably always existed; what is striking is that such grievances
were articulated into a coherent political movement by the claim
that a just leader (or maybe a *mahdi*, an eschatological savior) would
solve the problem. In other words, the Believers' movement, even as
late as the Second Civil War, brought with it the conviction that
such routine social injustices and oppression were no longer acceptable, that a new and more just order was attainable. The Believers'
movement thus mobilized people to act in ways designed, they believed, to resolve social and economic tensions that were more or less
endemic in premodern society (and maybe in all societies). In this
sense, we must see the ideology of the Believers' movement as the
prime cause of these historical developments, rather than the latent
economic and social tensions that the movement articulated, for such
tensions are always found.

The very fact that the civil wars were for the most part a struggle
within Quraysh over leadership means that the broader community
of early Believers—especially those non-Arabian Christians and Jews
who had joined in the movement—were not prominently visible in
these struggles. In the Second Civil War, there were moments when
Christians, at least, seem to have been involved. As we have seen,
the Umayyads' Christian administrator, Sarjun ibn Mansur was active in encouraging the Umayyads to make a bid for leadership
against Ibn al-Zubayr after the deaths of Yazid and Mu'awiya II. Did
he really feel himself to be an integral part of the Believers' movement, or was he just an employee solicitous of the interests of his
employers, the Umayyads, who buttered his bread? The evidence
is inadequate, but at least it is clear that people like Sarjun did not
feel that the movement he served was anti-Christian. The leaders of
the Kalb tribe, and many of their soldiers who formed an important
component of the Umayyads' troops, were also probably still Chris-

tian. We find no evidence, either, of any effort by Christians or Jews to exploit the disarray among the ruling elite to break away or overthrow the Believers' hegemony, perhaps because they may have felt themselves to be part of it. These factors suggest that the ecumenical qualities of the earliest Believers' movement was still alive through the period of the Second Civil War; but this situation was soon to change.

5

The Emergence of Islam

We have seen how Muhammad preached certain religious ideas that gave rise in western Arabia to an apocalyptically oriented pietistic movement which, following the name the members of the movement applied to themselves, we have termed the "Believers' movement."

We also examined the basic concepts of this movement, particularly its desire to establish a "community of the righteous" who could attain salvation on the Last Day and to spread the hegemony of this community as far as possible in order to realize a righteous political order—that is, a polity that was guided by the observance of God's revealed law—in preparation for the anticipated Last Day. We traced the community's rapid spread through much of the Near East during the seventh century C.E., led by a ruling elite of Arabian origin, and considered the relationship between this new community and the indigenous populations (mostly Christian, Jewish, or Zoroastrian) that it encountered and came to rule during its expansion. We also saw how disagreements over the question of leadership within the ruling elite resulted in two extended periods of brutal civil strife, with permanent repercussions.

In this chapter we shall see how, during the late first century AH/ seventh century C.E. and early second century AH/eighth century

C.E., the Believers' movement evolved into the religion we now know as Islam, through a process of refinement and redefinition of its basic concepts. Islam, as we understand it today, is thus the direct continuation or outgrowth of the Believers' movement rooted in the preachings of Muhammad and the actions of his early followers, even though it would be historically inaccurate to call the early Believers' movement "Islam."

The process by which Islam crystallized from the matrix of the Believers' movement following the civil wars was partially the result of intentional efforts made by the ruling Umayyad dynasty and its supporters and partially the result of a sea change in the perceptions within the community generally on matters of identity. For this reason, it seems to have been a transformation that took hold gradually and lasted for a considerable time—several decades at least, perhaps in some arenas as long as a century. While many aspects of this process of transformation remain murky, several dimensions of it are visible enough to be examined in more detail. These will form the main rubrics of this chapter. In general, however, we can say that the Believers, led by the Umayyad dynasty, particularly the *amir al-mu'minin* 'Abd al-Malik and his entourage, seem to have embarked on a renewed search for legitimacy, seeking ways to establish for themselves and for the world at large their right to claim political supremacy and their right to direct a regime based on what they understood to be God's word.

The Umayyad Restoration and Return to the Imperial Agenda

During the twelve years of the Second Civil War, neither the Umayyads nor any of the other contenders for leadership of the Believers' movement had enjoyed the calm or security needed to concentrate their energies on any of the Believers' fundamental concerns, other than settling the question of who should lead. The final defeat of 'Abd Allah ibn al-Zubayr in 73/autumn 692 marked the effective reunification, under the leadership of 'Abd al-Malik and the Marwanid branch of the Umayyad family, of the empire established by the early Believers. With that victory—indeed, even somewhat before it as its inevitability became clear and 'Abd al-Malik's position became secure—he began to pursue policies demonstrating his concern with resuming what he considered to be the Believers' fundamental agenda.

One activity that 'Abd al-Malik resumed, which had long been interrupted by the civil war, was the dispatching of raids and campaigns of conquest in an effort to further expand the borders of the empire and the writ of God's law. The Byzantines were the first to receive such attention. During the civil war, as we have seen, 'Abd al-Malik had been forced to buy peace from the Byzantine emperor on several occasions, including a treaty concluded as late as 70/689–690; but even before the final defeat of Ibn al-Zubayr, 'Abd al-Malik resumed the policy of launching regular raids during the summer deep into Byzantine territory. This policy was henceforth pursued vigorously by 'Abd al-Malik and his successors as *amir al-mu'minin*, particularly his sons al-Walid (ruled 86–96/705–715) and Sulayman (ruled 96–99/715–717). The latter, in fact, organized a massive land and sea assault on the Byzantine capital, Constantinople, that lasted more than a year (98–99/summer 717–summer 718) and almost captured the city. But the restored Umayyads also pursued a policy of expanding the empire in other areas as well, including significant campaigns in Tabaristan, Jurjan, Sijistan (Sistan), Khorezm, and beyond the Oxus River in the east and into the Iberian peninsula in the west. The latter region was largely subdued by the commander, Musa ibn Nusayr, and his lieutenant, Tariq ibn Ziyad, in 92–94/711–713. 'Abd al-Malik even dispatched a force to Sind (the Indus Valley, modern Pakistan), which resulted in the establishment of a colony of Believers there in 93/711, under the command of Muhammad ibn al-Qasim al-Thaqafi, a young protégé of 'Abd al-Malik's main general and govenor of Iraq, Hajjaj ibn Yusuf.

The campaigns of conquest, by this time, were as a matter of policy mounted regularly and on a large scale, both because they would spread the writ of God's law to new areas and because they were indispensable to the regime's finances: The booty and tax revenues (including regular levies of slaves) derived from such conquests provided the regime with the wealth it needed to pay its soldiers. It might be called a case of the dynasty "doing well by doing good," and it is very difficult to decide the relative importance of the material and the ideological or religious incentives, if indeed they can be separated. One cannot deny the immense material advantages of the expansion policy for the regime. But, it would be too facile to conclude that the religious motivation—the desire to extend recognition of God's word—was nothing more than a cover for the dynasty's cupidity. To do so would be to overlook the fact that the Believers' movement began and long continued to be one rooted in religious commitment. Moreover, there survive reports in the Islamic tradition (which is not generally well disposed to 'Abd al-Malik or to the Umayyads) that suggest that 'Abd al-Malik was devout and dedicated to acquiring religious learning in his early years. It therefore seems best to conclude that the expansion was driven by an indissoluble amalgam of religious and material motives.

Another key dimension of the early Believers' movement, as we have seen, was its focus on the coming of the Last Judgment, which many early Believers seem to have expected to be imminent. Such apocalyptic convictions may have been the force that impelled some Believers to abandon their usual day-to-day concerns and enlist in the distant and arduous campaigns to spread the writ of God's word that are usually called the "Islamic conquests." The pull of material incentives must also have played an important part in drawing people into the movement, of course, but would mainly have come into play after the process of expansion had developed obvious momentum;

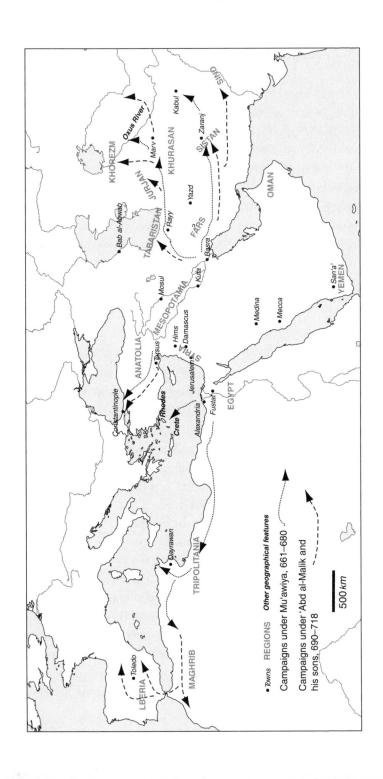

KHOREZM

Oxus River

Marv

KHURASAN

JURJAN

Kabul

Zaranj

SISTAN

SIND

Bab al-Abwab

TABARISTAN

Rayy

Yazd

FARS

Basra

OMAN

Mosul

MESOPOTAMIA

Kufa

ANATOLIA

Tarsus

Hims

Damascus

SYRIA

Medina

Mecca

San'a

YEMEN

Constantinople

Rhodes

Crete

Jerusalem

Alexandria

Fustat

EGYPT

Qayrawan

TRIPOLITANIA

Toledo

IBERIA

MAGHRIB

• *Towns*   REGIONS   *Other geographical features*

Campaigns under Mu'awiya, 661–680

Campaigns under 'Abd al-Malik and
his sons, 690–718

500 km

so it seems likely that the ideological motive—fear of the impending Last Judgment—was paramount in the movement's early years and only tapered off slowly. Indeed, as we have seen, the movement's very success in the mundane world probably heightened the religious fervor of some, who perceived in it a sign of God's favor for the Believers and an affirmation of their religious claims. The divisions of the civil wars may, likewise, have been viewed by some contemporaries as the tribulations *(fitan)* that were expected to usher in the Judgment, which may be why in later Islamic tradition the Qur'anic word *fitna* is used to refer to the civil wars. (Another reason was that the civil wars were seen, retrospectively, as occasions when some Believers had succumbed to the temptation or seduction—also called *fitna*—of worldly power.)

Once his position as *amir al-mu'minin* was secure, 'Abd al-Malik seems also to have wanted to remind the Believers of the reality, and perhaps the imminence, of the Last Judgment. He may even have wanted to advance for himself the claim to being that final, just ruler in whose day the Judgment would begin and who would deliver to God sovereignty over the world. After all, by resuming annual attacks on the Byzantines, he had again embarked on an active struggle against the unbelievers, as the final ruler was supposed to do. His desire to honor this scenario may have been what led him to order the construction of one of the most magnificent works of early Islamic architecture, the sumptuous building in Jerusalem usually called the "Dome of the Rock."

The Dome of the Rock has been the subject of extensive debate among scholars who wish to recover its original purpose and meaning. Some have argued that it was built by 'Abd al-Malik during the Second Civil War, when Mecca was controlled by his rival 'Abd Allah ibn al-Zubayr, in order to provide an alternative destination for pilgrims. Others have argued that its construction should be seen as

---

Map 6. Later campaigns of expansion

The Dome of the Rock. 'Abd al-Malik had this splendid monument built on Mount Moriah in Jerusalem—site of the Jews' Second Temple, destroyed centuries before by the Romans—in the 690s C.E. The building's extensive interior inscriptions are noteworthy for their anti-trinitarian emphasis; its octagonal plan suggests a commemorative building.

a "victory monument"—a statement of religious domination directed toward Christians (and, to a lesser extent, toward Jews), visible proof that the Believers were "here to stay" in the city that was most central to the other two faiths.

The Dome of the Rock poses numerous interpretive puzzles. It is not a mosque. It is constructed on the octagonal plan of a late antique Christian (and earlier pagan) martyrium—a design that was well known in the Byzantine architecture of the Near East. Yet the building was clearly not intended to be a Christian monument, because its interior is decorated with mosaics bearing lengthy passages and paraphrases from the Qur'an that reject the idea of the Trinity (about which we shall have more to say presently). Moreover, it was

Umm Qays. This town in northern Jordan, overlooking the Sea of Galilee, is the site of the late antique city of Gadara. It includes this octagonal martyrium, the plan of which resembles that used for the Dome of the Rock in Jerusalem, less than 100 km (62 mi) away.

constructed on Mount Moriah, the site of the Jewish Second Temple, where no Christian monument would have been; in the Byzantine period, as we have seen, the Christian authorities of Jerusalem had refused to construct any religious buildings on the Temple Mount and had ordered that the site be used as a dumping ground for trash. Nor can the Dome of the Rock, despite its location, be understood as an attempt actually to rebuild the Jewish temple; the description of the temple was well known from the Torah and bore little formal resemblance to a late antique martyrium.

It seems likely that 'Abd al-Malik, or his advisers, chose the martyrium plan because they knew that a building in that form would be immediately understood by anyone who saw it as a building having *religious* meaning. But what kind of religious meaning? It is possible that an assertion of religious supremacy was indeed involved. But recent research on the Dome and associated buildings suggests that it may also have been intended to symbolize or refer to paradise and resurrection, particularly as depicted in the Qur'an and in earlier late antique iconography. Jerusalem, we must recall, bears a very special relationship to paradise in Jewish, Christian, and later Islamic tradition, for they all consider Jerusalem—particularly Mount Moriah—to be the central locality in which the events of the Last Judgment will take place. It therefore seems plausible to suggest that the Dome of the Rock and attendant buildings may have been constructed to provide a suitably magnificent setting for the events of the Judgment—particularly, to be the locale in which 'Abd al-Malik (or one of his successors), as leaders of the righteous and God-fearing empire of the Believers, would hand over to God the symbols of sovereignty at the moment the Judgment was to begin. 'Abd al-Malik's magnificent monument, then, stands as testimony to the continuing force of the apocalyptic impetus of the early Believers' movement.

'Abd al-Malik thus resumed the basic agenda of the Believers' movement, interrupted by the civil wars: to spread the domain of God's kingdom by establishing God's law. His decree, issued shortly after the Second Civil War had been concluded, that all pigs in Syria and Mesopotamia be killed, seems to be an aspect of this policy. In this and other ways, such as building the Dome of the Rock, he was helping to prepare his community for the coming Last Judgment. After twelve years of civil war, however, he was doubtless keenly aware that he needed to do something more: he needed to find ways to unify the empire and the community of Believers morally, to refocus the Believers on the central goals of the mission that Muhammad had set them on, and to establish the legitimacy of his rule and that of the Umayyad family. We can see several of his policies as measures contributing to these broad goals of reunification and rededication to the Believers' original ideals. But with these policies came a subtle, but fundamental, redefinition of the movement itself, one with which we still live today, and it is to this that we must now turn.

The Redefinition of Key Terms

'Abd al-Malik seems to have encouraged the Arabian Believers to redefine themselves, and the Believers' movement, in a manner that was less ecumenical or confessional and open than it had been originally. The category of "Believer," which hitherto had included righteous monotheists of several confessions, came to be increasingly limited to those who followed Qur'anic law. A boundary began to be drawn between Qur'anic Believers and those righteous Christians and Jews who had formerly belonged to the Believers' movement, by redefining certain key terms that had been current in the community since the time of Muhammad—in particular, the words *mu'min* ("Believer") and *muslim*.

As we have seen, when the first generation of Believers came out of Arabia, sources tell us that they used two terms to refer to themselves: *mu'minun* (Believers) and *muhajirun*. The latter term (which, as we have seen, shows up in Greek and Syriac cognates) was a designation for those Believers who were militarily active and had made religiously motivated emigration, *hijra*, from Arabia. But as years passed, the term *muhajirun* eventually fell out of use. Why this happened is not clear. Perhaps it was because in the central areas of the empire, at least—Arabia, Syria, Iraq, and Egypt—the conquests were now over and the whole country was under the Believers' control, so one could not do *hijra* any longer, because *hijra* had the sense not just of emigration, but of emigration from an unbelieving society to a place held by Believers. Alternatively the term *muhajirun* may have been abandoned because one was now dealing not with the emigrants themselves but with the children or grandchildren of the original emigrants from Arabia or with local people who had no connection with Arabia at all but who had decided to follow the Believers in observing Qur'anic law. The only Qur'anic term that existed for these people was *muslim*, meaning "one who submits himself to God's ordinances" because he recognized God's oneness. In the Qur'an *muslim* basically means "monotheist," and it could therefore be applied also to Christians, Jews, and other monotheists. But, unlike the Arabian monotheists who followed Qur'anic law, Christians and Jews could also still be referred to as Christians or Jews. So gradually, the Qur'anic term *muslim* underwent a kind of shrinkage, so that it applied now only to those monotheists who followed Qur'anic law and no longer applied to Jews and Christians, the adherents of those earlier forms of God's revealed law, the *tawrat* (Torah) and *injil* (Gospel). In other words, the old Qur'anic term *muslim* acquired at last the meaning it retains until today, meaning a member of a religious confession that reveres the Qur'an, recognizes Muhammad as its prophet, and is distinct from other monotheists—a Muslim. At the same time, *mu'min* was taken to apply to *all* of those who followed Qur'anic law (not, as earlier, only to those who lived righteously), so that it became effectively synonymous with *muslim*.

In the present state of our knowledge, we can only speculate about why this shift in the identity of the Believers occurred. Perhaps this "hardening" of boundaries, which resulted in a clear-cut distinction between Muslims (that is, erstwhile Qur'anic Believers) and Christians or Jews (that is, former Believers who had observed Christian or Jewish laws), was a reaction against specific aspects of Christian or Jewish doctrine and the Christians' or Jews' unwillingness to relinquish those doctrinal obstacles—in particular, perhaps, the Christians' persistence in embracing the doctrine of the Trinity or both the Christians' and Jews' unwillingness to accept Muhammad's status as prophet and source of revelation. 'Abd al-Malik and his entourage may gradually have come to the conclusion that earlier expectations that Christians and Jews would abandon these beliefs were unrealistic.

Emphasis on Muhammad and the Qur'an

The central component of this rethinking of the Believers' identity involved an increased emphasis on the significance to the Believers of Muhammad and the Qur'an, and in this process 'Abd al-Malik seems to have played a decisive role. The earliest Believers knew from the Qur'an that God's word had been revealed numerous times in history to various prophets, of whom Muhammad was the most recent. This notion was consonant with the original ecumenical quality of the Believers' movement and is reflected in inscriptions and graffiti in which Believers appear to make statements of faith professing their reverence for God and several prophets, such as Muhammad and Jesus.

Beginning around the time of 'Abd al-Malik, however—in the last quarter of the first century AH/end of the seventh century C.E.—we find Muhammad's name mentioned with increasing frequency in the Believers' official documents; moreover, these references suggest that identification with Muhammad and his mission and revelation was coming to be seen as constitutive of the Believers' collective identity. The first inscriptions of any kind to carry the phrase "Muhammad is the Apostle of God" are coins from Bishapur (Fars), apparently issued in 66/685–686 and 67/686–687 by a governor for the Zubayrids, so it may be that the Umayyads were inspired to emphasize the role of the prophet by their rival 'Abdullah ibn al-Zubayr, known, as we have seen, for his stern piety. Whatever its inspiration, 'Abd al-Malik and his entourage seem to have advanced this process energetically and in several media. The Dome of the Rock inscriptions lay considerable emphasis on Muhammad's position as prophet; but more telling is the appearance on coins, from the time of 'Abd al-Malik onward, of the full "double *shahada*," that is, the combining of the phrase "There is no god but God" with the phrase "Muhammad is the apostle of God" as a decisive marker of the character of the issuing authority. The full double *shahada* becomes

increasingly frequent on later documents. The early Believers had
no doubt always recognized that their movement had been inaugurated by someone named Muhammad, but as we have seen it is not
clear how ready the Jews and Christians of the Near East were to
embrace the Arabian Believers' claim that Muhammad had been
truly a prophet. Emphasizing the importance to the Believers of
Muhammad's status as God's apostle was another way in which the
Umayyads and their advisers drew a clear line dividing Believers
from others—and drawing it unequivocally in such a way that
many Christians and Jews may have had difficulty remaining
within the Believers' fold. This increasing emphasis on the significance of Muhammad as prophet led, starting in the last quarter of
the first century AH/end of the seventh century C.E., to the cultivation and collection of sayings of the prophet (Arabic, *hadith*) as a
means of legitimating many practices and institutions within the
community.

Residual traces of this shift in terminology can be found in these
hadith collections. Some *hadiths* occur in two variants, one of which
appears more generally "Believerish" and the other more "Muslim."
For example, the collections record the prophet as giving two variant
responses to a questioner who asks, "what is the best of works?" One
variant has him answering, "Belief in God, and *jihad* in the path of
God," but the other has "Belief in God and His apostle, and *jihad*. . . ."
We can propose that, during the transmission of this *hadith*, the
second variant was generated by the addition of the apostle/prophet
to the first, in order to define "belief" in a way that included belief in
the prophet as an essential part, and not just belief in God.

Closely related to this emphasis on Muhammad's prophecy or
apostleship is an emphasis on the Qur'an itself, the Arabic revelation, which for Believers now assumes a status above those of the
earlier revelations, the *tawrat* (Torah) and the *injil* (Gospels). First
of all—although we know relatively little about it—'Abd al-Malik
ordered his governor in Iraq, Hajjaj, to prepare a re-edition of the

A letter from the Umayyad governor Qurra ibn Sharik. Early official letters, such as this one, were written in large format and majestic script. This letter fragment reveals Qurra adjudicating a dispute over property, referred to him by his subordinate in one of the villages of the Egyptian countryside.

Qur'an text that was provided for the first time with clear vowel and diacritical markings to ensure proper reading and recitation of the text. The fact that the *amir al-mu'minin* and his regime were distributing this "improved" version of the Qur'an—of God's word—to be used in key communities of Believers (particularly in the garrison towns) was one way in which ʿAbd al-Malik could emphasize the fact that the regime he headed was indeed that righteous "kingdom of God" that the earliest Believers had aimed to establish. But it also reaffirmed that the Believers' regime he headed was dedicated to the propagation and observance of God's revealed word, the Qur'an. The Dome of the Rock inscriptions are also instructive in this context. Just as they emphasized Muhammad's prophecy, they also emphasized the Qur'an, for the inscriptions contain extensive verbatim passages from, or close paraphrases of, parts of the Qur'an—showing that ʿAbd al-Malik and his circle were intent on emphasizing, in the most splendid construction he undertook, the primacy of the Arabic revelation as a source of religious legitimacy and guidance.

Similarly, ʿAbd al-Malik and his advisers instituted a thorough overhaul of the iconography of the empire's coinage, doing so in a way that projected the legitimating quality of the Qur'an. The earliest coins issued by the Believers had been based on the coinage of the Byzantine and Sasanian empires, whose dies they used, modified—if at all—not by replacing their characteristic images, but by the addition of some typically "Believerish" slogan, such as "There is no god but God." ʿAbd al-Malik, however, scrapped the old coin styles entirely and, after a short period of experimentation, began in 77/696–697 issuing coinage based on a radical new design. Unlike Byzantine and Sasanian coins with their images of rulers and religious insignia, such as the cross or a fire-temple, these new Umayyad coins were completely inscriptional and devoid of images of any kind. More important still, the inscriptions on these new coins—other than mint names, dates, and the name of the commander of the Believers or governor—included the full "double *shahada*" and Qur'anic verses as well, often verses emphasizing God's oneness and pointedly rejecting trinitarian concepts. Frequently found, for example, was the following passage from Qur'an 112:1–3: "God is one, the Lord of refuge, He neither begets nor is begotten." All of this was a way of proclaiming publicly that true Believers were those who revered Muhammad as God's prophet and the Arabic Qur'an as God's revelation.

Although it took some time to be implemented, the new reform coinage established a relatively standardized iconography for the empire, one that reflected consistently for the first time the Believers' values. It also established a greater uniformity in coin values, which presumably facilitated commerce. In a similar vein, 'Abd al-Malik standardized weights and measures of the empire, using as the new norm the traditional weight values of the Hijaz—a choice that reflects the importance of Muhammad and the holy cities, Mecca and Medina, in the minds of the Believers, and 'Abd al-Malik's concern to legitimate Umayyad rule by appealing to such sentiments. All these measures can be seen as efforts by 'Abd al-Malik (and by his Umayyad successors) to reunify the empire after the divisions of the civil wars. Moreover, they were attempting to bind the community in ways that self-consciously enunciated the guiding principles and beliefs of the Believers' movement and so contributed to the goal of establishing a righteous kingdom governed by God's law. But in doing so, they were clarifying or redefining the boundaries of the movement itself.

Another interesting measure taken by 'Abd al-Malik was his adoption, for a brief period, of the title *khalifat allah*, probably to be understood to mean "God's deputy," on a few transitional coin issues that, while remotely based on modified Byzantine prototypes, contained an image usually understood as a depiction of a standing figure in Arabian dress. (The figure on these so-called "standing caliph" coins has been interpreted variously as being either 'Abd al-Malik or the prophet himself.) The significance of this term, *khalifat allah*, has been much debated, but it seems likely that it was, once

Two coins of 'Abd al-Malik. 'Abd al-Malik presided over a radical transformation in the iconography of Umayyad coinage. The upper image shows a transitional issue, minted in Damascus in AH 75 (corresponding to 694–695 C.E.). It depicts, on the obverse, a standing, robed figure, girt with a sword, usually understood to be the *amir al-mu'minin* himself, but thought by some perhaps to represent the prophet Muhammad. The reverse is modeled on Byzantine issues showing a cross mounted on steps, but the crossbar has been left off to leave a post or staff on steps, thus negating the potent Christian symbolism of the cross. The inscription on the obverse reads, "In the name of God, there is no god but God alone; Muhammad is the apostle of God." The inscription on the reverse reads "In the name of God. This *dinar* was minted in the year 75." The lower coin shows a reform gold dinar, minted in AH 77 (696–697 C.E.); the mint is not given. All representational imagery has now been removed and replaced by verses from the Qur'an and religious slogans. On the obverse, the central inscription reads "There is no God but God alone, he has no associate." The marginal inscription reads "Muhammad is the apostle of God; [He] sent him with guidance and the true religion, to exalt it over every religion" (see Q. 9:33, 48:28, and 61:9). The central inscription on the reverse reads "God is one; God is everlasting; he begets not and is not begotten" (see Q. 112:1–3). The reverse margin reads, "In the name of God, this *dinar* was minted in the year 77."

again, an attempt by 'Abd al-Malik to legitimate his rule by referring to the Qur'an—in this case, specifically to Qur'an 38:26, in which God tells David, "O David! We did indeed make you a *khalifa* on earth, to judge between men in truth, so do not follow your vain passions." As the title *amir al-mu'minin* is not found in the Qur'an, we can speculate that 'Abd al-Malik was adopting the Qur'anic term *khalifat allah* in an effort to strengthen—or to establish—the perception that his rule had Qur'anic warrant. Perhaps 'Abd al-Malik also wanted to link himself with David, the founder of Jerusalem, because he was at the time constructing the Dome of the Rock there. In any case, these coins are the first documentary attestation of the application of the term *khalifa* ("caliph"); it eventually became the standard term for the leaders of the Islamic state. Although some have argued that the term *khalifa* was also applied to earlier *amir al-mu'minins*, such as 'Umar, 'Uthman, and 'Ali, there is no documentary support for such a view; although the number of such documents is limited, it is striking that of the roughly dozen documentary attestations to the leader of the community of Believers dating before the time of 'Abd al-Malik, *every one* refers to the leader as *amir al-mu'minin*—not once is he called *khalifa*.

It seems most plausible, then, to link the first use of *khalifa* to 'Abd al-Malik and his determined program of emphasizing the status of the Qur'an, and its legitimating value, among the Believers. It seems that this was part of 'Abd al-Malik's larger project aimed at restoring the authority of Umayyad rule, the legitimacy of which had been seriously eroded by the events (and the anti-Umayyad rhetoric) of the Second Civil War. He and the later Umayyads strove to do so especially by emphasizing the religious foundations of Umayyad rule, in particular, their status as successors to Muhammad as heads of the community of Believers and as rulers guided by the Qur'anic revelation Muhammad had received. In doing so, they essentially defined "Islam" as we know it today. Painful as they were, the two civil wars may thus have been the crucial catalyst for this historic development.

The Problem of the Trinity

The early Believers' sense of themselves as constituting a movement open to all who believed in God's oneness and in righteous living—what we have called the ecumenical character of the early Believers' movement—was probably always something that was open to debate. But we have seen that Jews and Christians could be, and some were, included within the Believers' movement. We have noted that early statements of faith (the "single *shahada*," "There is no god but God"), both inscriptional and literary, reflected this more inclusive outlook. Such testimony, and the persistent evidence that Christians at least were actively involved in some aspects of the Believers' community well into Umayyad times, as we have seen in previous chapters, shows that this confessionally open quality was a reality. The fact that many of the Christians encountered by the first Arabian Believers in the Near East were monophysites, whose formulations of trinitarian doctrine emphasized Christ's single nature, or Nestorians, who emphasized Christ's human nature and played down his divinity, may have meant that they aroused less immediate opposition from the Believers. It has been suggested that the Umayyads, ruling in and from Syria, may have been especially mindful of the concerns of Christians, some of whom were important supporters of the regime (including the Christians of the powerful Kalb tribe, who were intermarried with Mu'awiya's family and contributed troops to the Umayyad army). This may explain why the Believers in Syria appear to have placed considerable emphasis on the role of Jesus, whose "second coming" shows up in Islamic eschatological traditions dating to the Umayyad period. (Later, after the Umayyads had been overthrown and the Abbasids had moved the center of the empire to Iraq, this early emphasis on Jesus was abandoned by developing Islamic tradition, because Jews and Zoroastrians were more prominent and numerous in Iraq than Christians.)

But for those Believers who were inclined to be sticklers on the question of God's oneness, the Christian doctrine of the Trinity must always have been a problem. Indeed, we find even in the Qur'an a few passages in which the idea of the Trinity is decisively rejected: "They disbelieve who say: 'God is the third of three,' for there is no god but the one God . . ." [Q. 5:76]; "God is one, God is the Lord of refuge; He begets not, nor is He begotten . . ." [Q. 112:1–3].

The earliest surviving evidence (other than the Qur'an itself) that the ruling circles of the Believers' movement—the *amir al-mu'minin* and his key advisers—were inclined to turn against these Christian doctrines (the Trinity, Jesus as God's son, the divinity and resurrection of Jesus), is found on some early coins that the Believers issued in Syria, based on modified Byzantine coin types. The Byzantine coin issue that had shown a cross on steps (Christian symbol of Jesus' divine nature and resurrection) was modified to show only a vertical staff on steps—the crossbar is pointedly removed, and although the dating of these issues is debated, they appear to have been issued in the early years of 'Abd al-Malik's reign, if not earlier (possibly under Mu'awiya). More decisive evidence of an anti-trinitarian attitude among the ruling elite comes with 'Abd al-Malik's construction of the Dome of the Rock beginning in 72/692. The inscriptions in the Dome of the Rock include a selection of Qur'anic verses chosen specifically, it seems, to emphasize the unacceptability of the trinitarian idea and to reinforce the idea of God's indivisible unity. (See "Inscriptions in the Dome of the Rock, Jerusalem" in Appendix B.) As the Dome of the Rock was built on orders of the commander of the Believers in a prominent location and in sumptuous style, there can be little doubt that 'Abd al-Malik and his advisers wished to convey a powerful and unmistakable message. It seems fair to assume from this that 'Abd al-Malik and the Umayyad ruling elite were by this time, at the latest, reconsidering the status of Christians within the community of Believers, even though many Christians continued to serve the dynasty until its fall in 132/750. Or, to put it more precisely, the elite seems to have been engaged in rethinking their own identity as Believers and "drawing the line" between themselves and those who embraced any hint of trinitarian doctrines.

Elaboration of Islamic Cultic Practices

Yet another dimension of the process by which Islam coalesced from the early Believers' movement involved certain aspects of religious ritual; for even more than theological differences, it is differences in cultic practice that set one religious community apart from others. As we have seen, there is evidence that the early Believers from Arabia, as a religious movement, participated in the prayer practices of some of the Christian (and Jewish?) communities they encountered in Syria, Iraq, and possibly elsewhere—reports of the Believers "dividing" churches with Christians, and of an east-facing *qibla* or direction of prayer, were specifically noted. The evidence of the Cathisma Church, with its east-facing apse and south-facing *mihrab* or prayer niche added in the final phase of construction, presumably reflects architecturally the very moment when the Qur'anic Believers began to redefine themselves as "Muslims," distinct from their erstwhile Christian co-Believers. It is possible that the vague traditional reports about Muhammad himself changing the direction of prayer during his early years in Medina are a retouched, vestigial memory of this change, projected back to the time of the prophet to make it acceptable to later generations.

The similarity between some features of the Muslim Friday prayer service and certain aspects of both Christian and Jewish prayer rituals, discussed by various scholars, also suggests an initial stage in the development of Muslim ritual when the Believers' movement actually incorporated Christian or Jewish Believers. The complete absence in the Qur'an of any mention of the distinctive components of the Muslim Friday prayer—notably the *khutba* or sermon by the prayer leader, the *minbar* or pulpit from which it is delivered, or references to Friday prayer being in any way special—raise the question of whether the Friday prayer ritual existed at all before Umayyad times and the coalescence of the Umayyad state.

It is clear, however, that the Believers' basic ritual practices—ritual prayer, fasting during the month of Ramadan, and pilgrimage—go back to Muhammad's time and the very beginnings of the Believers' movement, because they are mentioned, if not always fully described, in the Qur'an text. But there is no doubt that these and other ritual practices were not at first so rigidly defined as they later became, so it seems likely that some of these rituals evolved under the influence of the practices of Jewish or Christian Believers of the Fertile Crescent (or even of Arabia in Muhammad's day). The number of prayers to be performed daily, for example, is not explicitly established by the Qur'an; later Muslim tradition eventually settled on five prayers per day as the requirement, but the question was clearly the subject of considerable discussion before this consensus was reached. The many sayings attributed to the prophet contained in the vast collections of *hadith*, which coalesced in the Muslim community in the second century AH/eighth century C.E.and third century AH/ninth century C.E., contains the residue of this and other debates in the community over just how various rituals were to be performed, revealing how numerous features of these rituals remained in flux for some time, as different practices or points of view were advanced by different *hadiths*.

The pilgrimage ritual or *hajj* also seems to have evolved during the early community's history. Reports of 'Abd al-Malik, as *amir al-mu'minin*, leading the *hajj* during his rule imply that details of the *hajj* ritual were still being settled during his day, and he is reported to have ordered a complete "restoration" of the Ka'ba, to purge it of additions made by 'Abd Allah ibn al-Zubayr. Similarly, 'Abd al-Malik's predecessor, the *amir al-mu'minin* Mu'awiya (ruled 41–60/661–680), was the moving spirit behind the construction of the first *maqsura* or

screen in the prayer hall to separate himself from the ranks of praying Believers (a construction perhaps somewhat similar in function
to the iconostasis or icon screen that sheltered Christian officiants
from their congregations in church).

The process of defining what became Muslim rituals thus lasted
for several—perhaps many—decades after the death of Muhammad.

Elaboration of the Islamic Origins Story

Another dimension of this transformation of the Believers' movement into Islam involved the construction of an origins story narrat-
ing the foundational events in the life of the community of Believ-
ers/Muslims. Many people in the community contributed to the
process of remembering, collecting, and reworking stories of what
had happened in the community in the days of Muhammad and
during the conquests and civil wars; but it is clear that the Umayyad
rulers, in particular, played a major role in encouraging this activity.
The Umayyads invited knowledgeable people to court and supported
them with patronage—a few of the foremost examples being Ibn
Shihab al-Zuhri and ʿUrwa ibn al-Zubayr, both of whom contributed
significantly to drawing up the first extant biography of Muhammad
and his prophetic career.

The Islamic origins story focused on several main themes and issues, which provided a detailed justification of the community's existence; and this story forms, to this day, one of the main sources of
information on which historians must draw to describe the events of
Islam's origins. Several themes clustered around the life of Muhammad; their overarching goal was to demonstrate Muhammad's prophetic status, in keeping with the model of the prophets who had
come before him, and to describe the manner in which he received
the Qurʾanic revelation. Other themes are concerned especially
with showing how Muhammad founded the original community of
Believers and how that community continued to exist and to cling to

its foundational values over the years and decades after the prophet's death. Still other themes provided a justification for the Believers'/ Muslims' hegemony over the vast areas and populations they ruled, framed by the twin propositions that the Believers' military victories over the Byzantines and Sasanians were signs of God's favor and that their rule was dedicated to the realization of God's law on Earth.

The goal of the origins narratives, as they coalesced, was thus to legitimate the community of Believers in general terms by affirming the details of how the community began for all Believers—especially those born too late to have known the prophet or to have witnessed the early days of the community's expansion. But it is also clear that this exercise in legitimation was directed not only inward, but also outward, at non-Believers/non-Muslims. The stories about Muhammad's prophecy made clear that one could not be a Believer (or Muslim) without recognizing Muhammad as one's prophet, and so it helped draw that line that came to distinguish Muslims from Christians and Jews, whose reservations about Muhammad's prophecy we have already noted. Similarly, the extensive conquest narratives, while emphasizing without fail the conquerors' religious motivations, consistently present them as *Muslims*—not as Believers or as *muhajirun*, the two terms that we know from Qur'anic and non-Islamic documentary evidence were the ones the conquerors had actually used to refer to themselves in the early years of the movement. This emphasis on the *Muslim* identity in the conquest narratives seems likely to be part of the process by which the Believers' movement excluded Christians and Jews and redefined itself as applying only to Believers following Qur'anic law—or as we would say, to Muslims.

The Coalescence of an "Arab" Political Identity

Another feature of the transformation of the Believers' movement into Islam was the articulation, for the first time, of a consciously

"Arab" political identity—that is, a collective identity that was not merely cultural, but that expressed itself loosely in the form of political claims. As a political identity, membership in this group gave one special political privileges, in particular, the right to be considered part of the ruling caste of the new Umayyad/Muslim empire.

It has sometimes been argued that the rise of Islam—what we prefer to understand as the first appearance and expansion of the Believers' movement—was essentially an "Arab" movement. The implication of such a view is that an "Arab" political identity existed on the eve of Muhammad's preaching and that it was the powerful desire to realize this latent collective identity as "Arabs" in political form that really generated the Believers' expansion and the creation of their empire. This view is, however, anachronistic and profoundly misleading. It usually represents the facile interpolation back into the seventh century C.E. of modern concepts of Arab nationalism that only came into existence in the late nineteenth century.

The Arabic-speaking peoples of Arabia and adjacent areas in the early seventh century (and, indeed, even in antiquity), were, to be sure, well aware of the fact that they spoke mutually intelligible forms of a common language; and there existed a common poetic language, the 'arabiyya, representing a literary ideal that was different from any particular spoken dialect. But this is to speak only of a vague linguistic, and perhaps cultural, identity, not of a political one as "Arabs." There is almost no evidence for the existence of a collective "Arab" political identity before the Believers created their empire. Moreover, the "Arab national" or "nativist" interpretation of the beginnings of the Believers' movement and Islam fails to take into account the Qur'an's deafening silence on the concept of an "Arab" political identity. In a few passages, the Qur'an refers to itself as an "Arabic Qur'an," but this is a linguistic statement and nothing more. Nowhere does the Qur'an advance, or even hint at, any kind of collective identity other than that of the Believers—an identity squarely based in faith and righteous action, not in ethnic or "national" or even cultural affiliation. Moreover, the few times the Qur'an mentions the *a'rab*—to be understood as nomads—it is with pejorative overtones; of "Arabs" (*'arab*) it speaks not at all.

The Arabic-speaking populations of the Near East were at this time divided into different tribes, and it was to their individual tribes that these people owed their primary identity—if it was not to their faith. In other words, we can no more speak of an "Arab" political identity at that time than we might speak today of Englishmen, Irishmen, Scots, Americans, Australians, Canadians, New Zealanders, Jamaicans, and so on, as having a common "Anglo" identity with significant political (rather than merely cultural) content. To argue that the Believers' movement was at heart a "national" or "nativist" or "Arab" movement is particularly misleading because it obscures the most important characteristic of the Believers' movement, visible in the Qur'an and in the few early documents we have—its nature as a movement rooted in religious faith—and substitutes for it a social impetus rooted in a presumed collective identity (as "Arabs") for which there is no credible evidence, only sketchy and unsupported extrapolation from present conditions.

Although there is thus no evidence that an "Arab" identity contributed to the early Believers' movement, it seems clear that with the passage of time the success of the Believers' movement in establishing an empire helped create an embryonic Arab political identity in the minds of the ruling elite. In other words, an Arab identity was an unintended result of the Believers' movement, not its cause. The historical accident that the movement began in Arabia meant that the ruling circles were dominated almost exclusively by Arabians (mostly, indeed, Hijazis) whose native language was Arabic. As the Believers spread into vast new areas and established their hegemony there—in Syria, Iraq, Iran, Egypt, and further afield—the leading cadres and the bulk of their soldiers, all Arabic-speaking and mostly from Arabia, could hardly have failed to notice that most of their subjects were not Arabic-speaking. The association of Arabic with political dominance thus may have generated a sense among Arabic speakers that the empire was an "Arab kingdom" and that all Arabic speakers were politically kin because of their shared dominant status in the new empire. But this "Arab" political identity remained weak (until the nineteenth century) and never seriously challenged the basic tribal identity of most Arabians.

This sense of an "Arab" identity that one imagines growing particularly among the upper echelons of the ruling elite is also expressed in the nascent historiographical tradition. The majority of the voluminous conquest narratives, following what we may call "reformed" vocabulary, speak in terms of Muslims conquering non-Muslims (rather than Believers and unbelievers); but there are some reports in which the confrontations are described as being between the "Arabs" on the one hand and the ʿajam (non-Arabic speakers), or Byzantines or Persians, on the other. This kind of vocabulary seems likely to reflect the identity categories of the age following this shift in conceptualizations, when the conquest narratives were compiled, rather than those of the conquest era itself.

Not only the experience of empire, but also the presence of the Arabic Qurʾan, provided an impetus for the crystallization of this nascent "Arab" identity in the Umayyad period. As the Believers' movement gradually evolved into Islam, there developed, as we have seen, an increased emphasis on Qurʾanic law as the decisive determinant of one's status as a Muslim. This increased emphasis on the Arabic Qurʾan, however, dovetailed well with the dawning awareness of an "Arab" political identity among a ruling elite that now preferred to identify itself as Muslims, rather than as Believers.

Official vs. Popular Change

The broad transformation just sketched, by which Islam crystallized out of the Believers' movement, was partly the result of intentional decisions made by the ruling Umayyad dynasty under 'Abd al-Malik and his successors and partly the result of changes of perspective among the rank and file of Believers themselves—both the Qur'an-oriented Believers of Arabian origin and those Jews and Christians who had been part of the early Believers' movement. The emergence of Islam and the demise of the original organizing conceptions of the Believers' movement thus combined changes that were quite sudden and radical with others that took shape only gradually and took decades, sometimes as much as a century, to reach completion. Official measures such as 'Abd al-Malik's coinage reform, with its emphasis on Qur'anic legitimation, or the building of the Dome of the Rock, with both its emphatic use of the "double *shahada*" and its strongly anti-trinitarian inscriptional message, can be dated quite precisely to within a few years. On the other hand, the more widespread and growing perception among Christian, Jewish, and Qur'anic Believers that perhaps only the latter were really part of the movement seems to have taken hold much more gradually. Moreover, the relationship between the two kinds of change is not obvious. Did the specific policy initiatives of the Umayyads (such as their attack on the Trinity) blaze the way for the reorientation of popular thinking? Or was the policy itself an official expression of changes in popular attitudes that were already underway? We cannot be sure, but we can say that a number of key policy initiatives that clearly conform to an intellectual shift from a more ecumenical Believers' movement to a more closely defined confessional identity as Muslims seems to cluster in the 70s/690s, in the time of 'Abd al-Malik. On the other hand, we cannot say that the shift from Believers' movement to Islam is complete at this time, because we continue to find evidence of close collaboration of some Christians (and perhaps some Jews) with the Muslims for many years thereafter. Wisdom sayings attributed to the Umayyad *amir al-mu'minin* 'Umar (II) ibn 'Abd al-'Aziz, who reigned between 99–101/717–720 and was renowned for his piety, suggest that he held Christian monks and holy men in high esteem, and he died while visiting the famous monastery of St. Simeon, in the hills near Aleppo, where his tomb can still be seen. The close association of Christian advisers with the later Umayyad caliphs—John of Damascus's service to Hisham is the best-known example—may also be a vestige of an earlier stage in which there was a fuller place in the leadership of the Believers' movement for righteous Christians and Jews. The continuing construction, or at least reconstruction, of Christian churches in geographical Syria into the late second century AH/eighth century C.E., datable by their excavated mosaic floors, also suggests that even for some time after the Believers' movement had given way to a self-consciously Muslim regime, that regime was not yet always harshly confessional in its policies.

There can be little doubt, however, that by the final years of the first century AH/seventh century C.E. and the beginning of the second century AH/eighth century C.E., the more open, "Believerish" character of the movement had begun to give way definitively to a firmer identity for those in the movement as belonging to a new religious confession, Islam. We can measure this by considering Christian religious polemics of the seventh and eighth centuries. Those written during the first century AH/seventh century C.E. are preoccupied, as earlier polemics had been, with attacking the errors of Judaism or of rival ("heretical") forms of Christianity—Nestorianism, monophysitism, or the Byzantine official doctrine. There are, as yet, no attacks on Islam in these polemics, even though a few of them mention in passing the presence of an *amir* or another representative of the *mhaggraye* at the disputation the text describes. These seventh-century Christian polemicists apparently did not yet recognize the Believers as constituting a separate religious creed that required theological refutation. Only in the very last years of the first century AH/seventh century C.E. and in the second century AH/eighth century C.E. do we begin to find Christian polemics that offer arguments attempting to refute Islam's main theological positions—

The Tomb of the *amir al-mu'minin* 'Umar II. This shrine is located just beside the cathedral and monastery complex of St. Simeon, where according to some traditions 'Umar is said to have died in 101/720.

evidence that by this time someone was presenting Islam in a way that depicted it as a creed distinct from Christianity. Yet the sense that the Believers' movement that becomes Islam was not entirely at odds with Christianity, at least, seems to survive in some ways even into the mid-eighth century, for it is then that John of Damascus— who, as a high administrator for the Umayyads, surely knew whereof he spoke—wrote his famous treatise on "The *Heresy* of the Ishmael-ites." In other words, he could still perceive nascent Islam as a form of Christian heresy, rather than as a fully independent religion.

It has long been recognized that Islam in the fully developed form we can see in the second and third centuries AH/eighth and ninth centuries C.E. was the result of a process of sustained development. Many have discussed the development of the institutions of the first

Islamic state, which began in Arabia with only rudimentary arrangements but within a century had acquired not only a standing army but also robust political, judicial, and administrative institutions. Others have discussed the development and refinement of the theological doctrines of Islam, building on the basic doctrines found in the Qur'an, a process that seems to get underway in earnest only in the late Umayyad period (first half of the second century AH/eighth century C.E.). These two processes of development, however, do not tell the full story. Just as important—indeed, perhaps more important—was a third process, by which Islam, as a distinct religious confession centered on reverence for the Qur'an as the latest revelation of God's eternal word and recognition of Muhammad as the final prophet and messenger of God's word, emerged from the more loosely defined Believers' movement inaugurated by Muhammad. It was this process, which we have attempted to trace in the preceding pages, that first truly established the lineaments of Islam.

APPENDIXES

NOTES AND GUIDE TO FURTHER READING

GLOSSARY

ILLUSTRATION CREDITS

INDEX

Appendix A:
The *umma* Document

The "*umma* document," sometimes also called the "Constitution of Medina," the "*sahifa* document," or the "*sunna jami'a*," is a group of connected documents or treaty clauses apparently concluded between the prophet Muhammad and the people of Yathrib. The original documents are now lost, but the text is preserved, with mostly minor variations, in two early Islamic literary texts: the *Sira* (a biography of the prophet) of Muhammad ibn Ishaq (died ca. 150/767), and the *Kitab al-amwal* (a book on property) of Abu 'Ubayd al-Qasim ibn Sallam (died 224/838). As with all literary texts compiled a century or more after the time of Muhammad, one can question the authenticity of this text; but the consensus of scholars, even those who are generally skeptical about the reliability of such late texts, is that the *umma* document is probably a fairly accurate transcription of an actual early document. This is because, both in form and content, it seems archaic and because it presents things in ways that do not conform to later idealizing views; hence it seems unlikely that it is a later invention.

The translation here follows mainly the text of Ibn Ishaq. I have relied heavily on earlier translations and analysis made by Alfred Guillaume, R. B. Serjeant, and Michael Lecker:

Alfred Guillaume, *The Life of Muhammad* (Oxford: Oxford University Press, 1955), 231–233.

R. B. Serjeant, "The "Sunnah Jami'ah," Pacts with the Yathrib Jews, and the "Tahrim" of Yathrib: Analysis an Translation of the Documents Comprised in the So-Called 'Constitution of Medina,'" *Bulletin of the School of Oriental and African Studies, University of London* 41 (1978): 1–42.

Michael Lecker, *The "Constitution of Medina": Muhammad's First Legal Document* (Princeton, NJ: Darwin, 2004).

The pious phrases that follow the names of God and Muhammad in most versions of the text have been omitted here.

The Text

This is a document from Muhammad the prophet (al-nabi), *between the Believers and the Muslims of Quraysh and Yathrib and those who follow them and attach themselves to them and struggle alongside them. Verily they are one community* (umma) *to the exclusion of [other] people.*

The muhajirun *from Quraysh [remain] in charge of their own affairs, arranging matters of blood-money among themselves, and ransoming their captives following custom and what is equitable among the Believers.*

Banu 'Awf [remain] in charge of their own affairs, arranging matters of their blood-money among themselves as before; every section of them ransoming their captives following custom and what is equitable among the Believers.

Banu al-Harith [remain] in charge of their own affairs, arranging matters of their blood-money among themselves as before; every section of them ransoming their captives following custom and what is equitable among the Believers.

Banu Sa'ida [remain] in charge of their own affairs, . . .

Banu Jusham [remain] in charge of their own affairs, . . .

Banu al-Najjar [remain] in charge of their own affairs, . . .

Banu ʿAmr ibn ʿAwf [remain] *in charge of their own affairs,* . . .

Banu al-Nabit [remain] *in charge of their own affairs,* . . .

Banu al-Aws [remain] *in charge of their own affairs,* . . .

The Believers shall not fail to give [aid] *to a debtor* [or: *pauper*] *among them in matters of ransom or blood-money, as is customary.*

A Believer shall not make an alliance with the client (mawla) *of* [another] *Believer to* [the latter's] *detriment* [or: *excluding him*].

The God-fearing Believers are against anyone among them who acts outrageously or [who] *practices extortion or* [spreads] *treachery or enmity or dissension among the Believers. Verily their hands shall be united against him, even if he is the son of one of them.*

A Believer shall not kill [another] *Believer for the sake of an unbeliever* (kafir), *nor shall he assist an unbeliever against a Believer.*

God's protection is one; the lowest of them [i.e., *of the Believers*] *may grant protection* [to outsiders] *that is binding upon all of them.*

The Believers are allies (mawali) *one to another, to the exclusion of other people.*

Whoever follows us among the Jews shall have assistance and equitable treatment; they shall not be oppressed, nor shall [any of us] *gang up against them.*

The peace of the Believers is indivisible. No Believer shall make a [separate] *peace to the exclusion of* [that is, without consulting?] [another] *Believer in fighting in the path of God, except on the basis of equity and justice among them.*

All raiding parties that set out on raiding with us shall follow one after another [that is, take turns?].

The Believers are to take vengeance for one another's blood shed in the path of God.

The God-fearing Believers are in accord with the best and truest of this [agreement?].

No polytheist (mushrik) shall grant protection to property belonging to Quraysh, nor to a person; nor shall he come between it/him against a Believer.

Whoever kills a Believer without good reason, [the murder being substantiated] on the basis of sound evidence, shall be slain in retaliation, unless the next of kin [of the slain] is satisfied [with blood-money]. All the Believers shall be against him; anything other than standing [united] against him shall not be allowed to them.

It is not permissible for the Believer who affirms what it is this treaty (sahifa), and believes in God and the Last Day, to aid a sinner [murderer?] or to give him refuge. Whosoever aids him or gives him refuge shall have upon him the curse of God and His wrath on the Day of Resurrection; and neither repentance nor ransom will be accepted from him.

Whatever matters you disagree on should be referred to God and to Muhammad [that is, for resolution].

The Jews shall pay [their] share with the Believers, as long as they are engaged in warfare [that is, alongside one another].

The Jews of Banu ʿAwf are a community [umma] with the Believers; the Jews have their religion/law (din) and the Muslims have their religion/law, their clients (mawali), and their persons, except that anyone who behaves unjustly and acts treacherously [or: acts sinfully] destroys only himself and his kinsmen.

The Jews of Banu l-Najjar have the same [rights and obligations] as the Jews of Banu ʿAwf.

The Jews of Banu l-Harith have the same. . . .

The Jews of Banu Saʿida have the same. . . .

The Jews of Banu Jusham have the same. . . .

The Jews of Banu l-Aws have the same. . . .

The Jews of Banu Thaʿlaba have the same [rights and obligations] as the Jews of Banu ʿAwf, except that anyone who behaves unjustly and acts treacherously [or: acts sinfully] destroys only himself and his kinsmen.

Jafna are a section of the Tha'laba and are [treated] like them.

The Banu l-Shutayba have the same [rights and obligations] as the Jews of Banu 'Awf.

The righteous person guards against treachery.

The clients (mawali) *of Tha'laba are [to be considered] just like them.*

The close associates of the Jews are as themselves.

No one of them may go out [from Yathrib? or from the umma? *or to war?], except with the permission of Muhammad.*

One shall not be prevented from taking revenge for a wound.

Whoever assassinates [someone], assassinates himself and his kinsmen, unless [the victim] be someone who acted wrongfully, for God supports the more righteous [party] in this (?).

The Jews owe their [share of] expenses, and the Muslims owe their [share of] expenses.

Between them is [mutual] assistance against whosoever declares war against the people of this treaty (sahifa).

Between them is sincere advice and counsel.

The righteous person guards against treachery.

A man shall not betray his ally, and assistance belongs to the person wronged.

The center (jawf) *of Yathrib is sacrosanct (or: a sacred area) for the people of this treaty* (sahifa).

The protected person (jar) *is like one's self, neither being harmed nor acting treacherously.*

A woman shall not be granted protection except with the permission of her family.

Whatever offense or disagreement there may be among the people of this treaty (sahifa), from which trouble may arise, should be referred to God and to Muhammad.

God supports whatever is most righteous and upright in this treaty.

No protection shall be extended to Quraysh, nor to anyone who assists them.

Between them [that is, the parties to the treaty] is [mutual] assistance against anyone who attacks Yathrib.

When they are called to conclude and observe a truce (sulh), they will conclude and observe it; and when they call [others] for the same, the Believers are obligated to grant them that, except whoever goes to war over religion/law (din).

All persons are responsible for their share of their side that is opposite them [?].

The Jews of al-'Aws, their clients (mawali) and themselves, are on the same basis as the people of this treaty (sahifa), with sincere loyalty from the people of this treaty.

The righteous person guards against treachery.

Whoever acquires [something, that is, for good or evil?] acquires it only for himself.

God supports the truest and most righteous of what is in this treaty.

This document does not protect anyone who acts unjustly or treacherously.

Whoever goes out is safe, and whoever remains in place is safe in the city [or: in Medina], except whoever acts unjustly or treacherously.

God is the protector of whoever is upright and righteous, and Muhammad is the apostle (rasul) of God.

The most worthy of those in this treaty (sahifa) are the sincerely righteous.

Appendix B:
Inscriptions in the Dome
of the Rock, Jerusalem

The inscriptions on the inner mosaics of the Dome of the Rock, constructed by order of the *amir al-mu'minin* 'Abd al-Malik, constitute the longest extant group of official inscriptions by the Believers from the first century AH. It is noteworthy for its inclusion of numerous quotations of, or close paraphrases of, selected verses of the Qur'an. The content is quite repetitive but conveys a strong theological message. The inscription itself is dated to the year 72/691, which must be close to the time the building was completed, because the decorations would be the last element in its construction. During the ninth century C.E., the caliph al-Ma'mun (ruled 198–218/813–833) ordered the inscription on the outer face of the arcade to be emended, replacing the name of 'Abd al-Malik with his own. However, he neglected to change the date of the inscription, so the attribution of the inscription and building to 'Abd al-Malik is certain. The section replaced is indicated in the translation below by underlining. The inscription generally lacks any punctuation, but sections on the inner face of the arcade are separated by medallions; in the translation below the location of each medallion is marked by an asterisk (*).

The translation is based on the careful transcription of the "Kufic" style script prepared by Christel Kessler in 1967 (Christel Kessler, "'Abd al-Malik's Inscription in the Dome of the Rock: A Reconsideration," *Journal of the Royal Asiatic Society* (1970): 2–14).

The Inscriptions

[A. Inner face of octagonal arcade]

In the name of God, the Compassionate, the Merciful. There is no god except God, alone; He has no partner. Sovereignty belongs to Him, and praise belongs to Him. He brings to life, and He takes life away, and He is powerful over every thing [see Q. 44:1 and Q. 42:2]. Muhammad is God's servant and His apostle (rasul). *Verily, God and His angels bless the prophet* (nabi). *O you who believe, bless him and offer greetings. May God bless him, and may peace and God's mercy be upon him. O people of the book, do not exaggerate in your religion* (din), *and speak of God only the truth. The Messiah Jesus son of Mary was only the apostle* (rasul) *of God and His word, which He cast unto Mary, and a spirit from Him. So believe in God and His apostles and do not say "three." Desist! [It is] better for you. God is one deity only, He is above having a son. Whatever is in the heavens and whatever is in the earth is His, and God is the best advocate [see Q. 4:171]. The Messiah would never disdain to be God's servant, nor would the closest angels; whoever disdains His service/worship and is arrogant, He will gather them all to Himself [that is, on the Day of Judgment; see Q. 4:172]. O God, bless Your apostle* (rasul) *and Your servant Jesus son of Mary; may peace be upon him on the day he was born, and the day he will die, and the day he will be resurrected alive [see Q. 19:15]. Thus is Jesus son of Mary, a statement of the truth that they doubt. It was not for God to take a son, glory be to Him. When He decrees a matter, He only says "be!" and it is. God is my lord* (rabb) *and your lord, so serve/worship Him; that is the straight path [see Q. 19:34–36]. God bears witness that there is no deity except Him, and the angels and men of knowledge [also bear witness], ordaining [matters] in justice* (qist); *there is no deity except Him, the Mighty, the Wise [see Q. 3:18]. Verily religion/law* (din) *with God is Islam. Those who received the book only differed after knowledge had come to them, due to envy among them. Whoever denies the signs (ayat) of God—God is swift of reckoning [see Q. 3.19].*

[B. Outer face of octagonal arcade]

In the name of God, the Compassionate, the Merciful: There is no deity except God alone, He has no partner. Say: He, God, is one, God the eternal; He did not beget nor was He begotten, and there is no equal to Him [see Q. 112]. Muhammad is the apostle (rasul) of God. May God bless him.* In the name of God, the Compassionate, the Merciful: there is no deity except God, alone; He has no partner. Muhammad is the apostle (rasul) of God. Verily God and His angels bless the prophet (al-nabi). O you who believe, bless him and offer greetings [see Q. 33:56].* In the name of God, the Compassionate, the Merciful: There is no deity except God, alone. Praise be to God, who did not take a son, and who has no partner in sovereignty (al-mulk), and who has no helper from the mundane (wali min al-dhull). So magnify Him greatly [see Q. 17:111]. Muhammad is the apostle (rasul) of God; may God and His angels and His messengers (rusul) bless him; peace upon him, and the blessings of God.* In the name of God, the Compassionate, the Merciful: there is no deity except God, alone, He has no partner. Sovereignty belongs to Him, and praise belongs to Him. He brings to life, and He takes life away, and He is powerful over every thing [see Q. 44:1 and Q. 42:2]. Muhammad is the apostle (rasul) of God, may God bless him and accept his intercession on the day of resurrection on behalf of his community (umma).* In the name of God, the Compassionate, the Merciful: There is no deity except God, alone, He has no partner. Muhammad is the apostle (rasul) of God, may God bless him.* The servant of God ʿAbd Allah the imam al-Maʾmun, amir al-muʾminin, built this dome in the year two and seventy; may God accept it from him and be pleased with him. Amen, Lord of the worlds, praise belongs to God.*

Notes and Guide to Further Reading

The following pages provide readers with some idea of where to go for further information on topics covered in this book. On occasion, they also provide supporting documentation, where it exists, for specialists and interested general readers alike. Matters are arranged more or less in the sequence in which they occur in each chapter.

The following abbreviations are used in the notes:

BSOAS   *Bulletin of the School of Oriental and African Studies*, University of London.

CCJ   Michael Maas, ed., *The Cambridge Companion to the Age of Justinian* (Cambridge: Cambridge University Press, 2005).

Donner, "Believers to Muslims"   Fred M. Donner, "From Believers to Muslims: Confessional Self-identity in the Early Islamic Community," *Al-Abhath* 50–51 (2002–2003): 9–53.

Donner, *Conquests*   Fred M. Donner, *The Early Islamic Conquests* (Princeton, NJ: Princeton University Press, 1981).

Donner, *Narratives*   Fred M. Donner, *Narratives of Islamic Origins: The Beginnings of Islamic Historical Writing* (Princeton, NJ: Darwin Press, 1998).

EI (2)   *Encyclopaedia of Islam*, 2nd ed. (Leiden: E. J. Brill, 1960–2002). Cited by the title of the article.

Guillaume, *Life* Alfred Guillaume, trans., *The Life of Muhammad* (Oxford: Oxford University Press, 1955).

Hoyland, *Seeing Islam* Robert Hoyland, *Seeing Islam As Others Saw It. A Survey and Evaluation of Christian, Jewish and Zoroastrian Writings on Early Islam* (Princeton, NJ: Darwin Press, 1997).

IJMES *International Journal of Middle Eastern Studies*

JSAI *Jerusalem Studies in Arabic and Islam*

Tab. Muhammad ibn Jarir al-Tabari, *Ta'rikh*, ed. Michaël Jan de Goeje (Leiden: E. J. Brill, 1879–1901). English translation *The History of al-Tabari*, 38 vols. (Albany: State University of New York Press, 1985–continuing). References are provided only to the Arabic text of the de Goeje edition; the de Goeje paginations are noted in the margins of the translation, so references can be traced in either version.

Preface

The quote is from Ernest Renan, "Mahomet and the Origins of Islamism," in his *Studies of Religious History* (London: Heinemann, 1893), 187. (French original *Études d'histoire religieuse* [Paris: M. Lévy, 1857].)

1.   The Near East on the Eve of Islam

For a general orientation into the Late Antique world, one can best begin with Peter Brown's classic *The World of Late Antiquity, AD 150–750* (London: Thames & Hudson, 1971), a short, brilliant overview. For greater detail, consult G. Bowersock, P. Brown, and O. Grabar, eds., *Late Antiquity: A Guide to the Postclassical World* (Cambridge, MA: Belknap Press of Harvard University Press, 1999), whose long essays and many shorter entries offer good orientations on most aspects of late antique history and life, including Byzantium, the early medieval West, the Sasanian Empire, and early Islam. Stephen Mitchell, *A History of the Later Roman Empire, AD 286–641: The Transformation of the Ancient World* (Oxford: Blackwell, 2007), covers both the eastern and western parts of the empire. Kevin

Butcher, *Roman Syria and the Near East* (London: British Museum Press, 2003), focuses on the East.

On the Byzantine Empire: Averil Cameron, *The Mediterranean World in Late Antiquity, AD 395–600* (London: Routledge, 1993), integrates recent work on social and economic history, as well as the more traditional foci of state and church institutions. *CCJ* includes a number of very helpful chapters. F. M. Donner, "The Background of Islam," *CCJ*, 510–533, offers a slightly more detailed discussion of some of the points covered here.

On the "last Byzantine emperor" idea, see Paul J. Alexander, *The Byzantine Apocalyptic Tradition* (Berkeley: University of California Press, 1985), 151–184; *idem*, "Byzantium and the Migration of Literary Works and Motifs: The Legend of the Last Roman Emperor," *Medievalia et Humanistica* n.s. 2 (1971): 47–68.

On the socioeconomic structure of the Byzantine world, see Cameron, *Mediterranean World*, chap. 4; Mitchell, *History of the Roman Empire*, chap. 10; and John F. Haldon, *Byzantium in the Seventh Century: The Transformation of a Culture* (Cambridge: Cambridge University Press, 1990), especially chaps. 3, 4, and 10. On the middle classes, see Linda Jones Hall, "The Case of Late Antique Berytus: Urban Wealth and Rural Sustenance—A Different Economic Dynamic," in Thomas S. Burns and John W. Eadie, eds., *Urban Centers and Rural Contexts in Late Antiquity* (East Lansing, MI: Michigan State University Press, 2001), 63–76. On the spread of ascetic Christianity and an egalitarian outlook, see Han J. W. Drijvers, "Saint as Symbol: Conceptions of the Person in Late Antiquity and Early Christianity," in Hans G. Kippenberg, Y. B. Kuiper, and A. F. Sanders, eds., *Concepts of Person* (Berlin: Mouton de Gruyter, 1990), 137–157. An excellent overview of developments in the third through the sixth centuries C.E. is Alan G. Walmsley, "Byzantine Palestine and Arabia: Urban Prosperity in Late Antiquity," in N. Christie and S. Loseby, eds., *Towns in Transition: Urban Evolution in Late Antiquity and the Early Middle Ages* (London: Scolar, 1996), 126–158.

On Christological disputes: F. M. Young, *From Nicaea to Chalcedon* (Philadelphia: Fortress, 1983) is the classic treatment; Patrick T. R. Gray, "The Legacy of Chalcedon: Christological Problems and Their Significance," in *CCJ*, 215–238, provides a clear, brief recounting of the tortuous debates and their consequences.

On Christian asceticism and monasticism: Derwas J. Chitty, *The Desert a City* (Oxford: Blackwell's, 1966) is a good introduction; Peter Brown, "The Rise and Function of the Holy Man in Late Antiquity," *Journal of Roman Studies* 61 (1971): 80–101, was a seminal contribution. Vincent L. Wimbush and Richard Valantasis, eds., *Asceticism* (New York: Oxford University Press, 1995), a massive tome, includes several useful chapters, particularly Averil Cameron's "Ascetic Closure and the End of Antiquity," pp. 147–161. On other aspects of Christian religiosity, see Derek Kruger, "Christian Piety and Practice in the Sixth Century," *CCJ*, 291–315.

On Late Antique apocalypticism (mainly Christian): A good introduction is the first fifty or so pages of Bernard McGinn, *Visions of the End: Apocalyptic Traditions in the Middle Ages* (New York: Columbia University Press, 1979). See also Alexander, *Byzantine Apocalyptic Tradition*, cited above; and chapters by G. Reinink and W. van Bekkum in Bernard H. Stolte and Gerrit J. Reinink, eds., *The Reign of Heraclius (610–641): Crisis and Confrontation* (Leuven, Belgium: Peeters, 2002).

On Late Antique Judaism: Nicholas de Lange, "Jews in the Age of Justinian," in *CCJ*, 401–426; Michael Avi-Yonah, *The Jews under Roman and Byzantine Rule: A Political History from the Bar Cochba War to the Arab Conquest*, 2nd ed. (Jerusalem: Magnes Press, 1984); Gilbert Dagron and Vincent Déroche, "Juifs et chrétiens dans l'Orient du VIIe siècle," *Travaux et Mémoires*, 11 (1991): 17–46; Gordon Darnell Newby, *A History of the Jews of Arabia* (Columbia, SC: University of South Carolina Press, 1988); Christian-Julien Robin, "Himyar et Israël," *Académie des Inscriptions et Belles-Lettres*, Comptes-Rendus des Séances de l'Année 2004, avril–juin, 831–908.

On Heraclius, Walter E. Kaegi, *Heraclius, Emperor of Byzantium* (Cambridge: Cambridge University Press, 2003), is the definitive study. Although detailed, it is quite readable.

On the Sasanian Empire, see Touraj Daryaee, *Sasanian Persia. The Rise and Fall of an Empire* (New York: I. B. Tauris, 2009). Also useful are the more technical presentations of Michael Morony, "Sasanids," *EI* (2), and (at much greater length) the *Cambridge History of Iran*, vol. III (Cambridge: Cambridge University Press, 1983), which contains many excellent chapters on aspects of Sasanian history (including, for example, their relations with Arabia and Byzantium). The Sasanians' use of Zoroastrian/Avestan myth to legitimize their claims to rule Iran is discussed in Touraj Daryaee, "Memory and History: The Construction of the Past in Late Antique Persia," *Name-ye Iran-e Bastan* 1:2 (2001–2002): 1–14. See also *Cambridge History of Iran*, III, 864–865, 409–410, and 692–696.

On Zoroastrianism: Mary Boyce, *Zoroastrians: Their Religious Beliefs and Practices* (London: Routledge and Kegan Paul, 1979) is the best introduction; Robert C. Zaehner, *The Dawn and Twilight of Zoroastrianism* (New York: Putnam, 1961); *idem, Zurvan: A Zoroastrian Dilemma* (Oxford: Clarendon Press, 1955).

On pre-Islamic Arabia: An excellent, readable general introduction is Robert G. Hoyland, *Arabia and the Arabs: From the Bronze Age to the Coming of Islam* (London: Routledge, 2001). See also many excellent articles in F. E. Peters, ed., *The Arabs and Arabia on the Eve of Islam* (Aldershot: Ashgate, 1999). The clearest brief overview of the internal politics of Mecca on the eve of Islam may still be that found in W. M. Watt, *Muhammad at Mecca* (Oxford: Clarendon Press, 1953), 4–16, but the reader should be aware that his discussions, elsewhere in the volume, of "tribal humanism" and his assumption that Mecca was the linchpin of international luxury trade have been decisively challenged in recent years—notably in Patricia Crone, *Meccan Trade and the Rise of Islam* (Princeton, NJ: Princeton University Press, 1987). Watt's *Muhammad at Medina* (Oxford: Clarendon Press, 1956), 151–174, offers a similarly useful overview of Medina before Islam, but now see also Michael Lecker, *Muslims, Jews, and Pagans: Studies on Early Islamic Medina* (Leiden: E. J. Brill, 1995).

On the empires' efforts to establish ties with Mecca and Yathrib, see M. Lecker, "The Levying of Taxes for the Sasanians in Pre-Islamic Medina (Yathrib)," *JSAI* 27 (2002): 109–126, and F. M. Donner, "The Background to Islam," in *CCJ*, 528, notes 16 and 17. Patricia Crone, "Making Sense of the Qurashi Leather Trade," *BSOAS* 70 (2007): 63–88, emphasizes the great military importance of Arabian leather to the Byzantine and Sasanian armies.

On Christians in the pre-Islamic Hijaz, see the suggestive reports in Guillaume, *Life*, 572: a Christian slave among the slain at Hunayn, and 552: pictures of Jesus and Mary inside the Ka'ba. The recent works that most emphatically advances the claim that Christians were found in the Hijaz are Günter Lüling's *Die Wiederentdeckung des Propheten Muhammad* (Erlangen: H. Lüling, 1981) and *Über den Ur-Qur'an* (Erlangen: H. Lüling, 1974), the latter now translated as *A Challenge to Islam for Reformation* (Delhi: Motilal Benarsidass, 2003).

On the Nazoreans, see François de Blois, "Nasrani (*Ναζωραιοσ*) and *hanif* (*εθνικος*): Studies on the Religious Vocabulary of Christianity and Islam," *BSOAS* 65 (2002): 1–30.

On the survival of prophecy: Rebecca Gray, *Prophetic Figures in Late Second Temple Jewish Palestine* (New York: Oxford University Press, 1993); on the Montanists, see Ronald E. Heine, ed., *The Montanist Oracles and Testimonia* (Macon, GA: Mercer University Press, 1989); on Manichaeism, see Samuel N. C. Lieu, *Manichaeism in the Later Roman Empire and Medieval China* (Tübingen: Mohr, 1992).

On the *ridda* wars, see Elias S. Shoufani, *Al-Riddah and the Muslim Conquest of Arabia* (Beirut: Arab Institute for Research and Publishing, and Toronto: University of Toronto Press, 1972).

2. Muhammad and the Believers' Movement

A readable overview of the traditional view of Muhammad's career, based closely on and replicating the general contours of the Islamic sources, is W. Montgomery Watt, *Muhammad, Prophet and Statesman* (Oxford: Oxford University Press, 1961)—which is based on his more detailed studies, *Muhammad at Mecca* and *Muhammad at Medina* (Oxford: Oxford University Press, 1953 and 1956). In shorter compass, see the article "Muhammad" in the *EI* (2) by F. Buhl as revised by A. T. Welch. Another account, which follows in its general outlines the traditional biography but is fully aware of the recent revisionist and skeptical critique, is F. E. Peters, *Muhammad and the Origins of Islam* (Albany: State University of New York, 1994). It also has the virtue of providing many relevant passages of traditional Arabic sources in English translation.

Many English translations of the Qur'an are available. Most are quite serviceable, but the new reader should try comparing two or more on a given passage to get some idea of the range of interpretations the text can support. Because the Qur'an does not, for the most part, present its material as connected narratives or gather all treatments of a particular issue in one place, new readers will find that a detailed index is an indispensable tool in exploring what the text says on a given subject and should consider the fullness of the index when buying a translation.

A readable account of some of the recent debates about the Qur'an among revisionist and traditionalist scholars is found in Toby Lester, "What is the Koran?", *Atlantic Monthly* (January 1999), 43–56. More up-to-date is F. M. Donner, "The Qur'an in Recent Scholarship: Challenges and Desiderata," in Gabriel Said Reynolds, ed., *The Qur'an in Its Historical Context* (London: Routledge, 2008), 29–50.

Western approaches to the traditional Islamic sources for the rise of Islam are surveyed and categorized in the introduction to Donner, *Narratives*. For the life of Muhammad specifically, see F. E. Peters, "The Quest of the Historical Muhammad," *IJMES* 23 (1991): 291–315, which has also been reprinted at the end of his *Muhammad and the Origins of Islam*, quoted above.

Recent revisionist views of Islam's origins were presented in P. Crone and M. Cook, *Hagarism* (Cambridge: Cambridge University Press, 1977) and in J. Wansbrough's *Qur'anic Studies* (Oxford: Oxford University Press, 1977), which first proposed the "late origin" theory of the Qur'an. The former, however, is not easy to follow, and the latter, even for specialists, is virtually incomprehensible. Wansbrough's ideas are best grasped by reading the work of one of his sympathizers, such as Andrew Rippin, "Literary Analysis of *Qur'an, Tafsir,* and *Sira:* The Methodologies of John Wansbrough," in *Approaches to Islam in Religious Studies*, ed. Richard C. Martin, 151–163 (Tucson: University of Arizona Press, 1985). I have offered a critique of Wansbrough's ideas on the Qur'an's date in chapter 1 of Donner, *Narratives*. The idea that the Qur'an may include "recycled" Arabian Christian materials that antedate the prophet was advanced by Günter Lüling (*Über den Ur-Qur'an* and *Wiederentdeckung*, cited near the end of the bibliography for chapter 1)—actually the earliest of the recent revisionists, although his ideas have little in common with the "English school" represented by Wansbrough, Crone, and Cook and have had far less impact to date. The publications of Christoph Luxenberg, starting with his *The Syro-Aramaic Reading of the Koran* (Berlin: Schiler, 2007; German original, 2000), with its thesis that significant parts of the Qur'an are not in Arabic, but Aramaic, created a great stir both because of its many specific reinterpretations of the text and because of the broader issues it raised concerning the relationship between the Qur'an and Christian tradition. A noteworthy contribution to the ongoing discussion of these issues is Gabriel Said Reynolds, *The Qur'an and Its Biblical Subtext* (New York: Routledge, forthcoming).

Many penetrating articles on early Islam have come from the pen of M. J. Kister; see his collection, *Studies in Jahiliyya and Early Islam* (London: Variorium, 1980), for a selection of these, or the journal *Jerusalem Studies in Arabic and Islam*, where many of his more recent pieces have appeared. A valuable study of the symbolic and legitimizing aspects in the narratives of a number of episodes in Muhammad's life (including numerological symbolism) is Uri Rubin, *In the Eye of the Beholder: The Life of Muhammad as Viewed by the Early Muslims* (Princeton, NJ: Darwin, 1995); it also refutes the assertion of some revisionists that many parts of Muhammad's biography are exegetical, that is, invented out of whole cloth to "explain" a certain passage in the Qur'an, showing instead that many accounts seem to be very early (which is not necessarily to say, of course, that they are accurate records of what happened). On Muhammad "feeding the multitudes" like Jesus, see Guillaume, *Life*, 451–452; for further cases of this sort, see Toufic Fahd, "Problèmes de typologie dans la «Sira» d'Ibn Ishaq," in *La vie du prophète Mahomet (Colloque de Strasbourg, octobre 1980)* (Paris: Presses Universitaires de France, 1983), 67–75.

The basic ideas presented in this chapter regarding the ecumenical character of the early Believers' movement are developed in a more specialized way in Donner, "Believers to Muslims."

Muhammad's calling his movement *hanifiyya* is noted by Jacques Waardenburg, "Towards a Periodization of Earliest Islam According to Its Relations with Other Religions," in *Proceedings of the Ninth Congress of the Union Européenne des Arabisants et Islamisants*, ed. R. Peters, 304–336 (Leiden: E. J. Brill, 1981), at p. 311.

The *umma* document, often misleadingly called the "Constitution of Medina," is discussed in a general way in R. B. Serjeant, "The Constitution of Medina," *Islamic Quarterly* 8 (1964): 3–16, and in greater detail in "The *Sunnah Jami'ah*, Pacts with the Yathrib Jews, and the *Tahrim* of Yathrib: Analysis and Translation of the Documents Comprised in the So-Called 'Constitution of Medina'," *BSOAS* 41 (1978): 1–42. See Michael Lecker, *The "Constitution of Medina": Muhammad's First Legal Document* (Princeton, NJ: Darwin, 2004), which studies it in great detail.

The idea that the Qur'an's invective against *mushrikun* may be directed not at pagans but rather at "soft" monotheists is advanced by G. Hawting, *The Idea of Idolatry and the Emergence of Islam* (Cambridge: Cambridge University Press, 1999); a similar notion was proposed by Raimund Köbert, "Zur Bedeutung der drei letzten Worte von Sure 22, 30/31," *Orientalia* 35 (1966): 28–32, and developed by Günter Lüling, *Über den Ur-Qur'an* (Erlangen: H. Lüling, 1974), esp. 202–203.

Qur'anic piety is discussed in Donner, *Narratives*, chapter 2. The original concept of *zakat* or *sadaqa* as a payment in expiation for sin, rather than alms, is brilliantly explored in Suliman Bashear, "On the Origins and Development of the Meaning of *Zakat* in Islam," *Arabica* 40 (1993): 84–113. For parallels between the Believers' piety and that of the late antique Christian tradition, see Ofer Livne-Kafri, "Early Muslim Ascetics and the World of Christian Monasticism," *JSAI* 20 (1996): 105–129. The quote about prayer as the fabric of religious life is by N. Hanif from the entry "Salat (Ritual Prayer)" in *Encyclopedia of the Holy Qur'an*, ed. N. K. Singh and A. R. Agwan, 1309 (Delhi: Global Vision, 2000).

For the Qur'anic data on ritual prayer, dozens of references could be provided, but the following will give the interested reader a start. Various prayer times: Q. 2:238, 4:103, 11:114, 20:30, 30:17–18, 52:48–49, 73:2–7, and 76:25–26. Standing, kneeling, sitting: Q. 2:43, 4:103, and 5:55. Prostration: Q. 50:40, and 9:112. Call to prayer: Q. 5:58. Ablutions: Q. 5:6.

On the *'ashura'* fast, see Suliman Bashear, "'Ashura', an Early Muslim Fast," *Zeitschrift der deutschen morgenländische Gesellschaft* 141 (1991): 281–316.

On Jewish converts to Islam, see Michael Lecker, "Hudhayfa b. al-Yaman and 'Ammar b. Yasir, Jewish Converts to Islam," *Quaderni di Studi*

Arabi 11 (1993): 149–162; *idem*, "'Amr ibn Hazm al-Ansari and Qur'an 2, 256: "No Compulsion Is There in Religion," *'Oriens* 35 (1996): 57–64; "Zayd b. Thabit, 'A Jew with Two Sidelocks': Judaism and Literacy in Pre-Islamic Medina (Yathrib)," *Journal of Near Eastern Studies* 56 (1997): 259–273.

On Jewish Christianity as antecedent for Qur'anic prophetology, including the notion of "seal of the prophets," see François de Blois, "Elchasai—Manes—Muhammad. Manichäismus und Islam in religionshistorischem Vergleich," *Der Islam* 81 (2004): 31–48. On prophecy in early Christianity, see Ernst Käsemann, "The Beginnings of Christian Theology," *Journal for Theology and the Church* 6 (1969): 17–46, esp. 27–29.

For the early community's eschatological and apocalyptic outlook, there is as yet no satisfactory comprehensive treatment, but for a few examples, see Lawrence I. Conrad, "Portents of the Hour: Hadith and Historiography in the First Century A.H.," *Der Islam* (forthcoming); Michael Cook, "The Heraclian Dynasty in Muslim Eschatology," *Al-Qantara* 13 (1992): 3–23; Suliman Bashear, "Apocalyptic and Other Materials on Early Muslim-Byzantine Wars: A Review of Arabic Sources," *Journal of the Royal Asiatic Society* 1 (1991): 173–207; and Wilferd Madelung, "'Abd Allah b. al-Zubayr and the Mahdi," *Journal of Near Eastern Studies* 40 (1981): 291–305. The idea that apocalyptic eschatology and realized eschatology might be found simultaneously may seem like a logical impossibility, but the coexistence of these concepts is known in other religious traditions, notably early Christianity; see David Aune, *The Cultic Setting of Realized Eschatology in Early Christianity* (Leiden: E. J. Brill, 1972). Some scholars claim that the apocalyptic tone is "not strong" in the Qur'an, but such statements ignore the forcefulness and immediacy of the apocalyptic imagery used in many of the Qur'an's shorter chapters. For some thoughtful reflections on Qur'anic eschatology, see Andrew Rippin, "The Commerce of Eschatology," in *The Qur'an as Text*, ed. Stefan Wild, 125–135 (Leiden: E. J. Brill, 1996). The quote about "easily visualized scenes" is from Bernard McGinn, *Visions of the End: Apocalyptic Traditions in the Middle Ages* (New York: Columbia University Press, 1979), 6.

My treatment of the Qur'an's attitudes toward militancy and activism is based on Reuven Firestone, *Jihad: The Origin of Holy War in Islam* (Oxford: Oxford University Press, 1999), which is both convincing and readable. On the Qur'an's use of "escape clauses," see F. M. Donner, "Fight for God—But Do So with Kindness: Reflections on War, Peace, and Communal Identity in Early Islam," in *War and Peace in the Ancient World,* ed. Kurt A. Raaflaub, 297–311 297–311 (Oxford: Blackwell's, 2007).

On the duty to "command good and forbid wrong" one may begin with Michael Cook, *Forbidding Wrong in Islam* (Cambridge: Cambridge University Press, 2003).

3. The Expansion of the Community of Believers

A brief overview of the Islamic conquests is F. M. Donner, "Islam, Expansion of" in J. Strayer, ed., *Dictionary of the Middle Ages.* A more detailed overview of the issues can be found in F. M. Donner, "The Islamic Conquests" in *Companion to Middle Eastern History,* ed. Youssef Choueiri, 28–51 (Malden, MA: Blackwell's, 2005). A readable older survey constructed within the parameters of the traditional paradigm is Francesco Gabrieli, *Muhammad and the Conquests of Islam* (New York: McGraw-Hill, 1968). The sketch of the expansion into Syria and Iraq provided here is based on Donner, *Conquests.*

On the reliability (or lack of it) of the conquest narratives, see Donner, *Narratives,* esp. chap. 7; Albrecht Noth and Lawrence I. Conrad, *The Early Arabic Historical Tradition: A Source-Critical Study* (Princeton, NJ: Darwin, 1994); and Chase F. Robinson, "The Conquest of Khuzistan: A Historiographical Reassessment," *BSOAS* 67 (2004): 14–39. On the questions of centralization and the general skepticism of some writers toward the early conquest narratives, see F. M. Donner, "Centralized Authority and Military Autonomy in the Early Islamic Conquests," in *The Byzantine and Early Islamic Near East, III: States, Resources and Armies,* ed. Averil Cameron, 337–360 (Princeton, NJ: Darwin, 1995).

On *ta'lif al-qulub/*"reconciling of hearts," see Watt, *Muhammad at Medina,* 348–353.

On 'Amr ibn al-'As's properties, see Michael Lecker, "The Estates of 'Amr b. al-'As in Palestine: Notes on a New Negev Inscription," *BSOAS* 52 (1989): 24–37.

The quote on Jerusalem is from Bernard McGinn, "The Meaning of the Millennium," *Encuentros* 13 (January 1996): 10 [Lectures published by the Inter-American Development Bank Cultural Center, Washington, DC].

On the *ridda* wars, see Elias S. Shoufani, *Al-Riddah and the Muslim Conquest of Arabia* (Beirut: Arab Institute for Research and Publishing, and Toronto: University of Toronto Press, 1972).

On the tribal composition of the early conquest armies in Syria and Iraq, see Donner, *Conquests*, appendices.

On the *ridda* wars as the crucial experience leading to the crystallization of standing armies, see F. M. Donner, "The Growth of Military Institutions in the Early Caliphate and Their Relation to Civilian Authority," *Al-Qantara* 14 (1993): 311–326.

On the *hima* at al-Rabadha, see Sa'd al-Din al-Rashid, *Rabadhah. A Portrait of Early Islamic Civilisation in Saudi Arabia* (Riyadh: King Saud University College of Arts, and Harlow, UK: Longmans, 1986), 1–7. Thick deposits of camel bones at al-Rabadha were reported to me in a personal communication in 1994 by one of the excavators. These are not mentioned in the report by al-Rashid, but the latter does mention (p. 88) that some inscriptions on camel bones were found (mostly business records).

The early Christian and other near-contemporary sources for Islam's origins are conveniently collected, translated, and discussed in Hoyland, *Seeing Islam*, which is indispensable.

Absence of archaeological evidence of destruction associated with the Islamic "conquests" is noted in Robert Schick, *The Christian Communities of Palestine from Byzantine to Islamic Rule* (Princeton, NJ: Darwin, 1995), *infra*, esp. 222–224. Specific examples: On Jerusalem, Meir Ben Dov, *In the Shadow of the Temple* (Jerusalem: Keter, 1985); on Jerash (Gerasa), Iain Browing, *Jerash and the Decapolis* (London: Chatto and Windus, 1982), 57–58; on Hama, Harald Ingholt, *Rapport Préliminaire sur sept campagnes de fouilles à Hama en Syrie (1932–1938)* (Copenhagen: Munksgaard, 1940), 136–139, on Level B, dated as Byzantine but probably Byzantine and early Islamic; on Asqalan/Ashkelon, Lawrence E. Stager, *Ashkelon Discovered* (Washington, DC: Biblical Archaeological Society, 1991), 53–54, discusses the transition but notes that no significant remains mark it. More generally, see Averil Cameron, "Interfaith Relations in the First Islamic Century,"

Bulletin of the Royal Institute for Inter-Faith Studies 1/2 (Autumn 1999), 1–12.

On churches established or rebuilt shortly following the "conquest," see Schick, *Christian Communities, infra.* Michele Piccirillo, *The Mosaics of Jordan* (Amman: American Center of Oriental Research, 1992) provides descriptions, mostly from churches dating from the sixth and seventh centuries, with sumptuous illustrations.

On early Christian texts mentioning Muhammad, see Robert Hoyland, "The Earliest Christian Writings on Muhammad: An Appraisal," in *The Biography of Muhammad: The Issue of the Sources,* ed. Harald Motzki, 276–297 (Leiden: E. J. Brill, 2000); also, especially, G. J. Reinink, "The Beginnings of Syriac Apologetic Literature in Response to Islam," *Oriens Christianus* 77 (1993): 165–187. On the evolving claims for Muhammad's prophecy and their relation to responses in the Jewish and Christian communities, see Sarah Stroumsa, "The Signs of Prophecy: The Emergence and Early Development of a Theme in Arabic Theological Literature," *Harvard Theological Review* 78 (1985): 101–114.

On the status of Zoroastrians, see Y. Friedmann, *Tolerance and Coercion in Islam* (New York: Cambridge University Press, 2003), 72–76 and 198.

On early *shahadas,* see Donner, "Believers to Muslims," 47–48. A. J. Wensinck, ed., *Concordance et indices de la tradition musulmane* (8 vols., Leiden: E. J. Brill, 1936–1988), lists under *shahada* many that mention only recognition of God's oneness—not of Muhammad's prophecy. M. J. Kister, ". . . *illa bi-haqqihi* . . . A Study of an Early *hadith*," *JSAI* 5 (1984): 33–52, deals with the debate over whether it is an adequate *shahada* to say only "There is no god but God," without reference to Muhammad's prophecy. Guillaume, *Life,* 668, has a report suggesting that the basis of true faith is recognition of God's oneness, prayer, alms, fasting, pilgrimage, and ritual purity, but recognition of Muhammad's status as prophet is pointedly missing. Hoyland, *Seeing Islam,* Excursus F (687–703), provides a tabulation of dated Muslim writings up to A.H. 135/752–753 C.E.

Text for the quote from the Nestorian patriarch is found in *Corpus Scriptorum Christianorum Orientalium,* Series III, vol. 64, 248–251; cf. Tor Andrae, "Der Ursprung des Islam und das Christentum," *Kyrkshistorisk årsskrift* 23 (1923): 167; cited also in Sebastian Brock, "Syriac Views of Emergent

Islam," in *Studies on the First Century of Islamic Society*, ed. G. H. A. Juynboll, 9–21 (Carbondale: Southern Illinois University Press, 1982), at p. 15.

On Muslim treaty texts, see Albrecht Noth, "Die literarische Überlieferten Verträge der Eroberungszeit . . . ," in *Studien zum Minderheitenproblem in Islam* I, ed. Tilman Nagel et al., 282–304 (Bonn: Selbstverlag des Orientalischen Seminars der Universität, 1973).

On Believers sharing worship space with Christians in churches, see Donner, "Believers to Muslims," 51–52; Philip K. Hitti, *The Origins of the Islamic State* (New York: Columbia University Press, 1916, 125 and 201, on Damascus and Hims; and Suliman Bashear, "*Qibla musharriqa* and the Early Muslim Prayer in Churches," *Muslim World* 81 (1991): 267–282. On the Cathisma Church, see Leah Di Segni, "Christian Epigraphy . . .", *Aram* 15 (2003): 247–267, at p. 248 (I thank Lennart Sundelin for bringing this reference to my attention).

On Jerusalem, see Heribert Busse, "'Omar b. al-Ḥattab in Jerusalem," *JSAI* 5 (1984): 73–119; Busse, "'Omar's Image as the Conqueror of Jerusalem," *JSAI* 8 (1986): 149–168; and Busse, "Die 'Umar-Moschee im östlichen Atrium der Grabeskirche," *Zeitschrift der Deutschen Palästina-Vereins* 109 (1993): 73–82. The relevant passage from Arculf is translated and discussed in Hoyland, *Seeing Islam*, 219–223.

The early conquest campaigns, as described by the Muslim narrative sources, are beautifully depicted in visual form on the map by Ulrich Rebstock in the *Tübinger Atlas des Vorderen Orients*, Map B.VII.2, "The Islamic Empire under the First Four Caliphs" (1989).

For the Zoroastrian tax collector, see Claude Cahen, "Fiscalité, Propriété, Antagonismes Sociaux en Haute-Mésopotamie au temps des premiers 'Abbasides d'apres Denys de Tell-Mahré," *Arabica* 1 (1954): 136–152.

On Mosul and the Jazira, see Chase F. Robinson, *Empire and Elites after the Muslim Conquest* (Cambridge: Cambridge University Press, 2000), esp. 33–41.

On centralization, see F. M. Donner, "Centralized Authority and Military Autonomy in the Early Islamic Conquests," in *The Byzantine and Early Islamic Near East* III: *States, Resources and Armies*, ed. Averil Cameron, 337–360 (Princeton: Darwin Press, 1995); for the Sebeos quote, see Holyand, *Seeing Islam*, 131.

On the *amsar*/garrison towns, see Donald Whitcomb, "Amsar in Syria? Syrian Cities after the Conquest," *Aram* 6 (1994): 13–33; for Ayla, see Whitcomb, "The Misr of Ayla: New Evidence for the Early Islamic City," in *Studies in the History and Archaeology of Jordan, V: Art and Technology throughout the Ages,* ed. G. Bisheh, 277–288 (Amman: Department of Antiquities, 1995). On the plan of Kufa, see Donner, *Conquests,* 226–236; and Hichem Djait, *Al-Kufa: naissance de la ville islamique* (Paris: G.-P. Maisonneuve et Larose, 1986). On Fustat, see Wladislaw Kubiak, *Al-Fustat: Its Foundation and Early Urban Development* (Cairo: American University in Cairo, 1987).

On the *diwan,* see Gerd-Rüdiger Puin, "Der Diwan des ʿUmar ibn al-Ḥattab: Ein Beitrag zur frühislamischen Verwaltungsgeschichte" (diss. Bonn, 1970).

On the *barid* in the conquest period, see Adam Silverstein, "A Neglected Chapter in the History of Caliphal State-Building," *JSAI* 30 (2005): 293–317.

On the countryside "running itself" after the conquests and forwarding taxes to the new regime, see Terry Wilfong, *Women of Jeme: Lives in a Coptic Town in Late Antique Egypt* (Ann Arbor: University of Michigan Press, 2002).

On settlement in Iraq and Syria, see Donner, *Conquests,* chap. 5, esp. 239–250.

4. The Struggle for Leadership of the Community, 37–73/655–692

The meaning of *ibn al-sabil* is discussed in G.-R. Puin, "Der Diwan des ʿUmar ibn al-Ḥatttab" (diss. Bonn, 1970).

On the *shura,* see Gernot Rotter, *Die Umayyaden und der zweite Bürgerkrieg (680–692)* (Wiesbaden: Franz Steiner, 1982), 7–16. The anecdote about ʿUmar on his deathbed is found in Tab. i/2778–2779.

On cutting stipends to soldiers, see Tab. i/2929.

On the complex questions of landholding and the distribution of conquered lands, one may begin with Michael G. Morony, "Landholding in Iraq," in *Land Tenure and Social Transformation in the Middle East,* ed.

Tarif Khalidi, 209–222 (Beirut: American University of Beirut, 1984). A helpful survey in Arabic is Faleh Husayn, "Al-Dawla al-ʿarabiyya al-islamiyya wa-l-ʾard al-maftuha khilal al-fatra al-rashida," *Dirasat* 22 (1995): 1807–1830.

On ʿUthman's changes to the pilgrimage rituals: Tab. i/2833–2835.

On the changing policies toward appointments among Abu Bakr, ʿUmar, and ʿUthman, see Martin Hinds, "The Murder of the Caliph ʿUthman," *IJMES* 3 (1972): 450–469.

On the codification of the Qurʾan text—a hotly debated issue today—see the surveys in W. M. Watt, *Bell's Introduction to the Qurʾan* (Edinburgh: Edinburgh University Press, 1970), 40–56; and *EI* (2), "Kurʾan," section 3, by A. T. Welch.

My description of the events of the First Civil War follows closely the detailed accounting given in Wilferd Madelung, *The Succession to Muhammad* (Cambridge: Cambridge University Press, 1997). Madelung, unfortunately, has allowed himself to become virtually a partisan in the conflict, unequivocally supporting the claims of ʿAli. My own summary treatment of these events, while based on Madelung's, thus differs significantly from his in its interpretation. Madelung emphasizes, in particular, the importance of ʿAli's close kinship to the prophet; a contrasting view is provided by Asma Afsaruddin, *Excellence and Precedence* (Leiden: E. J. Brill, 2002), 277–284, who contends that piety was more important than kinship.

The report of Yazid's Taghlibi troops marching with the cross and banner of St. Sergius comes from a poem of al-Akhtal, the Christian court poet of the Umayyads, cited in H. Lammens, "Le califat de Yazîd Iᵉʳ," *Mélanges de la faculté orientale de l'Université Saint-Joseph de Beirut* 5 (1911–1912): 229. Close ties of the tribe of Kalb with Quraysh even before Islam are noted in M. J. Kister, "Mecca and the Tribes of Arabia," in *Studies in Islamic History and Civilization in Honour of Professor David Ayalon*, ed. M. Sharon, 33–57 (Jerusalem: Cana, and Leiden: E. J. Brill, 1986), at 55–57.

On the quote from John bar Penkaye, see Donner "Believers to Muslims," 43–45; and G. J. Reinink, "The Beginnings of Syriac Apologetic Literature in Response to Islam," *Oriens Christianus* 77 (1993): 165–187.

On the inscriptions and other documents of Muʿawiya, *qadaʾ al-muʾminin*, and so on, see Hoyland, *Seeing Islam*, 687–703, nos. 7, 8, 9, 16;

Donner, "Believers to Muslims"; and Yusuf Ragib, "Une ère inconnue d'Égypte musulmane: l'ère de la jurisdiction des croyants," *Annales isla-mologiques* 41 (2007): 187–207.

On the conquest of North Africa, including the role of slave capture in it, see Jamil M. Abun-Nasr, *History of the Maghrib in the Islamic Period* (Cambridge: Cambridge University Press, 1987), 28–37; and Elizabeth Savage, *A Gateway to Hell, a Gateway to Paradise* (Princeton, NJ: Darwin, 1997). Also *EI* (2), "Kusayla" by M. Talbi.

On the confused biography of Sergius ibn Mansur and the importance of the family of John of Damascus as financial advisers to successive rulers, see M.-F. Auzépy, "De la Palestine à Constantinople (VIIe–IXe siècles): Étienne le Sabaïte et Jean Damascène," *Travaux et Mémoires du Centre de Recherche d'histoire et de la civilisation byzantines* 12 (1994): 183–218, at 193–204; also C. Mango and R. Scott, trans., *The Chronicle of Theophanes Confessor* (Oxford: Clarendon Press, 1997), 510, n. 4.

For a brief, clear survey of the events of the Second Civil War, see G. R. Hawting, *The First Dynasty of Islam: The Umayyad Caliphate AD 661–750* (London: Routledge, 1987), 46–57. More detailed reconstructions can be found in ʿAbd al-Ameer ʿAbd Dixon, *The Umayyad Caliphate 65–86/684–705: A Political Study* (London: Luzac, 1971); Gernot Rotter, *Die Umayyaden und der zweite Bürgerkrieg (680–692)* (Wiesbaden: Steiner, in Komm. für DMG, 1982); and Chase Robinson, *ʾAbd al-Malik* (Oxford: Oneworld, 2005).

Ibn al-Zubayr's sermon disparaging Yazid is mentioned in Ahmad ibn Jabir al-Baladhuri, *Ansab al-ashraf* IVB, ed. Max Schloessinger (Jerusalem: Hebrew University Press, 1938), 30.

The quote about al-Mukhtar is found in Tab. ii/650.

Pilgrimage leaders in 68/June 688: Tab. ii/782.

5. The Emergence of Islam

On ʿAbd al-Malik's religious learning, Ibn Saʿd, *Tabaqat*, ed. E. Sachau (Leiden: E. J. Brill, 1917–1940), V, 172–174. Robinson, *ʾAbd al-Malik*, 53–57, notes the difficulties of knowing about his person.

On the theme of prophecy in Islamic historiography, see Donner, *Narratives*, chap. 5.

On the Bishapur coins of the Zubayrids, see the discussion in Hoyland, *Seeing Islam*, 550–554.

On the "cross on steps" and reform coins of ʿAbd al-Malik, see Michael Bates, "History, Geography and Numismatics in the First Century of Islamic Coinage," *Revue Suisse de Numismatique* 65 (1986): 2310–2362; Sheila Blair, "What Is the Date of the Dome of the Rock?," in Raby and Johns, *Bayt al-Maqdis* I, 59–88; and Clive Foss, "The Coinage of the First Century of Islam," *Journal of Roman Archaeology* 16 (2003): 748–760.

On the iconography of the Dome of the Rock, see Myriam Rosen-Ayalon, *The Early Islamic Monuments of al-Haram al-Sharif: An Iconographic Study* (Jerusalem: Hebrew University of Jerusalem, 1989) [*Qedem*. Monographs of the Institute of Archaeology, Hebrew University of Jerusalem, No. 28.]

On the Dome of the Rock generally, see the essays in Julian Raby and Jeremy Johns, eds., *Bayt al-Maqdis: ʿAbd al-Malik's Jerusalem* and Jeremy Johns, ed., *Bayt al-Maqdis: Jerusalem and Early Islam* (Oxford: Oxford University Press, 1992 and 1999) [*Oxford Studies in Islamic Art*, IX, parts 1 and 2]; and Oleg Grabar, *The Shape of the Holy: Early Islamic Jerusalem* (Princeton, NJ: Princeton University Press, 1996). The inscriptions inside the Dome were published in facsimile by Christel Kessler, "ʿAbd al-Malik's Inscription in the Dome of the Rock: A Reconsideration," *Journal of the Royal Asiatic Society* (1970): 2–14; a translation is provided in Appendix B of this book. Recently, C. Luxenberg has retranslated the inscriptions in a manner that supports his view that they advance a pre-trinitarian form of Christianity, a view that has not received widespread support: C. Luxenberg, "Neudeutung der arabischen Inschrift im Felsendom zu Jerusalem," in *Die dunklen Anfänge: neue Forschungen zur Entstehung und frühen Geschichte des Islam*, ed. Karl-Heinz Ohlig and Gerd-R. Puin, 124–147 (Berlin: Schiler, 2005).

On early *shahadas*, see the references cited for Chapter 3 above. An inscription mentioning Muhammad, Jesus, and ʿUzayr is reported in Y. D. Nevo, Z. Cohen, and D. Heftmann, *Ancient Arab Inscriptions from the Negev* I ([Beersheba]: Ben-Gurion University/IPS, 1993), 54, no. ST

640(34). Another, dated 117/735, invokes "the Lord of Muhammad and Abraham"; see Moshe Sharon, "Arabic Rock Inscriptions from the Negev," in *Archaeological Survey of Israel, Ancient Rock Inscriptions, Supplement to Map of Har Nafha (196) 12–01* (Jerusalem: Israel Antiquities Authority, 1990), 22*, no. 66.I.

On parallels between Muslim, Christian, and Jewish prayer rituals, see C. H. Becker, "Zur Geschichte des islamischen Kultus," *Der Islam* 3 (1912): 374–399; E. Mittwoch, "Zur Entstehungsgeschichte des islamischen Gebets und Kultus," *Abhandlungen der königlichen Preussischen Akademie der Wissenschaften, Phil.-Hist. Classe* 1913 no. 2.

On the required five daily prayers, Uri Rubin, "Morning and Evening Prayers in Islam," *JSAI* 10 (1987): 40–64.

On the development of the Islamic origins story, see Donner, *Narratives*.

On interpretation of "standing caliph" coins, see Clive Foss, "A Syrian Coinage of Mu'awiya?," *Révue Numismatique* 158 (2002): 353–365; also Foss, "The Coinage of the First Century of Islam," *Journal of Roman Archaeology* 16 (2003): 748–760; and Michael Bates, "Byzantine Coinage and Its Imitations, Arab Coinage and Its Imitations: Arab-Byzantine Coinage," *Aram* 6 (1994): 381–403.

On the title *khalifat Allah* in literary sources, see Avraham Hakim, "'Umar ibn al-Khattab and the title *khalifat Allah*: A Textual Analysis," *JSAI* 30 (2005): 207–230; Wadad al-Qadi, "The Term '*khalifa*' in Early Exegetical Literature," *Die Welt des Islams* 28 (1988): 392–411; and Patricia Crone and Martin Hinds, *God's Caliph: Religious Authority in the First Centuries of Islam* (Cambridge: Cambridge University Press, 1986).

On the status of Jesus in early Islamic eschatology, see David Cook, *Studies in Muslim Apocalyptic* (Princeton, NJ: Darwin, 2002), 323–334, and Cook, "The Beginnings of Islam in Syria during the Umayyad Period" (diss. University of Chicago, 2001).

On the Umayyads "stressing their links to chains of earlier prophets as sources of authority," see Uri Rubin, "Prophets and Caliphs: The Biblical Foundations of the Umayyad Authority," in *Method and Theory in the Study of Islamic Origins*, ed. Herbert Berg, 73–99 (Leiden: E. J. Brill, 2003).

Glossary

agarenoi   See *muhajirun*.

ahl al-bayt   Literally, "people of the house," often a designation for members of the (extended) family of the prophet Muhammad; sometimes a designation for people associated with the Kaʿba in Mecca, called the "house of God."

ahl al-dhimma   Protected peoples, subjects of the Believers who paid special tax in exchange for the contract of protection *(dhimma)* by Believers.

ahl al-kitab   "Peoples of the book," that is, Christians and Jews, who were considered by Believers to have received God's revelations previously.

ʿamil   Finance director for a province, usually working in tandem with the *amir* or military governor.

amir   Arabic term for military commander of an expeditionary force or military governor of a province.

amir al-muʾminin   "Commander of the Believers," title given to successors to Muhammad as leaders of the community of Believers/Muslims.

amsar   See *misr*.

ansar   Literally, "helpers," the term for those people in Yathrib (later Medina) who joined Muhammad's movement.

'ashura'   The tenth day of the first month of the Muslim calendar, Muharram. On this day, Shi'a Muslims commemorate the death of Husayn ibn 'Ali at Karbala' in 61/680.

aya   A verse of the Qur'an; literally, "sign" (of God's favor).

barid   The official courier service maintained by the *amir al-mu'minin*s for the exchange of letters and intelligence information.

caliph   See *khalifa*.

dihqan   Middle Persian (Pahlavi) word for local gentry who dominated life in the Iranian countryside in the late antique and early Islamic periods.

diwan   In the early Believers' movement, the payroll or list of soldiers (and others) eligible to receive a salary from the regime. As the original *diwan* grew over time into a large bureaucracy to handle military pay and other matters, the term *diwan* later acquired the sense of "government bureau." It also means the collected works of a poet— the shared idea being that a *diwan* constitutes a listing or compilation of something.

dyophysite   Christians who believe that Jesus had two separate natures (Greek, *physis*), one human and one divine, that existed independently within him. Compare to monophysite.

fitna   Qur'anic word meaning "temptation"; used by later Islamic historiography to refer to the civil wars of the seventh century, because some of the protagonists were deemed to have succumbed to the temptation to seize worldly power.

futuh   Arabic word meaning "opening" and "act of divine grace," used in Islamic historiography to refer to the seizure of new areas or towns by the Believers' movement; often translated as "conquest."

hadith   A statement attributed to the prophet Muhammad, or a report about something he did, prefaced by a chain of transmitting authorities.

hajj   The annual pilgrimage in the twelfth month of the Muslim calendar, during which pilgrims engage in numerous rituals centered on Mt. 'Arafa and other sites near Mecca.

hanif   Somewhat obscure term in the Qur'an, evidently meaning a "natural" monotheist not belonging to one of the established monotheistic religions (for example, Christianity or Judaism).

haram In Arabian society of the seventh century, a sacred enclave or delimited sacred space. Mecca was a leading *haram* on the eve of Islam; Muhammad founded another *haram* in Yathrib after his emigration there in 622 C.E.

Hashim The clan or lineage within the Meccan tribe of Quraysh to which Muhammad the prophet belonged.

hijra Arabic word meaning "emigration," "taking refuge," and sometimes "settlement"; applied to the prophet Muhammad's move from Mecca to Medina (622 C.E.), which became year 1 of the Muslim calendar; also applied, in the early years of the Believers' movement, to the resettlement of Believers outside Arabia. See *muhajirun.*

hima Protected pasture, reserved by the *amir al-mu'minin* to maintain the livestock (especially camels) given as tax payments.

imam, imamate In ritual prayer, the person who prays in front of the others, with whose movements the other worshippers coordinate their own; in a more general sense, an *imam* is someone who is recognized as a leader in a particular context. Among the Shi'a, *imam* came by the second century AH to mean a God-guided leader of the whole community of Muslims, endowed with secret knowledge essential for the salvation of the community as a whole, and therefore the single Muslim who could rightly claim to be *amir al-mu'minin* (even though he did not actually hold that position).

jihad "Striving, exertion"; hence, in some contexts, "fighting against, struggling against, holy war."

Ka'ba The cubical stone structure in Mecca that is the central cult site for the Islamic faith and the focus of daily prayers.

kafir (plural, kafirun) An unbeliever; literally "ingrate," one who is not grateful to God for His bounties.

khalifa Qur'anic term adopted by the *amir al-mu'minin* 'Abd al-Malik (ruled 685–705) as alternative title for the head of state; anglicized as "caliph."

khawarij Literally, "those who go out," the original *khawarij* were ultra-pious members of the early community of Believers who broke with the *amir al-mu'minin* 'Ali ibn Abi Talib, whom they considered guilty of a grave sin (and therefore unqualified to lead) because of his decision to submit the question of leadership to arbitration.

khutba   The sermon delivered during the noontime prayer on Fridays.

Koran   See **Qur'an.**

kufr   Unbelief; see *kafir.*

magaritai   See *muhajirun.*

mawla (plural, mawali)   Client of an Arabian kin group, who though of different lineage is considered functionally a member of the kin group. New converts often held this status.

mhaggraye   See *muhajirun.*

mihrab   A niche in the wall of a mosque or place of prayer indicating the direction of the *qibla,* toward which one faces during prayer.

minbar   The elevated pulpit from which a prayer leader delivers the *khutba* or sermon during Friday prayers.

misr (plural, amsar)   Garrison towns that the military forces of the Believers' movement established as bases and which developed over time into major cities, including Kufa and Basra in Iraq, Fustat in Egypt, Qayrawan in North Africa, and Marv in Central Asia.

monophysite   Christians who believed that Jesus had only one nature (Greek, *physis*) that was simultaneously human and divine in character. The Byzantine "Orthodox" church condemned monophysitism at the Council of Chalcedon in 451 C.E. Compare to dyophysite.

muhajirun   Those who have made *hijra,* especially those Meccans who were early followers of the prophet Muhammad and migrated with him to Yathrib (Medina). It was also used to refer to Arabian Believers who migrated to lands outside Arabia during the first expansion of the movement. The term shows up in Greek and Syriac sources (Syriac, **mhaggraye**; Greek, *agarenoi* or *magaritai*) as the first designation for the Believers when they appear in the lands outside Arabia.

mu'min (plural, mu'minun)   Believer in the one God who lives righteously in accordance with God's revealed laws; in Qur'anic usage, can include righteous *ahl al-kitab* (Christians and Jews).

mushrik (plural, **mushrikun**) "Associators," those who associate other beings with God and hence deny His oneness.

muslim In the Qur'an, one who submits himself to God's will and law; perhaps specifically a follower of the Qur'an as revelation and law, rather than the Gospels or Torah.

nabi A prophet, sent by God to warn and guide a people. Compare to *rasul*.

qada', qadi The Qur'an uses *qada'* to refer to God's decree or decisive action; it came to be used for the jurisdiction exercised by those charged with deciding legal disputes on the basis of the Qur'an. These officials came to be called *qadis*.

qibla The direction toward the Ka'ba in Mecca, which Muslims face during prayers.

Qur'an (Koran) The sacred scripture of Muslims, believed by them to have been revealed to the prophet Muhammad (died 632 c.e.) by God. Often abbreviated as "Q." in this book.

Quraysh The tribe of Mecca to which Muhammad the prophet belonged.

rashidun "Rightly guided"; A retrospective term of later Islamic historiography, designating the first four successors to the prophet Muhammad: Abu Bakr (ruled 11–13/632–634), 'Umar (ruled 13–23/634–644), 'Uthman (ruled 23–35/644–656), and 'Ali (ruled 35–40/656–661). The term reflected the theological decision to make off-limits the debate on the rightfulness of these persons' claims, which was threatening to tear the community apart.

rasul Messenger or apostle, especially someone sent by God to be head of a religious community. Compare to *nabi*.

ridda An Arabic word meaning "going back," "replying," or "returning," used in later Islamic tradition as a pejorative term for the resistance within Arabia to the expansion of the Believers' community under the leadership of Abu Bakr (ruled 11–13/632–634). In later Islamic tradition, it carried the sense of "apostasy."

sabb The practice of cursing one's political opponents during the sermon in Friday prayer; practiced especially by the Umayyads and the 'Alids in their struggles for leadership.

sadaqa   Tax paid to the Believers' movement; sometimes equated with *zakat*, it seems in many sources to be especially linked to payments made by pastoral nomads.

sa'ifa   Summer raids launched by the Believers/Muslims, especially against Byzantine territory in Anatolia.

salah *or* salat   Ritual prayer for Believers/Muslims, constituting several *rak'a*s consisting of standing, bowing, prostrations, and certain recitations while facing the Ka'ba, performed at prescribed times of the day.

shahada   "Bearing witness," the basic statement of faith of Muslims: "There is no god except God, Muhammad is the apostle of God." Saying it became one of the five pillars or basic rituals of the Islamic faith.

shi'a, Shi'at 'Ali   Arabic *shi'a* basically means "party, faction." The party of 'Ali ibn Abi Talib, the prophet Muhammad's cousin and son-in-law, backed him during the First Civil War (656–661 C.E.). Later, his followers came to revere all of 'Ali's descendants and asserted that they had a special claim on leadership of the community. See *imam.*

shura   Consultative council of leading members of the community, convened to decide important matters, especially questions of leadership; traditionally, a *shura*'s members were to debate an issue until complete consensus was attained.

sura   A chapter of the Qur'an; all bear names ("The Cow," "Repentance," and so on) and are also traditionally given numbers (for example, "The Cow" is Sura 2).

tanzil   Literally, "sending down," this became the standard term for the process by which passages of the Qur'an were revealed by God to Muhammad. Hence, "[the process of] revelation."

tawwabun   "The penitents," a group of early Shi'a who regretted not supporting adequately the movement of Husayn ibn 'Ali, killed by an Umayyad governor at Karbala' in Iraq in 61/680.

thughur   The fortified border marches of the Believers' domains, especially those facing the Byzantine empire; literally, "gaps" or "spaces between the teeth" in Arabic, referring to the mountain passes that needed to be fortified against outside invasion.

umma   Community, particularly the community of Believers.

'umra   The "lesser pilgrimage" (compare to *hajj*), involving circumambulation of the Ka'ba and various other rituals in Mecca itself. These may be conducted at any time of the year.

zakat   In Islamic law, "alms, almsgiving," one of the "five pillars" or basic rituals of the faith. In Muhammad's time, a payment in expiation of past sins.

Illustration Credits

Page 6: Walls of Constantinople. Wikimedia/Nevit Dilmen, December 2000.

Page 8: Hagia Sophia. Wikimedia/"Bigdaddy 1204," June 2006.

Page 9: Roman road in Syria. Author photo, November 1966.

Page 12: Mar Saba. Wikimedia, January 2006.

Page 15: St. Simeon. Author photo, August 1974.

Page 19: Sasanian Throne-Hall at Ctesiphon. Author photo, May 1967.

Page 21: Triumph of Shapur, Bishapur. Courtesy of Touraj Daryaee.

Page 29: Bar'an Temple, Ma'rib. Wikimedia/Bernard Gagnon, August 1986.

Page 36: Jabrin oasis, Oman. Author photo, January 1977.

Page 37: The Ka'ba. Al-Sayyid 'Abd al-Ghaffar/C. Snouck Hurgronje, ca. 1890. Courtesy of E. J. Brill, Leiden.

Page 55: An Early Qur'an. Dar al-Makhtutat, San'a', Yemen, No. 01-25-1. Courtesy of Gerd-R. Puin.

Page 108: Floor from St. Menas, Rihab. Author photo. February 2001.

Page 113: Early coins. Courtesy of the American Numismatic Society, ANS 1977.71.13 and ANS 1954.112.5.

Page 138: Ayla. Author photo, March 2001; plan courtesy of Donald Whitcomb.

Page 187: Coins of rivals to the Umayyads. Courtesy of the American Numismatic Society, ANS 1951.148.3 and ANS 1953.9.4.

Page 200: Dome of the Rock, Jerusalem. Author photo, April 1967.

Page 201: Umm Qays. Author photo, February 2001.

Page 207: Letter of Qurra ibn Sharik. Courtesy of the Oriental Institute of the University of Chicago. OI 13756.

Page 210: Two coins of ʿAbd al-Malik. Courtesy of the American Numismatic Society, ANS 1970.63.1 and ANS 1002.1.406.

Page 223: Tomb of ʿUmar II. Author photo, August 2005.

Index